1

Media Discourses
Donald Matheson

Modernity and Postmodern Culture, 2nd edition
Jim McGuigan

Rethinking Cultural Policy
Jim McGuigan

Children, Media and Culture
Máire Messenger Davies

Critical Readings: Media and Audiences
Virginia Nightingale and Karen Ross (ed.)

Media and Audiences
Karen Ross and Virginia Nightingale

Sport, Culture and the Media, 2nd edition
David Rowe

Critical Readings: Sport, Culture and the Media
David Rowe (ed.)

Cities and Urban Cultures
Deborah Stevenson

Cultural Citizenship
Nick Stevenson

Compassion, Morality and the Media
Keith Tester

Critical Readings: Violence and the Media
C. Kay Weaver and Cynthia Carter (ed.)

Identity and Culture: Narratives of Difference and Belonging
Chris Weedon

CHILDREN, MEDIA AND CULTURE

ISSUES in CULTURAL and MEDIA STUDIES

Series editor: Stuart Allan

Published titles:

The Teletubbies. From left: Tinky Winky, Dipsy, Laa Laa and Po.

Image with permission of Ragdoll Productions Ltd.

CHILDREN, MEDIA AND CULTURE

Máire Messenger Davies

 Open University Press

Open University Press
McGraw-Hill Education
McGraw-Hill House
Shoppenhangers Road
Maidenhead
Berkshire
England
SL6 2QL

email: enquiries@openup.co.uk
world wide web: www.openup.co.uk

and Two Penn Plaza, New York, NY 10121–2289, USA

First published 2010

A catalogue record of this book is available from the British Library

ISBN10: 0 335 22920 4 (pb)   0 335 22919 0 (hb)
ISBN13: 978 0 335 22920 8 (pb)   978 0 335 22919 2 (hb)

Library of Congress Cataloging-in-Publication Data
CIP data applied for

Typeset by RefineCatch Limited, Bungay, Suffolk
Printed in the UK by Bell and Bain Ltd., Glasgow

Mixed Sources
Product group from well-managed
forests and other controlled sources
www.fsc.org Cert no. TT-COC-002769
© 1996 Forest Stewardship Council

The **McGraw·Hill** Companies

CONTENTS

SERIES EDITOR'S FOREWORD

When media attention is directed toward children, it often situates them as a problem demanding urgent intervention. Concerns may be raised about their behaviour (such as with regard to crime, truancy, eating disorders, spending habits or media tastes and preferences) or their vulnerability to those intent on taking advantage of them. Much less frequent are positive accounts of children's lives, leading some commentators to suggest that media interest in young people typically revolves around adult anxieties first and foremost.

Examples of how these sorts of tensions unfold are easy to identify when they spark sensational newspaper headlines, but they also appear in more everyday contexts. An example of the latter concerned a commercial for a diet soft drink featuring the Welsh popstar Duffy. In the commercial, Duffy is shown riding a bicycle through dark city streets before entering a supermarket, where she steers her way through the aisles (presumably in pursuit of the product). Some viewers were alarmed because Duffy appears to be riding at night without adequate safety gear, such as a proper light, reflective clothing or helmet, which led to complaints being made to the Advertising Standards Authority (ASA). At issue was whether the commercial was being irresponsible, namely because children could be encouraged to copy her dangerous example at serious risk to their personal well-being (a charge countered by the soft drink company, which insisted the advertisement represented 'Duffy's fantasy,' that is, 'a scenario that depicted her escape from the pressures of stardom [that was] far removed from the real world'). While the ASA decided in the end not to uphold the complaints, familiar debates were rehearsed in the press about public perceptions of media effects, especially where the power to unduly influence young, impressionable minds is concerned.

In making the case for an alternative conception of the relationship between the media and children, Máire Messenger Davies's *Children, Media and Culture* brings to bear a different perspective. In so doing, she offers an important reassessment of key tenets informing discussions about the role of popular media in children's lives. Children's culture, she observes, is regularly in the forefront of debates about how society is changing, thereby recurrently attracting a wide array of impassioned responses – both optimistic and pessimistic in their outlook. While today's media – such as video games, mobile telephones and iPods – are criticized by some for posing a threat to traditional norms and values, her research shows how such fears have long found expression vis-à-vis forms such as children's stories, fairy tales and playground games. Of particular interest to Messenger Davies are the ways in which communication technologies shape children's cultural experiences, not least their ideas of fun, as well as their sense of identity, beliefs in public service or feelings about community. In exploring how children may be seen as 'citizens-in-the-making' in complex media environments, she identifies and critiques a number of pressing issues. More specifically, she adopts a case study approach for different media forms – literature, film, television, screen adaptations, photography, computer games, websites, and so forth – in order to examine the everyday culture of childhood from multiple perspectives. Critical insights generated from close analyses are supplemented, in turn, with research based on interviews with media producers and consumers, the latter including families with children. *Children, Media and Culture* thus makes a major contribution to the formalization of this area of enquiry, helping to consolidate existing work with concrete strategies for pushing scholarship forward in imaginative, productive directions.

The *Issues in Cultural and Media Studies* series aims to facilitate a diverse range of critical investigations into pressing questions considered to be central to current thinking and research. In light of the remarkable speed at which the conceptual agendas of cultural and media studies are changing, the series is committed to contributing to what is an ongoing process of re-evaluation and critique. Each of the books is intended to provide a lively, innovative and comprehensive introduction to a specific topical issue from a fresh perspective. The reader is offered a thorough grounding in the most salient debates indicative of the book's subject, as well as important insights into how new modes of enquiry may be established for future explorations. Taken as a whole, then, the series is designed to cover the core components of cultural and media studies courses in an imaginatively distinctive and engaging manner.

Stuart Allan

LIST OF FIGURES, TABLES AND BOXES

Figures

Tables

Boxes

ACKNOWLEDGEMENTS

Particular thanks are due to the Arts and Humanities Research Council of the UK (AHRC) for funding a period of study leave during which I was able to do research for, and complete the writing of, this book. Thanks also to the Faculty of Arts at the University of Ulster (UU) for providing a period of matching leave for preliminary research and writing. Thanks to Professor Martin McLoone for taking over as the Director of the Centre for Media Research at UU while I was on leave. Other helpful colleagues at UU include Dr Amy Davis, whose research on Disney has been a stimulus to my study of fairy tales and of cartoons; Rowan Morrey, IT Systems Development Officer, for photographs and technical support; and my PhD student, Alexandra Cochrane, whose research on the politics and economics of preschool TV production, with special reference to *Sesame Tree* in Northern Ireland, has stimulated much thinking and research throughout the writing of this book.

Others who have been helpful in the background research for the book are:

Professor Dafna Lemish and colleagues at the Harvard Center for Research on Media and Child Health, Boston, and especially its head, Professor Michael Rich; Charlotte Cole and colleagues at Sesame Workshop, New York; Josh Selig, Heather Tilert, Tone Thyne and colleagues at Little Airplane Productions, New York; Professors William Uricchio, Erin Reilly and Scott Osterweil at the MIT Comparative Media Studies Program, Cambridge, Massachusetts; MIT MA student, Flourish Klink, for her introduction to the wonderful world of Harry Potter fan fiction at fictionalley.org; Professor Jeanette Steemers, University of Westminster and her co-organizers and contributors to the conference, 'Making television for young children: future prospects and issues', University of Westminster, 21 September 2008; Dr Cynthia Carter, Professor Stuart Allan,

Dr Kaitlynn Mendes, plus Roy Milani and Ian Prince (BBC), colleagues on an earlier research project on the BBC's *Newsround*, which has helped to keep me in touch with important issues of children's citizenship and participatory media as I worked on the book; the members of Save Kids TV, UK, and the Voice of the Listener and Viewer, for their untiring efforts to keep the cultural value of children's media to the forefront of public and government attention.

Thanks to the families, children and young people who have provided up-to-date information for me about their media habits: the Messenger/McAfees; Calum and Finn; Ishbel and Elandra; the young people in the Tuesday group at the Chicken Shed Theatre Company in Southgate, London, plus Mary Ward, Wendy Shillinglaw and Charlotte Bull at Chicken Shed; the children and staff of the Stepping Stones nursery at the University of Ulster; the children at Millstrand Integrated Primary School, Portstewart and at Dominican High School, Portstewart.

Thanks to Stuart Allan, the editor of the series, for his constructive and supportive comments in the preparation of the script and to Stephanie Frosch for help with picture research.

Special thanks to Ragdoll Productions; Sesame Workshop; Little Airplane Productions; Alf Wilkinson at burntcakes.com; Erin Reilly and Vinitha Nair at Zoey's Room website, for permission to reproduce images free of charge.

And, as always, thanks to my own – now very grown up – family of children: Tom, Hannah, Huw and Eli, and to my husband and critical friend, John.

PART 1
THE STUDY OF CHILDHOOD

DEFINING CHILDREN, MEDIA AND CULTURE

> The problem of working and street children lies in poverty, social exclusion, inequality and injustice ... Yet children and young people are a major resource for progress and the prime movers of innovation. Their imagination, idealism and collective energies form the creative impulse for the future of any nation.
>
> (Rahman 2001: 265)

Rahman's comments, in a book called *Youth, Citizenship and Empowerment*, summarize two pervasive media discourses about children and the young: the first, that they are a problem, particularly when they are poor, exploited and come from disadvantaged backgrounds, whether in the developing South – Africa, Asia, parts of Latin America – or whether they are in the rich, overfed cities of the developed North (Europe, USA) or in the prosperous developed societies of the geographical South and far East – Australia, New Zealand, Japan. The other perspective – and it can apply to the same group of disadvantaged children, as Rahman points out – is to see children as a source of hope and progress whose imagination, idealism and creativity are the foundation of the future of any society.

In academic and journalistic discussions of the relationship between media and children, both these positive and negative perspectives are apparent. One strand of discussion is culturally pessimistic – contemporary children are in a bad way; even when they are well off, our culture is degraded and children are corrupted by it. The other perspective is celebratory and more often than not driven by commercial interests – the bright, shiny, technologically-sophisticated media world of the 'kids'. This world is characterized as 'cool' and 'fun' (a favourite word on 'kids' websites). It provides the kinds of media, in the words of a promotional film from the commercial children's channel, Nickelodeon, which are: 'stuffed full of kids' programmes . . . wicked cartoons . . . brilliant live shows . . . and fantastic comedy' (quoted in Buckingham 2002: 3). This wonderful world replaced the rather staid cultural environment provided by earlier children's media, such as the BBC's offerings, which must conform to the public service criteria of 'information, education and entertainment' and must serve all ages and classes of the population. This worthy approach preceded the new consumer paradise of 'choice' provided by commercial subscription channels, mostly owned by American media conglomerates. Nickelodeon, with many international branches (including most recently, in China) is owned by a global media corporation: in this case, Viacom, who also own Paramount pictures and MTV. (See http://www.viacom.com/ourbrands/medianetworks/mtvnetworks/Pages/nickelodeon.aspx).

The BBC's public service offerings provide a third strand of discourse: the idea that children are *not* necessarily a problem and that cultural experiences should be offered to them which take them seriously – offerings which would produce, in presenter Zoe Ball's words, quoted in the same Buckingham article (2002), 'well-rounded individuals'. This public service discourse, sometimes described as **paternalistic**, expresses a position which accepts contemporary media such as television as potential forces for 'good' rather than corruption – but 'good' may sometimes be rather narrowly defined as what is good for the middle-class people running **public service broadcasting** organizations.

This book tries to steer a course between these discourses and also to branch out into some less well-trodden discourses on the topic of children and culture. The book originates in a course I have taught in a number of degree programmes, both in the USA and in different parts of the UK, called 'The Culture of Childhood'. In developing this course over the years, it became apparent that simply discussing the tradition of research on children and electronic media (primarily television) that constitutes the 'media effects' branch of media studies, did not begin to cover all that students wanted to learn about children and childhood. It did not cover everything I wanted to say about it either.

Young people in universities are not far removed from their own childhoods. Memories of books, games, jokes, crazes, relationships with family and friends, as well as TV programmes, popular music and films, were important to my students as a necessary background to their academic discussions about children and media. It was obvious, too, that childhoods were different in different countries and cultures. Postgraduate students from Africa wanted to pursue research on the ways in which the kinds of poor and exploited children discussed by Rhaman were – they claimed – inadequately reported in their home country's media. European, Welsh and Irish students wanted to focus on their own specific cultural identities and childhood traditions, different from those of the United States or Britain. Middle Eastern students were interested in the impact of Western consumer lifestyles on young people's attitudes to religious and social traditions.

As the course developed over time, imaginative student projects about fairy tales, children's literature, comic books and the representation of children in historical works of art, stimulated me to expand my own interests in these topics. A unit I introduced about language development proved to be of great interest to many students and required further contextualization around broader issues of child development: psychology, education and sociology were relevant here and so the course included brief introductions to theories of child development and their controversies.

The study of childhood, children, media and culture thus draws on academic and scholarly traditions which are very diverse and not always on good terms with each other. I hope this book will be useful to students from some of these other traditions, not just to students studying the media. Of course much has had to be left out in a relatively short volume; psychology students, for example, may find the material on their particular specialism – child development and child language – rather summary. Similarly, literary students will know that there is much more that can be said about children's literature and literature generally than has been possible here. Media students, I hope, will be relieved – as my students have been over the years – that they are not required only to dwell on the dystopic aspects of the relationship between children and media: the alleged destruction of childhood and its innocence by violent films, coarse TV programmes, sexy pop videos and pornographic websites. These issues and the body of research concerning them are addressed, but there are other more constructive aspects of the relationship between children and media that need to be acknowledged too. These aspects are also more supportive of students' own childhood pleasures and tastes.

A dangerous world

While I have been writing this book about 'children', 'media' and 'culture', not only street children in the developing world are represented in the media as problems; the world as a whole has been plunged into a major economic crisis, worse, many people say, even than the depression years of the 1930s, because it is truly global, whereas that depression affected primarily the western, non-communist world. Alongside this global economic collapse, this period also saw the 2008 attacks by Israel on Gaza, and continuing conflicts in Darfur,

Afghanistan, Iraq, Sri Lanka, Pakistan, the Congo and Chechnya, with dead, wounded, bereaved and traumatized children as the recurring public faces of these conflicts. Terrorism continues to haunt the world community in the form of Islamist suicide bombings; and even old conflicts that many thankfully thought had been settled have arisen again, as in the case of Northern Ireland, where two soldiers and a policeman were murdered at the beginning of 2009 by the Continuity IRA. In April 2009, disturbing memories of one of the worst crimes ever to involve children – the murder of 2-year-old James Bulger by two 10-year-old boys in Liverpool in 1993 – were revived with a similar crime being carried out by two Nottinghamshire 11-year-olds on two younger boys. In this case, the child victims did not die, but were very seriously injured. The child attackers were tried in an adult court, raising anew troubling questions about the status of children and childhood and to what extent 11-year-old children can be held responsible for their actions. At the same time, nearly every week brings another tragic case of a small child being killed by a parent or caretaker (for example the story of Baby Peter in London in 2009).

There is no denying the words of Mojibur Rahman that many children around the world, including 'migrants and refugees, the internally displaced, ethnic minorities and the poorest of the poor' live in 'families and environments where there is no choice, no possibility of alternatives and no respect for human rights' (2001: 265). Yet Rahman, writing specifically about **street children**, can still talk optimistically about children's 'imagination, idealism and collective energies'. For him, children are still 'a major resource for progress'. This is why, many scholars and cultural producers argue, the cultural and media products we offer them matter.

Defining terms

> The acquisition of societal rules and norms has always relied on culture . . . mythology, legends, storytelling and songs . . . since ancient times games, plays and toys have been an important part of the socialisation process . . . toys and games have an important function in teaching and consolidating social rules and norms, in establishing skills and transmitting social knowledge, in creating and reinforcing human relations and providing relaxation and entertainment.
>
> (Heller 2008: 271–2)

Maria Heller's comments, above, indicate how the three topics of this book are connected. But in defining them, and their relationship, controversies arise. 'Children' are regularly at the forefront of social and political debates on war, peace, economics, health, education, leisure, crime and presumed cultural decline. When the words 'children' and 'media' occur together, it is nearly always in the context of public anxiety about harmful effects, bad examples, corruption of innocence and cultural decline. 'Culture' is a more problematic word and, unlike the words 'children' and 'media', is less likely to appear in populist headlines. Among scholars in recent years, 'culture' has come to be applied to the topic of children and childhood coupled with the term 'construct'. The idea of 'childhood', as distinct from actual children, is, many scholars have argued, a 'cultural construct' – something which is not primarily rooted in biological reality, but which reflects the social, moral and political preoccupations of a particular time and place. Hence views of childhood, and how it should be defined and treated, will vary historically and geographically. These ideas will be examined in more detail in Chapters 2 and 3.

The structure of the book

Part 1: The study of childhood

The first section of the book deals with some of the ways in which children and childhood have been defined and studied by scholars from different disciplines. These disciplines include the non-media related ones of medicine (paediatrics, public health), history, psychology, sociology and political economy as well as media and cultural studies. It is relevant to look at these approaches to the study of children and childhood because, like all branches of human knowledge, they too are part of culture. Whereas it is possible to study the culture of adults without these adults' social or medical status being considered too, this is not the case for children. Children are seen as vulnerable, because of their youth and dependency, and the ways in which this vulnerability (both physical and emotional) is defined affect everything we say about them and their culture. For instance, doctors such as those at the Harvard Center on Media and Child Health will be concerned about unhealthy food advertising. Creative producers of children's educational and entertainment media are concerned to understand children's cognitive and emotional capacities. In addition to all this, the knowledge and information generated by other disciplines comes to the rest of us via media – whether through publishing, the press, film and television or, increasingly, the Internet. Media scholars need to be aware of how stories about child health, child development and child welfare are reported in relation to current scientific and social-scientific knowledge.

Part 2: Children in media, children's media

The second section of the book deals with specific media produced for children. Although a great deal has been written about the effects of media on children, there has been comparatively little critical attention to actual media products. This is even true of children's literature, which is usually seen as more culturally respectable than electronic media such as television and videogames. As professor of children's literature Peter Hunt has put it: 'children's literature is . . . at the bottom of the heap'. (1992: 2) The position is worse even than that for other branches of children's culture, such as television, the Internet and computer games. These are often defined primarily as commodities, only of interest insofar as they represent either cultural imperialism – the flooding of European and world markets with American cartoons – or the regrettable commercialization (and, it is implied, corruption) of unsullied childhood by the media marketplace. Jack Zipes writes gloomily (2002: xi):

> Everything we do to, with and for our children is influenced by capitalist market conditions and the hegemonic interests of ruling corporate elites . . . Children are expected to sort out the contradictions that are inevitable and intolerable in our society, and our vested interests drive them forward into hysteria, violence and bewilderment.

What is the evidence for this?

This book looks at some specific media products in its second section, beginning with traditional tales, some very ancient but still echoed in contemporary storytelling, moving on through the kinds of print literature discussed by Peter Hunt and Jack Zipes, to film, television, digital media and the Internet. The outputs, of children's television particularly, are vast and I have had to be selective in the material I have chosen to discuss. The scope of the Internet is similarly vast, and fluctuating all the time, with new information being added every nanosecond, and earlier information disappearing just as quickly. Nevertheless, important and influential claims are being made by some scholars for its 'empowering' and 'participatory' functions for children, and this is influencing the 'corporate elites' mentioned by Zipes in the way that they invest, or not, in media products for children. Are these shifts in investment in the interests of children?

In discussing specific cultural products, it becomes clear that historical, psychological, sociological and other academic 'constructions' of childhood can often be revealed in the kinds of entertainment products people have offered their children down the ages. Children learn about the society they live in, and how to adapt to it, from the cultural products offered to them by that society. Some of these products, of course, were, and are, not intended for children; folk tales are a good example. So are horror films. But what is it they offer children?

The aim of this book is to introduce students from different disciplines who have an interest in the topics of children, media and culture – whether individually, or combined – to the ways in which these topics have been researched and discussed by scholars. It aims to introduce (or re-introduce) students to some classic studies and authorities in these various fields, as well as to draw attention to new scholarly work appearing more recently. Much of the research discussed emanates from either the USA or the UK, partly because this is where the great bulk of scholarship in this field has been carried out, and partly because these countries are where I have done much of my own work. But wherever possible I have tried to make sure that relevant international examples and studies are cited too.

Since the terms 'children', 'media' and 'culture' are all capable of different interpretations, I will start by defining the ways in which they will be used in this book.

What is a child?

When I have taught my course on 'The culture of childhood', I've always started off by asking the students to define 'a child'. My students find it surprisingly difficult. To help, I suggested they try to explain what 'a child' is to a visitor from another planet. How would such a visitor identify 'a child' in order to distinguish him/her from other categories of human being? Because it's necessary in any project to be clear about definitions, I am going to attempt to come up with an Ockham's razor definition of 'a child'[1] – a definition that could not apply to anybody else *but* a child.

1 Babies and where they come from

A human child is the product of human conception, usually via sexual intercourse between an adult male and an adult female which results in the fertilization of the female ovum by the male sperm. Although we may not always think of an unborn and newborn baby as relevant to studies of 'media and culture', not to do so is a mistake; babies start acquiring and demonstrating the characteristics of 'childness' through cultural experiences from day one of their existence, and we will hear more about this in Chapter 3.

2 Genetic contributions

Fifty per cent of the fertilized embryo's genetic makeup (his/her own unique individuality which makes him/her different from anybody else) comes from the father, and 50 per cent from the mother. Many characteristics are genetically determined, including colouring, handedness, height, facial appearance, predisposition to some illnesses and disability, and probably some human talents such as music or maths. Psychological qualities such as a tendency to depression, hyperactivity, and – especially – intelligence have also been attributed to genetic causes.

3 Prenatal and natal experiences

The unborn child spends approximately nine months growing and developing in the mother's uterus, during which time he/she can be seriously adversely affected by environmental factors, particularly the mother's health and diet, and by habits such as smoking. Again, these habits are culturally determined, with poorer mothers having poorer diets and being exposed to more environmental hazards. Birth has traditionally been very hazardous for both mothers and babies. Cultural developments produced by modernity – modern midwifery, health care and obstetrics – minimize risks to both infant and mother, so that in developed countries, maternal death rates are low – four per thousand – and infant death rates are on average six to eight per thousand. In poorer countries, death rates can be over 100 per thousand. Such easily preventable loss of young life is one of the worst features of global inequality: an example of how culture – the prioritizing, or not, of maternity and paediatric care, arising from socio-political decisions – intersects with 'nature' – the supposedly 'natural' processes of reproduction.

4 Size

A child is smaller than most adults, and he/she starts life *very* small, weighing only about 3.2 kg (7 lb) on average, and measuring about 54 cm (21 inches) in length. A child is differentially proportioned than an adult: his/her head is bigger in proportion to the body, and other proportions vary too, and these proportions change as the child grows (see Tanner 1990).

5 Growth

Linked to size, there is growth – a key marker of 'childness': unlike an adult, a child is growing very rapidly. Rates of growth fluctuate at particular periods of life: in the first year the growth curve is steep, between the ages of 2 and 5 it becomes less steep, and then between 5 and around 11 the curve almost flattens. It becomes steep again when adolescence starts at around the age of 10 to 12 in girls, a year or two later in boys. These kinds of growth spurts and fluctuations do not occur in adults.

6 Sex and gender distinctions

Boys and girls grow and develop along pretty much the same lines before the adolescent growth spurt (see Figures 3.1 and 3.2, pages 39–40). As Simone de Beauvoir put it in *The Second Sex* ([1949] 1988: 295) 'up to the age of twelve the little girl is as strong as her brothers and she shows the same mental powers: there is no field where she is debarred from engaging in rivalry with them'. At puberty, some time between 10 and 14 years of age, boys and girls start to become markedly different in their physical and sexual characteristics and this unavoidable biological development has all kinds of implications for social and cultural behaviour, which both media and cultural products have to take account of.

7 Maturation

A child is *developing*: alongside physical growth, muscles, nervous system, bone structure and brain are all becoming more physiologically complex in order to become more specialized in function. A very obvious example is the way a small child's hands, which are quite pudgy and clumsy in babyhood, become able to pick up tiny objects and manipulate them in the second and third years of life. Such delicate and purposeful movements are not possible in the first year, because the child's perceptual, nervous and muscular systems have not sufficiently matured to enable such movements. Damage to any of these systems during these complex developmental processes can have lifelong harmful effects, the most harmful being brain damage at, or soon after, birth. Conversely, recent research suggests that the optimum physical development of the brain and nervous system in the early months of life is facilitated by affectionate and consistent nurturing from parents/caretakers.

8 Cognition

Linked to these physiological and neurological developments are cognitive developments – a child is *learning* rapidly and extensively. Although we all go on learning throughout life, so looking for this characteristic by itself wouldn't necessarily help an interplanetary visitor to identify a child, nearly all basic human skills – motor skills, communicative skills, social skills – are acquired in the first five years.

9 Language

A child is someone who acquires language, without special instruction, at a stage of life when he or she is physically very immature. In all cultures a child's first language is fully acquired by around age 4, regardless of grammatical variation and complexity. This is an impressive achievement and we could argue that the rapid acquisition of language at a very early and dependent stage of life is another essential marker of 'childness'.

10 Dependence

A young child is dependent for survival on caretaking adults. The age at which a child is able to live independently can vary – a child could survive on its own by the age of 5, if it were an exceptional child and there are cases of this. But most could not, and under that age survival would be unlikely if the child were abandoned. Street children in the cities of some developing countries – children abandoned by their families – can survive in groups, but the risks of them dying from malnutrition, disease, accidents and crime are massively higher than for children whose families take care of them until they are grown up.

11 Sexual immaturity

Human children do not acquire the capacity for sexual reproduction until they are in their early teens (on average – again there are exceptions). They do not finish growing physically until they are in their twenties. In this they are unique among animal species. No other animal takes so many years to reach sexual and physical maturity. This delayed maturation increases the need for dependence on adults (see point 10 above); this dependence in turn has consequences for the wider organization of human societies – for instance, in the need for adults to provide children with extended preparation for adult life. This has particularly significant implications for the status of women.

For all these reasons, it is never appropriate to write about 'children' without specifying what you mean by the term, because of the great developmental and other variations encompassed in it. A recognition of these realities also influences public policy and legislation relating to children. Dafna Lemish sums up the general position in her book *Children and Television: A Global Perspective* (2007):

There does seem to be agreement that in all societies round the world children are perceived to be the most vulnerable members: they are smaller and physically weaker, they need protection, care, feeding, fostering and socialization to the adult world; they lack life experience and knowledge; they think differently than do adults and they lack social and economical resources.

(p. 70)

Chronological age versus maturity

How we define childhood is strongly linked to chronological age in ways that are not always consistent. If you are currently a high school student, you are *still* a child politically and economically because you may not be old enough to vote (at age 18) and because you are financially dependent. This may be very irksome to you, as you almost certainly have the looks and body of an adult, you may be sexually active, (legally permissible in the UK, the USA and other developed countries at age 16, younger in some other countries) and you may even be a parent already. You may believe, possibly with good reason, that you have the judgement and intellectual maturity to make your own decisions rather than have parents and teachers make them for you. But legally, you are still that discursive construction – 'a child.'

Box 1.1 gives some examples of how, in contemporary developed societies such as the UK, maturity is linked with age.

Box 1.1: When can you do this?

- private drinking of alcohol (age 5);
- opening a bank account (age 7);
- criminal responsibility (age 10);
- buying a pet (age 12);
- part-time employment (age 13);
- film/video-watching (12, 15, 18 years);
- age of sexual consent (16);
- licence to drive a car (age 17, 16 in some states of the USA);
- legal adulthood, including the right to vote (age 18).
  Source: At What Age Can I? A Guide to Age-Based Legislation. The Children's Legal Centre, University of Essex, 2008 edition, updated by Joanne Claridge

---

The age at which you can fight and die for your country also varies. The CIA (Central Intelligence Agency of the USA) website at [https://www.cia.gov/

library/publications/the-world-factbook/fields/2024.html] gives information about the minimum age required for military service in every country in the world. This ranges from 16 years for voluntary service in Bangladesh, Burundi, Liberia, the Netherlands Antilles and (with parental permission) the United Kingdom, to 22 years in Afghanistan.[2]

What are media?

In the first place 'media' is a plural noun. Print is a 'medium'; television is a 'medium'. Print, television, film and the Internet are 'media'.

The term 'media' will be unpacked in more detail in the second half of the book, when different media addressed to children will be discussed. At this point, we simply need to recognize that a 'medium' is a communicative form, in other words a channel or conduit through which information is passed. There are many complex models of communications media. Where children are concerned, 'media' have to be defined in the broadest possible sense, because children are exposed to all kinds of communicative forms from the day that they are born; for new babies, *everything* is a communicative form. From their first day they will be attempting to interpret and make sense of these forms; they will be making what the psychologist Frederick Bartlett called 'effort after meaning' ([1932] 1995: xii). Media are all the means whereby children (and all of us) learn about and define the world we live in. Media thus include: spoken language; sign language and gestures; written language; computer language; music; sounds; images; scents; objects; maps; musical notation; books; comics; TV programmes; films; telephones; advertising posters; paintings; sculptures; designs; and artefacts of all kinds.

To the extent that all these objects, experiences and cultural products convey information and meanings, they are media. To the extent that, through everyday objects and behaviours, the child learns meanings, almost everything is 'media'. This book will touch on these broader aspects of media, but, to keep its scope manageable, the term 'media' will mainly be used in its more conventional sense, to talk about published forms of narrative and information in the print and electronic media.

What is culture?

In *Keywords* (1976) Raymond Williams described 'culture' as 'one of the two or three most complicated words in the English language' (1976: 76). In the context of 'children' and 'media', the term culture has a very specific and functional aspect. A helpfully parsimonious definition (parsimony is another principle of Ockham's razor) is given by Melvyn De Fleur and Sandra Ball Rokeach (1988: 6): '[Culture is] solutions to problems of living, that are passed on to following generations.' This definition highlights the usefulness of culture (and media) to children. It suggests that culture, far from being mainly about the refinements of adult civilized life, such as art, music and poetry, is essential because it is functional. From the moment they are born, human children are faced with an immense number of 'problems of living'. Culture, interacting with 'nature' in the form of children's inborn human capacities, is what enables children to do all this. Thus, culture includes relatively simple things, like learning how to drink from a cup, as well as very complex things, like learning how to write essays, or to read and play music, or, indeed, to design and manufacture a cup.

Culture also has a broader definition in the sense that it encompasses the rules and regulations, the customs and traditions, of the society into which the child is born – and every child *is* born into such a network. These rules and customs include religious (or non-religious) beliefs and practices; other moral and ethical codes; political affiliations; approaches to eating, cooking, clothing, decoration, entertainment; customs facilitating birth, marriage, death, trade; laws about property, safety, inheritance; institutions to provide financial services, education, health care, transport, communication, laws, regulation, warfare, diplomatic relations with other cultures; sport and other games; governmental arrangements, whether democratic or otherwise, to manage all the rest, and so on and on. All societies, including what would once have been described as 'primitive' ones, are cultured – in other words they provide these arrangements and they have regular procedures for enabling their young to become part of their social structures, and eventually to perpetuate – or, when necessary, modify – these structures.

Culture came into being in human societies in order to enable each generation to do this: we could say that the whole point of culture is to enable the human child to carry on, and when necessary, to change, her society's traditions after older generations have passed on. Hence, one of the main arguments of this book is that the terms 'culture' and 'children' are always intrinsically linked. And one of the primary ways in which they are linked is through 'media'.

CHILDHOOD, HISTORY AND MEDIA

As discussed in Chapter 1, there are certain characteristics of 'a child' that do not change over time and space (size, growth, maturation and dependency). Nevertheless 'childhood' as a concept has been defined in different ways by scholars. Historians have been particularly apt to challenge the idea that 'childhood' is a fixed concept that can be universally characterized, regardless of historical period or geographical location. In order to understand how children, media and culture are related, it is necessary to take a historical perspective because many of our ideas about these concepts are historically rooted – and historically variable.

Children in the past two thousand years – a period of history which has produced many written and visual historical records about adults – have left very few traces of what their lives were like. Were their lives unimaginably different from the lives of children today? Or do children at every stage of history have characteristics in common? It's certainly true that children at earlier periods would have demonstrated the physiological changes of growth and development discussed in Chapter 1, as child skeletons found in archaeological sites indicate.

Children's rights

Our contemporary concerns with children and their media tend to focus particularly on their relationship with 'new' media. Children being themselves 'new', and in the process of discovering the world, this connection seems persuasive. But there are broader discourses around the subject of childhood in the

modern world which we also need to be aware of. A major source of contemporary ideas about childhood is the notion of children as a group of people
that has 'rights' and childhood as a period in which special rights are applicable,
which do not apply to adults. This is a particularly twentieth-century idea,
partly linked to the foundation of the United Nations and the universal doc-
trine on human rights. It shows how attitudes to children, childhood and their
status do indeed change historically. In 1989, the UN produced a Convention
on The Rights of the Child, to which the majority of nations in the world
have signed up – even if, in practice, they do not carry out all of its provisions
(see Figure 2.1).

In the twentieth and twenty-first centuries, children are seen as deserving of
special legal and political attention. This has not always been the case.

The historical 'invention' of childhood

The special status of children and childhood, it has been argued by sociologists
such as Neil Selwyn, is 'a discursive invention of the past hundred years or so'
(2003: 353). This provocative statement raises a number of questions. Did people in earlier periods of history really have no 'discursive' concept of 'childhood'
and how do we know? If they lacked the concept, how did they deal with the
flesh and blood reality of 'children?' How were children brought into the world
and 'safeguarded' sufficiently well to reach adulthood, to use the UN's term, if
there was no 'discursive' construction of childhood as a period of life needing
special protection?

Or perhaps they were not safeguarded. Historical evidence, drawn from parish and other official registers, and also from gravestones like the one illustrated
in Figure 2.2, suggests that child mortality rates in the past were very high.
According to the *Encyclopedia of Children and Childhood in History and
Society* (2009), 'it seems probable that through much of human history 30 to
40 percent of all infants born died before they could celebrate their first birthdays'. Most of these deaths would be preventable now, (although in some
poorer countries of the world, high infant and child death rates – inexcusably,
given modern knowledge – continue.) But there is also evidence of deliberate
infanticide, child abandonment, child labour and child slavery, which could
suggest that people in earlier periods of history did not care much about children at all. Neil Postman in *The Disappearance of Childhood* (1994) states that
the ancient Greeks, while valuing education, did not have special words for
children. Infanticide was permitted in their society, and children were not represented artistically. In 374 AD, Postman notes, there was the first law against
infanticide in Western Europe.

Figure 2.1 The UN Convention on the Rights of the Child poster (in child-friendly language!) © UNICEF Canada

Figure 2.2 Children's gravestone, credit: www.burntcakes.com

The cultural construction of childhood: Philippe Aries

The scholar generally acknowledged with launching the history of childhood as a major area of research is the French demographic historian, Philippe Aries, whose *La Vie Familiale sous l'Ancien Regime* ('Family Life under the Old Regime', translated into English as *Centuries of Childhood*), was first published in 1962. Aries declared that before the seventeenth century: 'Nobody thought as we ordinarily think today that every child already contained a man's personality' ([1962] 1996: 37). In his introduction to the 1996 reprinting of *Centuries of Childhood*, psychotherapist Adam Phillips states that 'it was the virtual revelation of Aries' book that childhood had been . . .

invented. Before the 17th century people had been children, but before the 17th century there was no such thing as childhood' ([1962] 1996: 5).

How is it possible for twentieth-century historians to know what childhood was like in the past? This is where cultural artefacts – 'media' – come into play. Aries drew much of his evidence for his view that the past had no concept of childhood from European paintings. He asserted:

> Medieval art until about the 12th century did not know childhood and did not attempt to portray it. It is hard to believe that this neglect was due to incompetence or incapacity. It seems more probable that there was no place for childhood in the medieval world.
>
> (Aries [1962] 1996: 31)

However his book also incorporates research drawn from official documents, or at least such documents as there were. In *Centuries of Childhood*, he points out that concepts such as age, birthdate, name, parish registers, and so on are relatively recent in Europe. King Francois the first introduced the practice of recording births in France in the sixteenth century, but 'It was only in the 18th century [in France] that parish priests began keeping their registers with the exactness which a modern state requires of its registrars' (1996: 14). This was because, according to Aries:

> The personal importance of the idea of age must have grown in proportion as religious and civic reformers imposed it in documentary form, beginning with the more educated social strata, that is to say in the sixteenth century, those who had a college education.
>
> ([1962] 1996: 14)

There are obvious reasons why state authorities need to know how many people have been born, who they are and when they die, not least for the purposes of calling them up for military service. In England, the state's requirement to record important events in individuals' lives, as in France, began to be formalized in the sixteenth century, in the reign of Henry VIII. In 1538 the clergy of each parish were ordered to keep a book recording all baptisms, marriages and burials. In 1597 special registers were bought by each parish and annual returns had to be sent to a diocesan registrar. Later, it became clear that parish records were not an adequate way of keeping track of the whole population since many people, including non-conformists and Catholics, were not baptized in Church of England parishes. In 1837 at the beginning of Queen Victoria's reign, official registration by special state-employed registrars was introduced; everybody's births and deaths were officially recorded. (See the Home Office General Register office at [http://www.gro.gov.uk/gro/content].) This system continues.

Children in culture

According to Aries, children became worth talking, writing and painting about – in other words, they entered the culture (or at least the culture of pre-revolutionary France, and to some extent the rest of Europe) – in the seventeenth century. In this period, children became a new source of pleasure, and 'a new source of imagery'. They became, in a sense, the toys of adults. Aries describes how, in the seventeenth and eighteenth centuries, there was the gradual introduction of 'coddling' – caressing, even eroticization of the child. In the past, Aries argues, people often did not know how old they were, so 'age' was not considered to be a particularly important concept – and this contrasts with the very precise ages at which children in our culture are deemed to be able to do things. Nevertheless, even if they could not tell you their birthdays, people in the past could hardly have failed to notice that the life cycle involves systematic processes of observable change. In fact Aries acknowledges another print-based piece of evidence about the recognition of childhood and its special status which appeared in 1556: *Le Grand Proprietaire*.

Le Grand Proprietaire, 1556, adapted from Aries ([1962] 1996: 19):

1. Childhood, when the teeth are planted.
2. From seven onwards – 'pueritia', 'like the pupil in the eye' – goes up to 14.
3. Adolescence which ends in the twenty-first year, but may go up to 28 or even 35 – 'the person grows in this age to the size allotted to him by nature' – according to historical authorities.
4. Youth – a person in his greatest strength.
5. Senectitude or gravity.
6. Old age – up to 70.
7. 'Senies' – or senility, coughing, spitting and dirtying.

Le Grand Proprietaire is a developmental account of human life, based on observations of biological growth and ageing. Aries is not very complimentary about this: he says that nowadays we may think such 'jargon' is 'empty and verbose' – whereas in fact, it seems quite recognizable.

Evidence from painting

In addition to demographic registers, such as parish records and public documents Aries uses cultural evidence, especially painting, to illustrate how childhood has only comparatively recently come into existence. In the past, he claims that children were part of the adult world by the age of 7. They wore the same clothes, had the same pastimes, and were expected to work. He argues that: 'Medieval art until about the 12th century did not know childhood or did not attempt to portray it' (Aries 1996: 31). Children were represented as miniature men and women, not with their correct proportions. 'Childhood was a period of time which passed quickly and was just as quickly forgotten' (p. 32). In the thirteenth century, childhood enters the form of pictorial representation, in the form of Jesus with the Virgin Mary, as in the example in Figure 2.3 by Fra Filippo Lippi in the Palazzo Medici-Riccardi, Florence. These images proliferated throughout the next two hundred years, and included other holy childhoods, such as portraits of the young John the Baptist. There were also many representations of children in groups and crowds, and among adult scenes.

Figure 2.3 Madonna col bambino, Fra Filippo Lippi, Palazzo Medici Riccardi, 15th century. Image thanks to Art RenewalCenter® www.artrenewal.org

Despite there being obvious sensibility and intimacy towards the child in the kind of tender images shown in the Lippi painting, Aries suggests that there was a *new* sensibility in the seventeenth century, which led to an increase in for instance, pet names for children, and a change in the way that children were represented in portraits – on their own, or as the centre of other groups.

A key ingredient of childhood's increasing importance is an increasing recognition of women in the public and literary sphere. In 1671 Madame de Sevigné wrote: 'Our daughter is a dark-haired little beauty . . . she shrugs her shoulders, she dances, she strokes, she holds her chin . . . I watch her for hours on end' (quoted in Aries [1962] 1996: 47). Aries cites this as evidence of increasing public awareness of the charm of children, but shows little sympathy for de Sevigné's sentiments: he calls it 'a genre picture with the pretty affectation of late 17th century engravers . . . Countless mothers and nannies had already felt the same way. But not a single one had admitted that these feelings were worthy of being expressed in such an ambitious form' ([1962] 1996: 47).

The explanation for the failure of 'countless mothers and nannies' to express their affection for their children comes several chapters later on page 318 when Aries reminds us that 'schooling remained the monopoly of one sex'. Mme de Sevigné could write, and so she was able to leave us an account of her experience of motherhood. Most mothers and nannies could not write – and so they left no record. In most of Europe and North America this was the case at least until the end of the nineteenth century and is still the case in many parts of the world today. Hence the story of childhood – which tends to be the primary responsibility of women – does not get told by those closest to it. Children, too, were not in a position to tell their own story in forms which have survived in printed or pictorial records; however, many games, jokes, riddles and urban myths enjoyed by children down the ages *have* survived. There will be more about them in Chapter 7.

'Ba's, faunts and striplings' – medieval children: Nicholas Orme

Although Aries' most important idea – of 'childhood' as a cultural construct, rather than an immutable biological reality – continues to be influential, other historians since Aries have contested the view that earlier historical periods did not have a concept of 'childhood' similar to our own. Nicholas Orme, in his 2001 book *Medieval Children*, is troubled by the fact that Aries' views have entered 'popular thought': 'When I talk about medieval children to people who are not historians of the subject, their most frequent response is to ask if such children were regarded as small adults, or to assert that this was so' (2001: 3). Orme goes on to challenge this negative view of the past by citing a number of more recent historians who 'have gathered copious evidence to show that adults regarded childhood as a distinct phase or phases of life, that parents treated children like children . . . that they did so with care and sympathy and that children had cultural activities and possessions of their own' (p. 5). Drawing on evidence from published texts, songs and lullabies, he points out, for example, that 'special words applied to children included: baby, infant, faunt, damsel, stripling, youth, knave, lad, girl, wench' (p. 6).

Orme's lavishly illustrated book, like Aries', partly relies on paintings and other artworks to provide evidence for his arguments (see Bruegel's painting of children's play, Figure 2.4), but he also looks more widely at other sources of information about medieval childhood: tombstones; church registers; legal documents; books, including early printed books; and children's games and toys. He also provides evidence of 'baby talk' surviving in songs and rhymes – the kinds of sounds and babblings still used today. 'The practice may be be as old as homo sapiens', says Orme, 'and it was noted in the mid 13ᵗʰ century by Bartholomew in his encyclopedia' (p. 130). Song writers depicted the infant Jesus saying 'ba-bay' to his mother and her saying 'by by' to him in return. (Ba is a universal first sound made by babies today – and presumably in the middle ages too.)

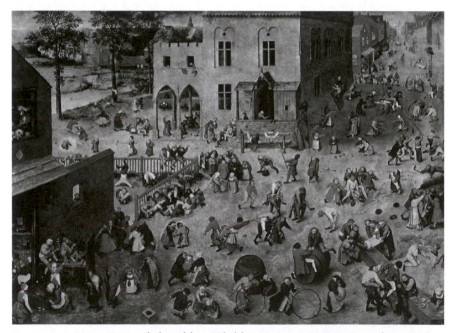

Figure 2.4 Pieter Bruegel the Elder, 'Children's games' 1560, Kunsthistorisches Museum, Vienna. Image thanks to Art RenewalCenter® www.artrenewal.org

The 'invention' of childhood by printing: Neil Postman

For Neil Postman, it was the invention of printing in the late fifteenth century in Europe (although the Chinese had developed it much earlier) and the resultant spread of literacy that 'invented' modern childhood. In *The Disappearance of Childhood* (1994) Postman argues that the spread of literacy through schooling and formal methods of teaching gave rise to our modern concept of a stage-related childhood. Learning to read, he argues, has to happen in stages, in 'grades' – and hence the process of acquiring literacy skills, and the grades through which children passed to reach full literacy, became literally classes or classrooms. Children were divided into different classes depending on the stage they had reached (usually related to age) and they could not leave the first grade until their skills were up to second grade standard.

The conception of the constructed child as deriving from print literacy is an example of discussing the capacities of the human mind in terms of communications technology. Printing for Postman consists entirely of the printed word – the widespread dissemination of images which printing also brought about seems not to have concerned him. To decipher the printed word requires linear thought – and it is linear, logical thought that is privileged in Postman's view of the young, developing human mind. Being able to process complex written arguments is seen as the highest function of the human intellect – and this process was brought about above all by the spread of literacy, in turn facilitated by printing. The other great advantage of print literacy, argues Postman, is that it made adult knowledge – especially 'shameful' knowledge, related to sexuality – inaccessible to those who could not read, that is, most young children. For Postman, 'shame' is an essential ingredient of the 'invention of childhood' and the necessary barrier between adult knowledge and childhood innocence, says Postman, was erected by literacy. In his book, he claims that this childhood innocence has been destroyed by the medium of television.

The problem of controlling the images of adult behaviour to which children are exposed now (in the 2000s) has far transcended anything that children might have seen on television, Postman's main target, in the 1960s to the 1990s, now that there is widespread dissemination of pornography and erotic material on the Internet. Many young children are still sufficiently 'childlike' to find this material objectionable and disturbing. Buckingham et al., in their literature review of academic research for the British Government's **Byron Review** on children and new technology (Byron 2008) state: 'the Internet has made it more likely that children will be exposed to pornographic or sexually explicit material . . . a sizeable minority do not like it and do not wish to see it' (2007: 35).

From a historical perspective, the key point to recognize is that protecting children from adult knowledge and behaviours, including sexual knowledge, is now generally accepted as desirable in our society, despite the fact that there is tension in the opposite direction from commercial trends towards the early sexualization of children, particularly young girls (see Holland 2004). The concept of childhood as a protected period of relative innocence is, says Postman, an invention of modernity, and modernity – including scientific, technological and social development – is a function of the ease with which knowledge could be disseminated, brought about by the invention of printing. He argues that this period of history has now been brought to an end by electronic media. These new media enable the young to have almost universal access to every kind of knowledge, both desirable and taboo. Hence the so-called 'disappearance of childhood.'

The Romantic child: Jean-Jacques Rousseau (1712–1778)

At the end of the eighteenth century, an idea of childhood as innately innocent and morally superior to adulthood began to be expressed in the cultural products of the Romantic literary and cultural movement. A key exponent of this view was the French writer Jean-Jacques Rousseau. In his classic work about the development of a child, *Emile*, published in 1762, Rousseau presented a portrait of the child as 'noble savage'. This was linked to contemporary ideas of primitive races as 'noble savages' too. Innocence was seen as better than experience and this view of unspoiled Nature, defiled by human progress, was a major tenet of late eighteenth-century and early nineteenth-century **Romanticism**, a reaction to the spread of industrialization and its ugliness, overcrowding and pollution. It is a view that to some extent survives in the environmental movement of today. In *Emile* Rousseau argued that the interventions of parents and teachers 'mar and distort the natural succession of the changes of childhood; the child that man raises is almost certain to be inferior to the child that nature raises'. Rousseau himself had his own children committed to a foundling hospital – so he never had to put this rather idealistic view of child rearing into practice: an example of the philosophy of child rearing being divorced from the actual practice of it.

The nineteenth century: the Child Study movement

A major change came in the nineteenth century when theories of child rearing began to derive from actual observation of children, and to be linked to the care and welfare of children. As child mortality declined, the psychological and developmental study of children emerged in the new academic disciplines of psychology and sociology (see Butterworth and Harris, 2003). As already discussed, people had always had a sense of how children grew and changed, based on observation, for example, the sixteenth-century Proprietaire, quoted by Aries, but in the nineteenth century there arose a medical/psychological model of childhood, based on systematic observation and treatment of actual children, for example Charles Darwin's *Biographical Sketch of an Infant*, published in 1877. This growth in the scientific study of childhood accompanied the rapid development of the natural sciences generally (physics, chemistry, biology) and the technological developments arising from industrialization in the West.

Despite acute poverty, unsanitary and disease-ridden living conditions, and abuse of children of every kind, including child prostitution and child labour, the nineteenth century was actually a time when the conditions of children began to improve in Western societies (see Horn 1999). Infant mortality fell, and children began to survive to adulthood in greater numbers. Industrialization and urbanization required greater organization and registration of families and individuals and the needs, conditions and problems of children were noticed and began to be addressed by social reformers and legislators, for example the Factory Acts in England in 1833 and 1844 raising the legal age below which children could not work to 8 and then to 10. Compulsory schooling accompanied these changes, with Education Acts in both Britain and the USA from the 1870s to the 1890s raising the school leaving age progressively to 10, 11 and 12. In both countries it is now 16–17. Medical discoveries, such as those of Louis Pasteur's identification of germs in France in the 1860s, contributed to a greater recognition of the importance of hygiene. The status of women improved and as it did so, so children's health and welfare became more publicly prominent and eventually the subject of legislation such as the 1911 National Insurance Act (see Lewis 1980).

The child's point of view in literature

In the middle of the nineteenth century, children and their needs and woes also began to appear prominently in popular adult fiction, with the child's perspective, often in the form of first-person narration, seen as privileged in comparison to the adults': examples are Charles Dickens' *Oliver Twist* (serialized 1837–1839) and *David Copperfield* (serialized 1849–1850); Charlotte Brontë's *Jane Eyre* (published 1847) and George Eliot's *The Mill on the Floss*, published in 1860. One of the great classic novels of American fiction, *Huckleberry Finn* by Mark Twain (1886), is told entirely in the colloquial voice of its vagabond boy narrator. And at the end of the nineteenth century, children's fiction as a separate literary genre, with children increasingly becoming cultural consumers in their own right, developed a momentum leading to what has sometimes been called a **Golden Age** of childhood. (See Chapter 8.)

The model of childhood emerging during the nineteenth century constructs childhood as a vulnerable, dependent state in need not only of physical protection, and occasional strict discipline (including physical punishment) but also (more importantly from a cultural point of view) of psychological understanding. The model has frequently been criticized as inadequate and too Western-oriented, for example by David Buckingham (1995). He argues:

> The discursive and institutional definition of children as a distinct social group is a comparatively recent development in Western industrialised societies. As numerous social historians have shown, the removal of children from the workforce and the imposition of compulsory schooling during the 19th century were fundamental pre-requisites of the modern construction of childhood as a discrete stage of human development with its own unique characteristics.
>
> (1995: 17)

But it is necessary to remember that these developments, as well as creating a perhaps restrictive 'discursive and institutional definition' of childhood, were primarily intended to improve the lot of children as a whole. The model was to a large extent created, and is still sustained, by childcare professionals, including the health professions – paediatricians, health visitors, psychologists – and educators – teachers, and educational psychologists, whose goals tend to be predominantly practical in terms of nurturing and teaching children, rather than simply conceptual. This is not to deny that specific ideologies of the 'right' and 'wrong' way to conceptualize childhood underlie these professional practices; only to point out that if childcare professionals (as distinct from academic commentators such as myself) do anything (or fail to do anything) that results in harm to children, they will be held to account. (See, for example, the case of Baby Peter, in the Times Online, at [http://www.timesonline.co.uk/tol/life_and_style/health/child_health/article6276211.ece], accessed 13 May 2009).

This medical/psychological model does now seem to be the dominant contemporary model of childhood; a conception of childhood as a period of life when children, defined as people from birth to 18 by the **UN Convention on the Rights of the Child**, need to be nurtured and protected from the full demands of adult breadwinning, sexual commitment, reproduction and parental responsibility. This is viewed by some commentators as a 'colonization' and professionalization of childhood and as such, not necessarily benevolent. Nevertheless, for parents, to live in a society where infant mortality is 8 per thousand or lower, as it is in most European countries, compared to the situation in the Victorian era when 25 per cent of all deaths in England and Wales were of infants under 1, must be preferable. Modern children may have less freedom to work and earn money, and they may grumble about being forced to go to school, but most of them live to grow up. Parents in developing countries where child death rates are over 100 per thousand would certainly welcome similar advantages.

Conclusion: studying 'children'

With the growth of the **Child Study movement** and the medical/psychological model of childhood, the historical focus of child studies becomes not on 'childhood' but on 'children.' It is within this protectionist model of childhood that the relationship of children with modern mass media has primarily been studied: children are seen as vulnerable and dependent, and mass media threaten them with various 'toxic', 'narcotic', corrupting and damaging influences, from which they need to be protected, or about which they need to be 'educated' and made 'literate'. The supposed danger to the young of new communications media is, in fact, a long-standing discourse with deep historical roots (see Chapter 5). In the next chapter we look more closely at some of the theories and practices involved in the scientific and social-scientific study of actual 'children', and how this impacts on our notions of children's relationships with media and culture.

Further reading

The classic work on the history of childhood is Philippe Aries, ([1962] 1996 translated R. Baldick) *Centuries of Childhood*, London: Pimlico. Nicholas Orme's (2001) *Medieval Childhood*, New Haven and London: Yale University Press, is a more sympathetic account of childhood and parenthood in the past, producing evidence to suggest that medieval families were not so different from our own. The classic dystopian view of media's impact on childhood is Neil Postman's (1994) *The Disappearance of Childhood*, New York: Allen and Unwin. For historical information about child development studies see Butterworth, G. and Harris, M. (2003) *Principles of Developmental Psychology*, Hove: Psychology Press. See also classic novels with child protagonists and/or narrators: *Jane Eyre*; *David Copperfield*; *Oliver Twist*; *The Mill on the Floss*; *Huckleberry Finn*; *Tom Sawyer*.

3 | THE SCIENCE OF CHILDHOOD

'Feed them and love them.'
(Richard Lansdown, paediatrician and psychologist, Great
Ormond Street Hospital for Sick Children, personal
communication/interview, 1984)

'Love 'em, feed 'em, keep 'em out of traffic.'
(Michael J. Fox, interview, *The Guardian*, 11 April, 2009)

As noted in the last chapter, a key distinction for the scientific/social scientific study of childhood is an emphasis on 'children' as potentially vulnerable, or, conversely, potential-filled, individuals, or groups of individuals. They may be characterized as patients, pupils or simply as young small people, but the scientific study of childhood emphasizes characteristics drawn from studies of many children, rather than conceptual ideas of 'childhood innocence' or 'humanity' and its 'nature'. 'Science' may seem objectively detached from value judgements about such qualities as 'innocence', but, like all human activities, it is part of culture, and as such is subject to historical shifts in priorities and in political agendas. What seem like stable scientific theories and ideas may also prove to be 'wrong', or at least incomplete, and hence in need of a 'paradigm shift'. (Still the most enlightening account of how scientific thought can change historically is Thomas Kuhn's *The Structure of Scientific Revolutions* 1996, first published in 1962.)

It helps for us to remember that science, regardless of historical and cultural shifts in its theories and agendas, is a *method*. Scientific inquiry is based on evidence; on systematic observation and standardized procedures collectively agreed on. It depends on the testing of hypotheses, to destruction if necessary, and on collaborative efforts by several people, before even provisional conclusions can be reached. Replication of findings is a key component of scientific procedure: only when you get the same result at least twice can you suggest that you might have discovered something. In social science, of course, when we are trying to 'measure' and 'test' human emotions, behaviour and intellectual capacity, such procedures can be more difficult to carry out in standardized ways, given the huge individual and social variations between human beings. Nevertheless, the early scientific and social scientific study of children was based on empirical observation, measurement and testing of thousands of actual children. These have provided useful baselines for us to understand children's development generally, and how even this, too, changes with circumstances – for example, with improved nutrition, average height increases and puberty may be earlier.

What best facilitates children's optimum development in all aspects of life is open to great variation of opinion and practice, as a quick search of the Internet or a magazine rack in a bookstore will reveal; theories of child rearing are big media business. They also have a long and varied history (see Hardyment [1983] 2008). Child-rearing practices are highly culturally determined, but certain priorities are common across cultures.

Food and love

The simplest and most succinct definition of the needs of children I have heard is the advice above, from Dr Richard Lansdown, whom I interviewed when writing a book for Great Ormond Street Hospital (Hilton and Messenger Davies 1990). I was intrigued to see the movie actor, Michael J. Fox, use almost the exact same words about his own three children in a 2009 newspaper interview. According to this view, the two basic necessities for healthy child development are enough food, and affectionate nurturing, Everything else is variable – child rearing practices can, and do, vary culturally, historically and over an individual's lifetime, but if the child is given enough food and love, by and large, argued Lansdown, culturally variable practices will all work equally well in rearing the child to adulthood, one way or another.

The reason he and his colleagues at the Hospital for Sick Children emphasized these two ingredients is because without them, children simply fail to grow – or to use the more technical term, they exhibit 'failure to thrive' and if food and love are denied for a sufficiently long time, these children will die.[1] For paediatricians and child psychologists at leading research and treatment hospitals like Great Ormond Street, physical growth is a major indicator of every kind of well-being (see Tanner 1990).

The contributions of culture

However, even such an apparently straightforward outcome as 'food and love' cannot easily be achieved. Most of the obstacles to achieving the healthy rearing of children are not medical, nor even personal (despite the crucial importance of parental care) – but political and cultural. No matter how loving the parents, children cannot thrive in the midst of famine, war or social breakdown. Hence, in discussing the subject of 'childhood', the disciplines of paediatric medicine (the physiological care of children), psychology (the emotional and intellectual development and welfare of children and their families), education (the teaching and training of children), sociology and anthropology (the study of social structures which affect children, including critiquing these other disciplines) – all intersect. As media scholars, we also need to bear in mind that much of this knowledge – from whatever scholarly tradition – is conveyed to most of us through the mass media. The book that Tessa Hilton and I wrote on behalf of Great Ormond Street Hospital is an example, as are the parenting magazines such as the one on which I began my career as a journalist writing about children, *Mother & Baby*. The raising of children is a matter of concern to everybody, but particularly to parents, and to children themselves. One central question to media scholars of childhood, therefore, needs to be how, and whether, the voices of those most intimately concerned with children and childhood can be represented effectively in the media.

Defining childhood scientifically

In a paper entitled 'Culture-nature and the construction of childhood' (2008: 24–5), sociologist Alan Prout gives a pared-down biological definition of childhood:

> [biological childhood is] an extended period of juvenility in humans, longer than that found even in other primates; [it] is a key feature of the evolution of the human species and is associated with other species characteristics such as the development of sophisticated linguistic communication and the use of tools . . . the human child uses an enormous proportion of metabolic effort on brain development, greater even than chimps and this continues rapidly after birth . . . a pattern involving very extended juvenility, the intense acquisition of skills and a prolonged period of

socialisation and developmental plasticity . . . this allows mothers to share care of young with other competent members of the social group, freeing them to give birth to other young.

This modern way of defining childhood draws heavily on the theory of evolution, explaining what we might see as cultural phenomena ('the acquisition of skills'; 'the care of the young') purely in terms of their biological evolutionary advantages. From an evolutionary point of view, human children do need an extended period of childhood – 'juvenility' – in order to grow and maximize their body and brain development, and this in turn requires 'a prolonged period of socialisation', in other words the intense involvement of other people.

Prout then goes on to outline the growth of the Child Study movement, which accelerated in the late nineteenth century, partly under the impetus of the new insights provided by evolutionary biology, and partly in tandem with other social developments for the welfare of children, such as the banning of child labour and the introduction of universal schooling (see Chapter 2). Charles Darwin, the founder of the theory of evolution, studied his own children scientifically, and published *The Biographical Sketch of an Infant* in 1877.

But Prout then introduces a divergence in the ways in which childhood has been studied, between those scholars who emphasize biology (which, in turn, has a direct bearing on the care and treatment of children) and those who continue the philosophical tradition of studying childhood more as a 'construct', with less direct practical bearing on childcare. This sets up the 'childhood as biological state' versus 'childhood as a cultural construct' antithesis, summed up by Neil Selwyn (2003: 353) as follows:

> [N]otions of the child are inherently political in nature. Childhood is of course a discursive invention of the past hundred years or so and the child has been used as a 'potent political metaphor' throughout post war society . . . the figure of the innocent child is central to almost all contemporary forms of politics.

Alan Prout quotes his and Allison James's influential book, *Constructing and Reconstructing Childhood* (James and Prout 1997) in setting out the sociological claim that 'childhood' is emphatically not the same as biological immaturity:

> Childhood is understood as social construction . . childhood as distinct from biological immaturity, is neither a natural nor universal feature of human groups but appears as a specific structural and cultural component of many societies.

(p. 29)

So we have on the one hand, a biological definition of childhood as a period of 'juvenility', requiring prolonged interventions of various kinds on the part of adult social institutions such as medicine and education. On the other hand, there is the view of childhood as a 'construct', with what Prout calls 'social and cultural ramifications', (p. 25), in which these adult interventions are critiqued from a political, cultural and ideological perspective, and quite often found wanting. This socio-cultural approach to the study of childhood looks at the ways in which, for example, the discipline of medicine does not just cure children's illnesses, but 'colonizes' childhood itself, and seeks to define it. The 'New Sociology of Childhood', as the work of Prout, James and their colleagues has come to be called, (see James and Prout 1997) also criticizes the discipline of academic psychology for trying to create 'norms' of social and cognitive development which can apply to all children everywhere. New Sociology's relativist notion of childhood occupies a similar paradigm to Philippe Aries' historically relativist approach, described in Chapter 2.

'Childhood' in this branch of academic study is not directly concerned with actual children, and in reading these diverse scholarly accounts, children's own voices are noticeably absent (as are those of their parents). Surprisingly, the 'new' sociologists also say very little about media and culture, as Prout himself acknowledges in his 2008 article (Prout 2008). Yet the interaction between the biological model of human childhood and its social context is entirely mediated through cultural means. Biological children are brought up culturally.

Nature and nurture

> [W]e cry as we enter the world, filling our lungs with air and announcing our coming as beings with selves and needs . . . our first attempts to talk are made with vowels, 'aah' and 'ooh'. Next we add consonants . . . later we double the syllables and vary them; at last, after ten or eleven months we produce our first real words in the language of those around us. We now speak English, French or Japanese.
>
> (Orme 2001: 130)

These are the words of Nicholas Orme, the historian discussed in Chapter 2. Orme goes on to say: 'All this [language development] is *natural* [my italics] and must have happened in medieval England in a manner and time frame similar to those of today' (2001:130).

In using the term 'natural' Orme brings into the topic of culture and media and children's relationship with them, a longstanding intellectual controversy: what is often described as 'the **nature/nurture**' argument. Are we born or are we made? Are our good and bad qualities and abilities innate, inherited, the product of our 'nature', and hence, not very easy to change? Or are they the product of 'nurture' – the way we are brought up, and the influences of the social structures of the society within which we find ourselves when we utter that first cry? If they are the former ('nature'), there is not much we can do about them. But if our qualities come from the latter ('nurture') then they are amenable to influence; it means we can be 'moulded' to fit different social and ideological ways of being.

Within this debate are deep political, religious and ideological divisions: we could argue that to take a pro-nature or 'nativist' position, makes you a conservative: there is a natural order (perhaps as a result of 'God's will') which humans are powerless, and probably unwise, to challenge. To take an 'environmentalist' or pro-nurture position, is to argue that no human faculty is immutable or the product of divine will: we have control over our environment and we can improve it, reform it and – sometimes – violently revolutionize it. Thanks to recent advances in the study of genetics, we can even modify what was once seen as immutable: our 'nature' – or genes. We can also destroy our environment – as we see from the evidence of global warming. This is the basis of modernity and modernist thought, arising from the scientific revolutions of the seventeenth and eighteenth centuries in Europe; this view believes in progress and the ever-increasing benefits of scientific discovery – including benefits to children.

Because children are the raw material of human activity and progress (or lack of it), the ways in which they are brought up have inevitably been central to political and ideological debates like these, as Neil Selwyn (2003) pointed out. But what *is* attributable to 'nature'? Physical examples would be a child's colouring or physique, or the workings of his or her digestive system, or the construction of the brain into right and left hemispheres with specialized areas for language, vision and handedness. Intelligence has been argued to be genetic, but intellectual performance is so closely correlated with social background and schooling, that there is plenty of evidence for the importance of 'nurture' too. Predispositions to certain diseases, such as sickle cell disease, are genetic. Personality appears to have genetic components and although gender (maleness and femaleness) can be 'culturally constructed', physical sexual characteristics – our genital organs – are formed genetically.

Conversely, we also need to know what is *not* attributable to 'nature' and which can be modified. Gender is a good example. We may not be able to change our sexual organs, except with a great deal of complex surgery – but we can behave in diverse ways along a continuum of 'masculinity' and 'femininity'. Women can join the army; men can look after babies. Both can dress up in clothes usually seen as appropriate for the other sex if they feel like it. Culturally, human beings are extremely malleable – but to be malleable, or to have 'plasticity' to use Prout's term, above – is also part of our 'nature'.

Theories of social and educational development

Children and childhood have long been the subject of discussion among society's intellectuals. As we discussed in the chapter on history, much of this discussion was divorced from the actual care of children (which was and is often undertaken by people who were illiterate, so could not write down their practices and advice), but philosophical and intellectual views on the development of the human race have also influenced the practical care of children in various ways. It is in this way that medical and social care is inevitably part of culture.

Philosophical beginnings

Plato 427–347 BC: In *The Republic*, the Greek philosopher set out a hierarchical view of human society so he could be described as more on the 'nature' than the nurture side of the debate. He argued that we have natural gifts that determine our pre-ordained place in society: intellectual (philosopher kings); auxiliaries (civil servants – the bourgeoisie); producers (craftsmen, tradesmen, etc.). Plato did not attribute much influence to environment, and he was writing within a society which, although 'democratic', still excluded women and slaves from these various pre-ordained social roles. Since children were likely to be cared for and taught by women and slaves, Plato's social hierarchy was only tangentially related to actual child care and welfare. However, he did have a view about the influence of stories – which he did not approve of. He argued that the influence of early stories became 'indelibly fixed' and hence young children should not be exposed to 'bad examples'.

John Locke (1632–1704): The seventeenth-century philosopher John Locke emphasized not natural gifts, but the environment. He coined the term 'tabula rasa' – blank slate – to describe the mental and social state of the new baby. Hence children become what we make of them; they are totally shaped by their environment. Many people have found the blank slate view – that children are what we make them – attractive. However, creative writers and mythmakers have produced many warnings that this is a view with drawbacks. The conflict between free will in human individuals, versus overweening power which seeks to remove this freedom, or agency, is a theme of some of the best children's stories, for example Philip Pullman's *His Dark Materials* and Gillian Cross's *Demon Headmaster* series and of course, the Harry Potter series. It is implied in any story in which children are the main protagonists (see Chapter 8).

The establishment of 'norms': the Child Study movement

In his chapter on culture-nature and the construction of childhood, Alan Prout outlines the development of what he calls 'panoptical' procedures for studying children, which began with the Child Study movement in the nineteenth century and gathered momentum in developed societies in the twentieth. Key developments included Arnold Gesell's work in the early years of the twentieth century at Yale University, making systematic observations of perceptual, motor and social behaviour of American infants, indicating 'norms'. This work was published as a best selling book, *The Child from Five to Ten* (Gesell et al. [1946] 1977). In 1905 came the Binet-Simon scale (1905), the first IQ test, aiming to be diagnostic and to identify learning difficulties. Test items were grouped by the age at which must children could complete them. Some sample items are given in Table 3.1.

'Panoptic' procedures, to use Prout's term, include medical developmental checks carried out by doctors and health visitors, and later, surveys of child-care practices carried out by researchers looking at education, economic circumstances and behaviour in large numbers of children, over extended periods of time.[2] Through these large scale collections of data from thousands of individual babies and children, 'norms' of growth and development could be built up and established, against which other individual children could be measured.[3] The growth charts shown here (see Figures 3.1 and 3.2) are examples of such norms; they show, too, the quite wide variations of height and weight contained within the 'normal'. Boys at age 2 can range between 81.3 cm (32 inches) and 91.4 cm (36 inches) in height and at age 20 between 1.65 m (65 inches or five feet five inches) and 1.9 m (75 inches or six feet three) in height. Girls start off at similar lengths as boys when they are 2, but by the time they reach 20, they are, on average, shorter than boys by several centimetres. Of all the measures that are taken of children's growth and development, normal physical growth is the single most reliable indicator of a child's well-being. This is what Richard Lansdown meant by the importance of 'enough to eat' and 'love'. Without these two things, children do not grow and eventually, they die.

These growth charts are also revealing in their graphic shape. They look like a very steep cliff – and thus they clearly indicate the vertical nature of the human 'developmental climb', from the minuscule starting point of the helpless newborn, to the fully-fledged socially and culturally functioning adult. They are a graphic illustration of the amount of work the human infant has to do to grow up.

The primary goal of developing clinical and **developmental norms** was (and is) to identify problems in children's growth and development; they can indicate children who are, for example, not putting on enough weight, and could be

Table 3.1 Sample items from the 1911 Binet Simon test

AGE	TASK
Three years	Shows nose, eyes and mouth.
	Repeats two digits.
	Describes objects in a picture.
	Gives family name.
	Repeats a sentence of six syllables.
Four years	Gives own sex.
	Names key, knife, and penny.
	Repeats three digits.
	Compares the length of two lines.
Five years	Compares two weights.
	Copies a square.
	Repeats a sentence of ten syllables.
	Counts four pennies.
Six years	Distinguishes between morning and afternoon.
	Defines objects in terms of their use.
	Copies a shape.
	Counts 13 pennies.
	Compares faces from the aesthetic point of view.
Seven years	Identifies right hand and left ear.
	Describes a picture.
	Follows precise directions.
	Names four colors.

Source: Alfred Binet and Théodore Simon, *A Method of Measuring the Development of the Intelligence of Young Children*, 1911 (translated by Clara H. Town, 1913).

malnourished, or – as is more likely in twenty-first-century Britain and North America – children who are putting on far too much weight and are clinically obese. Developmental checks on speech, hearing, movement, hand-eye coordination and social interactions can also help to identify problems in a child's growth and well-being. These checks are particularly helpful for babies who may have been born prematurely, or who have health problems or disabilities. The sooner a health problem in babyhood is identified, the more easily it can be treated. The later it is left, the harder correction becomes. This is why the early years of human life (broadly the first three to four, where the 'climb' in the growth charts is steepest) are so crucial and hence, subject to regular professional checkups. Prout calls this 'surveillance', with the implication that there is

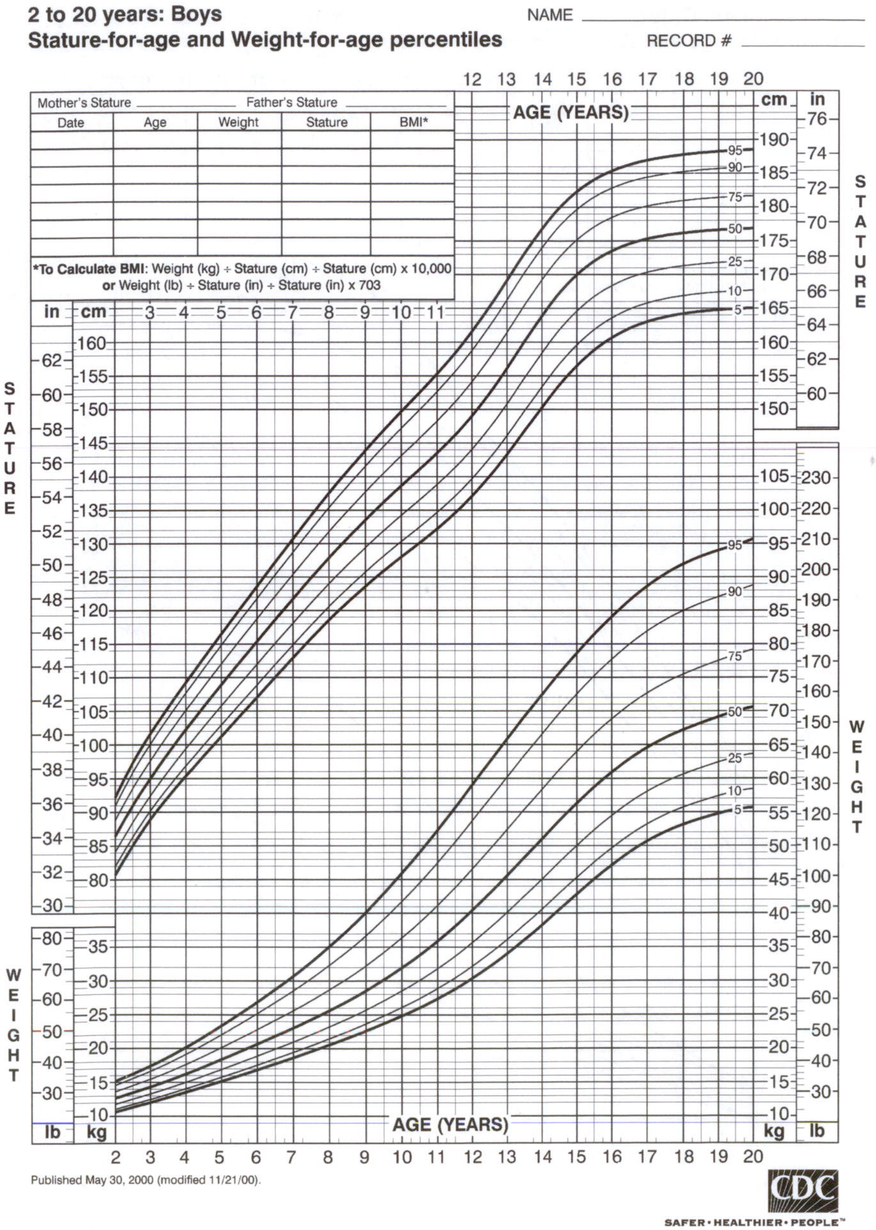
2 to 20 years: Boys
Stature-for-age and Weight-for-age percentiles
NAME
RECORD #
Mother's Stature
Father's Stature
Date
Age
Weight
Stature
BMI*
*To Calculate BMI: Weight (kg) ÷ Stature (cm) ÷ Stature (cm) x 10,000
or Weight (lb) ÷ Stature (in) ÷ Stature (in) x 703
AGE (YEARS)
STATURE
WEIGHT
in
cm
lb
kg
95
90
75
50
25
10
5
AGE (YEARS)
Published May 30, 2000 (modified 11/21/00).
CDC
SAFER • HEALTHIER • PEOPLE™

Figure 3.1 Growth chart from 2–20, boys, developed by the National Center for Health Statistics in collaboration with the National Center for Chronic Disease Prevention and Health Promotion (2000), http://www.cdc.gov/growthcharts

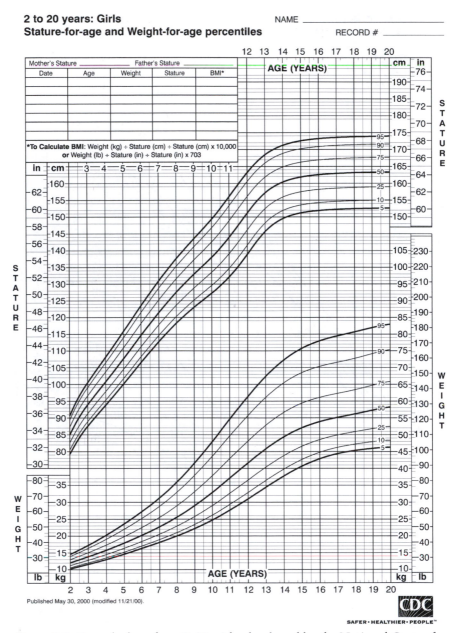

2 to 20 years: Girls
Stature-for-age and Weight-for-age percentiles

NAME _____

RECORD # _____

Published May 30, 2000 (modified 11/21/00).

Figure 3.2 Growth chart from 2–20, girls, developed by the National Center for Health Statistics in collaboration with the National Center for Chronic Disease Prevention and Health Promotion (2000), http://www.cdc.gov/growthcharts

something rather sinister about it: 'an enormous terrain for panoptical practices' (Prout 2008: 25). But early years developmental checks have saved many children's lives. Conducted sympathetically, these checks can also be very supportive for isolated and inexperienced young parents.

I have emphasized the importance of physical development because it is the foundation of everything else in childhood – whether social, emotional or cultural. It is also important for people studying, or working for and with children (which includes media producers) to understand the 'nature' of the people they are dealing with. Growth and physical change are so crucial, and size, height, weight and rate of growth are so bound up with children's own sense of themselves as they get older, that we should never forget the sheer extraordinariness of how rapidly, and in what complex ways, a human child *changes* as he or she grows. Children themselves are very aware of it. Dealing with being big or small, or weak or powerful, coping with startling transformations from beast to beauty and vice versa, are at the heart of many of the stories we tell to children – and in some cases, to ourselves as adults. This will be discussed in more detail in Chapter 7, on traditional stories and fairy tales.

Three key theorists of child development

As well as philosophers speculating on what human 'nature' might be, and later, medical practitioners and scientists creating panoptic 'norms' of what human children are observed to be and perhaps *ought* to be, other thinkers have produced theories of child development that are both philosophical and have had practical application. The following are three of the most important who have also been significant in studies of media and culture.

Sigmund Freud, 1856–1939

Freud is one of the most influential thinkers of the modern age. He was a doctor in Vienna who studied adult patients with emotional and psychological problems, and drew inferences from his work with them about the influence of their childhood experiences on their later neuroses. He did not work with, or observe, children directly, unlike his daughter, Anna Freud (1895–1982) and some of his later followers, such as Melanie Klein (1882–1960).

Freud stressed the importance of the biological, instinctive forces which drive us: the libido (sexuality); self-preservation (hunger, pain) and dominance (aggression). He called the storehouse for this instinctual energy 'the id' – and he argued that a baby is almost all 'id'; more recent studies with babies have suggested otherwise. As awareness of environment develops, argued Freud, the ego also develops; this is the 'executive part' of the personality. Then at around age 4 to 6 years, the superego develops, adding ideals, conscience and the demands of society. The conflict between the id and the demands imposed by the ego and superego can lead to neurotic problems, which are sometimes 'repressed' into Freud's most famous concept – the unconscious.

Freud used the technique of **psychoanalysis** (a one-to-one talking session with the patient) to access these early repressed experiences, in order to release the person from their neurotic conflicts. From this work he developed his theories, including a major one which does have some bearing on our constructs of 'childhood': the Oedipal theory. This theory suggests that the very young child is attracted to the parent of the opposite sex (Oedipus in Greek mythology killed his father and married his mother). As a result they can be murderously jealous of the parent of the same sex. They will therefore also be jealous of siblings who displace their privileged relationship with the loved parent.

Freud's theories have been profoundly influential, not just in psychology (indeed, more recent psychology has moved away from Freudian models of the personality), but also culturally and aesthetically. Freudian ideas have been important in film theory, for instance (see Richard Allen on 'Psychoanalytic film theory', 2003). As we will see later in discussing fairytales, Freud's ideas have also proved an explanatory tool for exploring the hidden symbols and motifs of these enduring stories. Freud's ideas are powerful and intellectually challenging – especially his concept of the 'unconscious' in helping to explain puzzling aspects of human behaviour. A major argument against his theories is that they are difficult to prove (or disprove, as a scientist would want to do). They also have nothing to do with 'normal' development, with the physical and social behaviours of babies as they generally grow, and as indicated by accumulated measurements from thousands of children over time. We cannot know what is 'normal' – that is, what is to be expected from any particular child or group of children as they grow up – only from studying adult psychiatric patients. This is where detailed observation of a full range of children needs to be undertaken.

Jean Piaget, 1896–1980

This kind of detailed observation was done (following in the footsteps of Darwin) by one of the most famous authorities on child development of the twentieth century, Jean Piaget. Piaget was a Swiss zoologist who became a cognitive psychologist and his theories, deriving from detailed observation of children, especially his own, have been very influential in education and in educational media. Piaget argued that children developed according to systematic cognitive stages; and for him, as an empirical former zoologist, cognition

Box 3.1: Piaget's four main stages of cognitive development

1. **Sensori motor stage: birth to around 2 years**
    The child learns about the world through physical and sensory experience, in terms of the activities he/she can perform
2. **Pre-operational stage: 2–7 years**
    Still learning through experience, not yet fully able to perform abstract logical thinking
3. **Concrete operational stage: 7–12 years**
    The child is able to think logically about 'concrete', immediate problems. Thought becomes 'reversible' and can return to its starting point.
4. **Formal operational stage: adolescence onwards**
    Thinking about abstract or hypothetical problems, for instance scientific reasoning, deducing from hypotheses.
    (Adapted from Butterworth and Harris, 2003: 19)

was not divorced from physical/animal behaviour. From Piaget, we have received the idea of 'readiness' – the view that children cannot acquire certain skills before they are mentally ready. He studied the *behaviour* of children, especially his own children, and made notes of what they could, and could not, do at different ages. He devised theories based on 'stage' development, starting with 'sensori motor' and ending with abstract, formal operations (see Box 3.1). Piaget wrote a series of highly influential works on child development, including *The Language and Thought of the Child* (1923); *The Construction of Reality in the Child* (1937) and *The Child's Conception of Number* (Piaget and Szeminska 1941). Later developmental scholars have challenged some of Piaget's theories about the stages of development. The idea that intellectual development is rigidly linked to age and biological stage is now seen as too simplistic a view; social and cultural experiences are seen as having a greater influence and there is an emphasis on 'nurture' rather than 'nature'. Usha Goswami (2008) in a review of current literature on children's intellectual development, describes contemporary thinking on this issue:

> [K]nowledge construction, language acquisition and memory, do not show marked functional differences with age. . . . Piaget's theory that children think and reason in qualitatively different ways at different ages is no longer accepted. . . . Gaining self-regulatory skills and reflective awareness of one's own cognition are major developmental achievements, and are still unfolding during adolescence.
>
> (Goswami 2008: 33)

Nevertheless, as Butterworth and Harris (2003) point out, Jean Piaget remains a toweringly influential figure in our thinking about how children learn and develop, and his ideas have influenced generations of educators, including those involved in producing educational and entertainment media. 'One measure of how much impact ideas have in science is how much new research they generate . . . there is no doubt that he has acted as a catalyst for some of the most exciting work in the field' (Butterworth and Harris 2003: 16).

Despite some criticism by the 'new sociologists' (see James and Prout [1997] 2005), Piaget's ideas about the stages of development and his sympathetic understanding of how to evaluate children's skills in imaginative ways, continue to provide useful rules of thumb in the nursery and on the ground. His pains-taking research is still a baseline against which other, more recent studies can be measured. It still influences producers of educational material for children, including media producers, for instance in recognizing the importance of the 'concrete' and the tactile, for very young children. Although we may lament the commercial exploitation of children when it comes to the myriad forms of merchandising associated with children's TV programming, these do have a positive aspect. Piaget's ideas and methods showed us how young children learn, not just by listening and watching, but also by interacting with *things*, and by exploring their physical environment. Concrete objects like toys help them to do this. Piaget has also provided useful models of expectation for media researchers, such as Grant Noble (1975) and the originators of *Sesame Street* (Gerald Lesser 1974).

John Bowlby, 1907–1990

Another important area of study in the twentieth century was concerned with **attachment** – how children learned to relate to and 'love' other people. Bowlby was a clinical psychologist who wrote a series of influential books, under the overall title of *Attachment and Loss*, based on research he had conducted with children uprooted and separated from their families after the Second World War. Many of these were delinquent and had ended up in penal institutions. Bowlby found that what he called 'affectionless individuals' lacked 'mothering' – that is, consistent, affectionate care in their early years. Like many other researchers on early childhood, particularly those concerned with preventing stress and distress in children, Bowlby emphasized the psychological import-ance of consistent affectionate bonding with significant carers. These were usually, but not inevitably, mothers. His research has been widely misinter-preted in the media, and elsewhere, as implying that all mothers should spend all day with their babies and children and should never go out to work – or even out with their partners in the evening. This misinterpretation is to diminish the key importance of Bowlby's insights into young children's psychological makeup – insights which Freud had only speculated upon in his work with neurotic adult patients. Bowlby argued that children are innately capable of producing behaviours which elicit attachment from parents. This is necessary for survival – a combination of evolutionary and psychological theory. Usha Guswami (2008: 42), summarized and expanded on Bowlby's ideas, emphasizing the importance of the 'self-concept' as an outcome of parenting. Like Bowlby, she stresses the importance of attachment for future well-being. Children with secure attachments 'do better at school, and are at lower risk for later mental health problems' (p. 42).

Early years

Freud, Piaget and Bowlby, as with many other child psychologists, all emphasized the importance of early years; the foundation of healthy physical, psychological and emotional development is laid in the first few years of life. If things go wrong then, there could be problems later – though the origins of these problems may be lost to conscious memory, as Freud argues.

From the point of view of media and culture, whatever school of thought you espouse when it comes to studying the development of young children, it is obvious that humans in their early years are highly malleable; they can be profoundly influenced physiologically, neurologically and psychologically by the way they are treated, and they are extraordinarily rapid learners. Hence the concern about the bombardment of media information that they are now continually exposed to almost from the day they are born.

The Center on Media and Child Health at Harvard Medical School in the United States has been set up to examine these influences from a health and development perspective. Their database of research on media effects and child health is at [www.cmch.tv]. An example of their research looked at the effects of food marketing on children's preferences, with a view to raising public awareness of the damaging influences of 'junk food' advertising on TV (Chernin 2008); American children aged between 5 and 11 were shown cereal and soft drink commercials embedded in programme material, and it was found later that the children were significantly more likely to say that they preferred the specific advertised products, compared with other products. This is a very typical experimental design for studying the effects of media on children in the tradition of **psychological/medical** research.

Evolutionary psychology and language: Barrett, Dunbar and Lycett (2002)

Research into child development has come full circle, with the relatively recent discipline of evolutionary psychology. The theory of evolution, first articulated by Charles Darwin in *The Origin of Species* in 1859, has been applied to explain the variations we find in human beings, particularly in the way they grow and develop, and the ways in which culture plays a part in this. Barrett et al. (2002) sum this up as follows:

1. All individuals show variation in their behaviour and physical traits – their 'phenotype'.
2. Part of this variation between individuals is 'heritable' and will be passed on to offspring.
3. Because of competition between different organisms for food, mates, housing and so on, some variants allow individuals to compete more effectively.

Hence, successful individuals have a better chance of reproducing, produce more offspring, and thus these successful traits are handed on.

Barrett et al. (2002) emphasize that this is not necessarily a *genetic* process. The theory of evolution is just as much about behavioural (cultural) adaptations, as about genetic variation. Humans are successful because they have learned to adapt their environments to help them eat, stay warm, stay sheltered, be comfortable, and to learn and to hand on their learning. Above all, human beings have evolved to use language – symbolic communication.

The importance of language

Language – the use of specific meaningful sounds (words), in rule-governed combinations (sentences) – is what enables us to teach our children effectively how to cope with their environment; it bypasses the long drawn-out necessity of them having to achieve effective survival tactics solely via reproductive success, which would take generations. Language enables media and culture – 'the solutions to the problems of living'. Barrett et al. (2002: 322–3) argue:

> Language may be the single most important feature that distinguishes humans from other animals . . . making it possible for one individual to influence how another sees the world . . . The speed with which children acquire language points to a highly-organised faculty. Between the ages of 18 months and six years children acquire a vocabulary of around 15,000 words, which represents one new word for every 90 minutes of their

waking day. By the age of six years they are more or less fully competent in the grammar of their particular language community.

Like the historian Nicholas Orme, these evolutionary psychologists stress that the culture of childhood – specifically the ways in which children begin to communicate – is rooted in the species-specific function of language.

Language is the foundation of all communication systems and as such, of interest and concern to those studying communications media. The developmental chart in Box 3.2 shows the broad stages at which human children acquire language and these stages are generally true for all children everywhere, and, as Orme points out, were probably true throughout known human history.

Box 3.2: Key stages in speech and language development

0–2 months, discomfort cries: 'Waa'

2–4 months, pleasure sounds: 'Ooh'

4–9 months, babbling: 'baba, gaga, didi' (these are universal in all languages)

9–12 months, vocalizations with meaning: 'da-dog' (linguistic differentiation begins, English babies say 'dog', French ones say 'chien')

12–15 months, first single words: 'daddy; doggie'

18–30 months, word phrases: 'biscuit gone'

$2\frac{1}{2}$–4 years, developing syntax (rule-governed 'mistakes'): 'I hitted the dog'; 'I seed some mouses'

4–6 years, adult syntax: 'This dog's feeling a bit sick because he ate a whole packet of biscuits this morning' (2009: 72) (Understanding of cause and effect, past and present tenses, use of adjectives – 'whole', anaphoric reference – 'this'; adverbial phrases – 'a bit sick')

(Adapted from Sheridan [1973] 2009; see also Messenger Davies et al. 1987)

Nature or nurture?: Chomsky and Skinner

The fact that language develops so early in humans, (it's nearly all there by the fourth year of life) and in similar stages for everyone, suggests that it is 'natural' – something which is innate and genetic. And to the extent that all humans, even deaf ones, manage to develop it (in their case through signing) without formal teaching, it clearly is 'species-specific' – something we've evolved biologically to do by ourselves.

But the problem with seeing it as entirely genetic is obvious: languages differ; dialects and accents differ. We don't just inherit our language skills; we *learn* from the people around us to speak the way that they speak. A child's environment does have an effect on language acquisition. There is evidence that children who are not spoken to very much suffer delay in language development, and have more limited vocabularies than children in more verbally-rich homes (see Bernstein [1971] 2003.). This is sometimes related to social class – but is not invariably so. And even these children don't lack language altogether; they still follow the basic developmental steps listed above.

Language may be a universal human trait, but it is also something that divides us. The world currently has over 6000 different languages, and most of us cannot understand most of the rest of us; many of us can only speak our own language, although Sheridan ([1973] 2008) argues that 'on a world scale, monolingualism is unusual' ([1973] 2008: 73). All this looks like evidence that language derives primarily from 'nurture' rather than nature. In the middle of the twentieth century, there was a fierce debate within psychology and linguistics about how living creatures, including human beings, learned. **Behaviourism** – the view that people learn primarily in response to external stimulus, to positive or negative 'reinforcement' – was a dominant view in psychology. Behaviourism was 'nurture' carried to extremes; intrinsic capacities for learning were not acknowledged, only the way in which people behaved in response to environmental experiences.

The fact that very small children learn language within a few short months was a problem for behaviourist theory; one of the most eloquent rebuttals of the behaviourist view was given by Noam Chomsky, whose own theories on language acquisition (themselves also much debated) inclined more to 'nature' – the existence of innate ability (he proposed an internal 'Language Acquisition Device' in the brain). Students interested in language should acquaint themselves with Chomsky's classic article, which sets out the issues most clearly: his Review of B.F. Skinner's *Verbal Behavior* originally published in the journal *Language* in 1959, available online at [http://www.chomsky.info/articles/1967----.htm].

Chomsky argued:

It is simply not true that children can learn language only through 'meticulous care' on the part of adults who shape their verbal repertoire through careful differential reinforcement, though it may be that such care is often the custom in academic families. It is a common observation that a young child of immigrant parents may learn a second language in the streets, from other children, with amazing rapidity, and that his speech may be completely fluent and correct to the last allophone, while the subtleties that become second nature to the child may elude his parents despite high motivation and continued practice. A child may pick up a large part of his vocabulary and 'feel' for sentence structure from television, from reading, from listening to adults, etc.

(1959: 31)

Conclusions: language and the foundation of media codes

Languages are not just a means of interpersonal communication (although this is one of their most valuable functions); they are also cultural systems. Languages don't remain static; they change as a result of social and cultural practices whose origins are still quite mysterious, for example the 'great vowel shift' in medieval England. In every language, new words are constantly coined, old words are dropped; grammatical constructions become modified. What was once seen as a mistake becomes accepted as normal usage; for instance, 'Media' as a singular noun is now accepted in quite up-market publications.

The study of language is an important area of study in its own right, not just so that we can understand children better, but also so that we can understand human thought and cognition – what Chomsky called 'speculation as to the higher mental processes' (1959: 42). Linguistic capacity – the ability to make sense of symbols and to create new ones – underlies all human creative activity, including the production and the understanding of all kinds of media. Art, film, TV, advertising, all have their own codes, conventions, vocabularies and grammars which children have to learn as they are exposed to them. This is a significant area of study for media scholars, which we will hear more about in Chapter 5.

Further reading

For good historical summaries of important theories of child development, see Butterworth, G. and Harris, M. ([1994] 2003) *Principles of Developmental Psychology*, Hove: Psychology Press.

Noam Chomsky's (1959) review of B.F. Skinner's *Verbal Behavior*, in *Language*, 35(1): 26–58, is a classic piece of academic criticism worth reading for its intellectual clarity and as an example of how to do academic criticism.

Allison James and Allan Prout's (1997, e-book, 2005) *Constructing and Reconstructing Childhood*, London: Falmer Press, is one of the founding texts of the 'New Sociology of Childhood'.

THE POLITICS OF CHILDREN AND MEDIA

The last chapter discussed some of the ways in which the development and welfare of children have been studied, defined and (for industrialized countries) improved over time. To a great extent, the improvements in children's welfare are due to nineteenth- and twentieth-century improvements in scientific knowledge, but they are also a cultural achievement, brought about by the educational dissemination and the political *applications* of this knowledge. Both the status of this scientific knowledge and the ways in which it has been applied have been contested by scholars: for instance, some have questioned the 'colonization' of childhood by medical and psychological 'norms' based on Western criteria, rather than taking a more global and culturally variable view of childhood (see Chapter 3). Children's well-being is always a political issue and in this chapter we look at the ways in which children's relationship with media and culture intersects with political action: in other words, we look at aspects of this relationship which have found their way into public campaigns, official reports, legislation and professional agendas such as schools curricula.

The global perspective

But first, to get away from the Western bias: what is the global situation as far as children's welfare is concerned? In a 2008 report on the state of the world's children, The United Nations Children's Fund (UNICEF) pointed out: 'Child mortality is a sensitive indicator of a country's development . . . Investing in the health of children and their mothers is not only a human rights imperative, it is a sound economic decision and one of the surest ways for a country to set its

Figure 4.1 Cover of UNICEF's report, 'The state of the world's children', 2008
© UNICEF

course towards a better future' (2008: vi). The report points out that in 2006
9.7 million children died (from preventable causes) before their fifth birthdays,
most in the early weeks of life, and these deaths were primarily in the poorer
countries of the world. It states:

> [T]he causes of and solutions to child deaths are well known. Simple reliable and affordable interventions with the potential to save the lives of millions of children are readily available. The challenge is to ensure that these remedies . . . reach the millions of children and families who so far, have been passed by.
>
> (UNICEF 2008: vi)

The question is: why don't they?

This book is not about the politics and economics of child and family health – but primarily about children's relationship with media and culture. However, the broader context within which children live – and the context within which the rest of us *learn* about children's lives, including the shocking global disparities which lead to so many preventable deaths, are constantly inflected by, and reported through, media representations. Organizations like UNICEF know the importance of media publicity in circulating their reports (and this one was widely reported).

A further heavily-mediated UNICEF report appeared in February 2007, (*Report Card 7, Child Poverty in Perspective: An Overview of Child Well-being in Rich Countries*). This time it addressed the well-being of children and young people in 21 industrialized – that is, prosperous – countries. It received widespread media coverage and led, again, to concerns about what 'we' are doing to 'our' young people. The chair of the UK Children's Society (who themselves produced yet another pessimistic report entitled 'Good Childhood', at the beginning of 2009) was quoted as saying: 'We simply cannot ignore these shocking findings. UNICEF's report is a wake-up call to the fact that, despite being a rich country, the UK is failing children and young people in a number of crucial ways' (Bob Reitemeier, The Children's Society's chief executive, UNICEF news release, 14 February 2007). North European countries dominated the top half of the table, with child well-being at its highest in the Netherlands, Sweden, Denmark and Finland. The UK's youth were particularly liable to risk-taking behaviour with far more UK young people than in any other countries reporting being drunk, being involved in violence and having under-age sex, leading to high levels of teenage pregnancy.

Interestingly, despite successive **moral panics** about the harmful effects of media over the years, and the view that contemporary mass media are responsible for 'the disappearance of childhood', media do not make an appearance in any of these major evaluations of the state and well-being of the world's children. Media access, or representation, is not a component of the six indicators of well-being specified in the UNICEF 2007 report which are:

- material well-being
- health and safety

- education
- peer and family relationships
- behaviours and risks, and
- young people's own subjective sense of their own well-being.

Nor do the media appear in the 40 sub-sectors of these six categories. Nevertheless, the politics of children and media continue to include media aspects in public discourse.

'Toxic childhood'

In 2006 an ex-teacher and writer, Sue Palmer, hit the headlines with a book called *Toxic Childhood*. She was in no doubt as to the cause of some of these disturbing statistics about the state of young people in wealthy countries: it is a 'clash between our technology driven culture and our biological heritage [which] is now damaging children's ability to think, learn and behave' (2006: 3). Palmer's targets were several; they included junk food diets; over-stretched parents with not enough time for their children (also blamed in the Children's Society 'Good Childhood' report of 2009) and particularly, the screen-based culture of television and computers, which has now invaded a majority of children's bedrooms, leaving them 'cocooned in a virtual world'. But, she warns, 'in a pack animal like homo sapiens, the long term risks of widespread social isolation are as yet unknown' (p. 259). Nevertheless they are assumed to be very unpleasant.

A number of well-known public figures joined Palmer in writing to the *Daily Telegraph* in September 2006, deploring the 'toxicity' of contemporary childhood. And In February 2009, one of these experts, Baroness Susan Greenfield, a distinguished neuro-scientist, told the British House of Lords that children's experiences on **social networking** sites 'are devoid of cohesive narrative and long-term significance. As a consequence, the mid-21st century mind might almost be infantilised, characterised by short attention spans, sensationalism, inability to empathise and a shaky sense of identity.'[1] From the fact that this announcement was made to the House of Lords, the upper house of the British Parliament, we can see that children's relationship with media *does* have a political dimension which is not always recognized in scholarship on the politics and economics of the media.[2] Yet, in the long history of the tussle between the media and state and religious authorities – whether in terms of freedom of speech, of the 'protection' of citizens from 'unsuitable' material, of 'bias', of 'stereotyping', or in terms of the pragmatic questions of licensing, technological innovation, distribution, marketing and advertising – the needs and vulnerabilities of children have been in the forefront of every kind of public and media discourse (see Starker 1989; Postman 1994; Gauntlett 1995; Barker and Petley 1997; Springhall 1998; Buckingham 2000; Messenger Davies 2001; Winn 2002; Comstock and Scharrer 2007; the archive of publications at the Center on Media and Child Health, Boston [www.cmch.tv]).

Recent scholarship on the sociology of childhood draws attention to the potential, but neglected, role of children as citizens. Allison James and Adrian James (2005) comment: 'though as minors children may not have any political rights, as people they are not spared from the effects of political acts that adults perpetrate' (2005: 3). Aldridge and Cross (2008) stress the role of the media in defining and constructing contemporary images of childhood:

> [J]ournalists and news media have a responsibility towards children and young people that has yet to be realised in news reporting on childhood and youth issues which currently sees an emphasis on 'yobbishness' and anti-social behaviour. This responsibility extends to allowing children and young people much more agency in media discourses as well as acknowledging their rights.
>
> (2008: 215)

These comments illustrate the 'double bind' in which children and young people find themselves with regard to their relationship with the media. On the one hand, they are beneficiaries of the twentieth-century discourse of 'rights' (see Chapter 2) and are expected to learn to act responsibly and increasingly to participate in the media as young 'citizen journalists' (see Mendes et al. 2009). On the other hand, their occasional anti-social behaviour (or conversely their status as victims of shocking abuse) make them threats to the social order – and as such, good journalistic copy. The most common plea from children themselves, interviewed in our research into children's relationship with news since the early 2000s, is summed up by this 12-year-old girl interviewed in Glasgow in 2003: 'Children are shown as a responsibility in adult news . . . something which commits teenage crimes and eats unhealthily. THIS IS NOT RIGHT' (Carter and Messenger Davies 2005).

Public and academic policy debate about the role of media in children's lives thus tends to fall into two categories: on the one hand, the protective discourse of keeping them safe: the nineteenth-century **Child Rescue** philosophy has now come to be applied to the 'toxic' cultures of the screen in the twentieth and twenty-first centuries. On the other hand, there is an alternative policy discourse around the relationship of children and media concerning 'empowerment': enabling children to exercise their *rights* when it comes to participation in their culture (see Wells 2008).

The UN Convention on The Rights of the Child has a number of Articles specifically relating to the media. Article 12 provides for the 'right of the child to express an opinion and to have that opinion taken into account, in any matter or procedure affecting the child.' Article 17 stresses the importance of 'protection' in the State's responsibility towards children and outlines: 'the role of the media in disseminating information to children that is consistent with moral well-being and knowledge and understanding among peoples and respects the child's cultural background.' Article 13 provides for the child's right to freedom of expression and information: 'to seek, receive and impart information and ideas of all kinds, regardless of frontiers, either orally, in writing or in print, in the form of art, or through any other media of the child's choice'.

The World Summits on children and media

Building on these internationally-accepted (if not necessarily put into practice) rights, a number of movements have sprung up to advance them. Prominent among these is the **World Summits on Children and Media** movement [http://www.wsmcf.com/].

The first World Summit in Melbourne, Australia in 1995, was attended by hundreds of media producers, activists, educators and academics from 71 countries; it was hosted by the Australian Children's Television Foundation, a non-profit organization to support children's media, and Telstra, the tele-communications company (see http://www.wsmcf.com/past_summits/pdf/finrep1.pdf). At this first summit, a charter was produced, asserting children's rights to their own media products.

The Children's Television Charter

The Children's Television Charter (see Box 4.1) remains the 'mission statement' of the movement, although the advent of 'new media' has meant that the summit organizers and speakers have had to broaden their remit. The charter has also been modified by different regions, for instance the African version of it at [http://www.nordicom.gu.se/clearinghouse.php?portal=linkdb&main=africacharter7.php&] includes radio, and emphasizes educational needs and protection from commercial exploitation. The original Charter is set out in Box 4.1.

Obviously different countries have different agendas and different broadcasting arrangements, and – as at any other kind of 'summit' – the charter points were only agreed after considerable argument and negotiation. Key issues common to all contributors – and even more applicable in the deregulated, digital media world of the 2000s – are the importance of *indigenous* production and audiences; the *accessibility* of material to all children, regardless of background; the promotion of 'high standards' (money and Government support);

Box 4.1: The Children's Television Charter

Drafted at the World Summit on Children and Television, Melbourne, March 1995

Approved at the PRIX JEUNESSE Round Table Munich, May 1995

Children should have programmes of high quality which are made specifically for them, and which do not exploit them. These programmes, in addition to entertaining, should allow children to develop physically, mentally and socially to their fullest potential.

Children should hear, see and express themselves, their culture, their languages and their life experiences, through television programmes which affirm their sense of self, community and place.

Children's programmes should promote an awareness and appreciation of other cultures in parallel with the child's own cultural background.

Children's programmes should be wide-ranging in genre and content, but should not include gratuitous scenes of violence and sex.

Children's programmes should be aired in regular slots at times when children are available to view, and/or distributed via other widely accessible media or technologies.

Sufficient funds must be made available to make these programmes to the highest possible standards.

Governments, production, distribution and funding organizations should recognize both the importance and vulnerability of indigenous children's television, and take steps to support and protect it.

(http://www.nordicom.gu.se/clearinghouse.php?portal=
linkdb&main=ctc4.php&)

---

and the core elements of public service – protection from 'gratuitous' violent and sexual material, combined with educational and 'self-affirming' content.

   Other summits have followed at three-yearly intervals in London (1998); Thessaloniki (2001); Rio (2004) and Johannesburg (2007), with regional 'summit' conferences being held in Africa, Asia and Canada in intervening years. The politics of this international 'movement' are mixed, with children's producers clearly having a specific professional agenda in order to support their own work and livelihoods. Educators are primarily concerned to promote children's intellectual and emotional well-being and to put pressure on producers to provide public service material, as well as being concerned with media education in schools. For academics the summits have been an opportunity to study the broader agendas of sociological, psychological and cultural constructions of children and the media in conjunction with direct contact with media producers, a useful reality check. For commercial sponsors these huge events offer effective advertising and public relations opportunities. These combinations of interests have led to some productive cross-fertilizations of ideas and have certainly placed the rights, needs and pleasures of children, their media and culture, into the international public domain. All of the Summits have generated considerable publicity and political attention in their host countries.

Children's summit in South Africa

The most recent World Summit was a huge event in Johannesburg in 2007, in which over a thousand adult delegates and over a thousand children from 88 countries participated (see [http://www.5wsmc.com/]). This was an exceptional event in its emphasis on children's agency; a parallel children's conference, including practical media workshops and performances, was held alongside the main conference events.

Figure 4.2 Children celebrating at the 5th World Summit on Children and Media, Johannesburg, South Africa, April, 2007

Photograph: Rowan Morrey, CMR

Figure 4.3 Young people from the Republic of Ireland, contributing to the conference entertainment at 5th World Summit on Children and Media, Johannesburg, South Africa, April 2007.

Photograph: Rowan Morrey, CMR

The World Summit series has its problems – both of organization and of varying ideologies – but it is certainly a truly global and inclusive cultural phenomenon with regard to children, of a kind which is unprecedented. I attended the Johannesburg event, and during the five days of the conference, could not do justice to the wealth and variety of cultural outputs on show there. The theme of the conference was an overtly political one: 'peace and democracy'. Alongside entertaining animations made by children, co-existing with a sophisticated film about cooperation and harmony from the Disney studio, presented by keynote speaker Roy Disney, there were more localized and politically-challenging presentations on child soldiers; victims of famine; girl victims of rape; poverty; conflict resolution; HIV/AIDS and drugs. Many panels included eloquent child speakers from developing countries – voices rarely heard at other large-scale media-related events.

Figure 4.4 Children addressing the Fifth World Summit on Children and Media, Johannesburg, 2007.

Photograph: Rowan Morrey, CMR
(See report and links at http://cmr.ulster.ac.uk/pdf/policy/publicserv.pdf)

Commercialism and the growth of the child consumer

Notwithstanding the language of entitlement and rights contained in the Charter, ('children should have . . .') the fact remains that television and other entertainment media are major global industries, operated by multi-media conglomerates in nearly all countries of the world, in order to make profits. Hence, the other international influence on children and the politics of the media is commercial globalization, with children's media products being significant global media commodities. Along with health and educational developments noted in earlier sections of this book, the nineteenth century also saw the rise of the child as a consumer, and as a stimulus to adult consumption. Daniel Thomas Cook traces the rise of the child consumer through an historical examination of the baby and child clothing industry and its location in special 'infant departments' within that other new nineteenth-century marketing phenomenon, the department store. In his book, *The Commodification of Childhood* (2004), he claims that 'Markets have not invaded childhood . . . They provide, rather, indispensable and unavoidable means by which class-specific, historically situated childhoods are made material and tangible' (2004: 144). In other words, the marketplace, including the media marketplace, is a key site for our contemporary constructions of childhood.

The market as socializer

In cultural terms, the marketplace is not just a useful mechanism for providing children and their families with essential commodities, and persuading them to buy less essential ones. According to Steven Kline the market is 'a growing force within the matrix of socialization' (1993: 13) His book, *Out of the Garden* (1993) is a primarily negative analysis of how the toy industry, working through television programming and advertising (in the USA) teaches children 'roles, attitudes and sentiments that reinforce consumer culture' (1993: 13). Kline deplores the linking of toys, books and other products for children as an aspect of vertical and horizontal integration of business operations and a corrupting influence on the young. In contrast, Marsha Kinder in *Playing with Power in Movies, Television and Video Games* (1991) points out how Saturday morning television in the USA with its 'transmedia intertextuality' among television, movies and toys, enhances a form of '**media literacy**' (a further policy agenda, of which more below). 'Even when young viewers do not recognize many of the specific [intertextual] allusions, they still gain an entrance into a system of reading narrative – a means of structuring characters, genres, voices and visual conventions into paradigms' (1991: 41).

   The pure negative view of commercialism presupposes that buying things which have been advertised on television is bad for children, but it can be difficult for parents and children to know what, in an industrialized society, is the alternative. Currently (2009), I am writing at a time when the world market as an economic system is on the verge of collapse, following the 2008 'credit crunch'. Both the USA and the UK have pumped billions of dollars into the banking sector to try to revive lending and liquidity but even so, companies continue to go out of business for lack of capital and householders continue to lose their homes as a result of 'toxic mortgages'. One solution to this is supposedly increased consumption. The so-called digital economy, based on 'new' communications technology, has been proposed as a solution to current economic problems (see Carter 2009) but this economy can only be effective if consumers accept the 'need' to go on acquiring 'new' media products.

The 'junk food' advertising ban

An issue that has brought the two political/ideological ways of constructing the child media consumer into direct conflict is the advertising of 'junk food' – or food which is 'HFSS' (high in fat, salt or sugar) as defined by the UK Food Standards Agency. The empowered child consumer ought to be able to 'choose' for him/herself which messages to heed, and which to ignore, including advertising promotions; but the vulnerable child who needs protection (the same child) is assumed to be susceptible to the persuasion of HFSS ads, and is more likely to spend pocket money on crisps, fizzy drinks, sweets and burgers, or to persuade parents to do so. Fuelling this concern (which is worldwide – see www.chinaview.cn, 9 May, reporting an Australian contributor to a conference on obesity in Amsterdam) is a coalition of health and other organizations particularly concerned about an epidemic of childhood obesity in the Westernized countries of the world.[3] This problem is in stark contrast to the children who die of preventable starvation and disease described in UNICEF's report above.

The **Ofcom** ban on 'junk food' advertising in Britain in 2006 most particularly affected ITV, the main commercial broadcaster, which lost around £39 million in annual advertising revenue. This loss of revenue led to a cancellation of its children's production – a reduction, instead of an improvement, in services to children.

The 'junk food ban' regulations require the following (from Ofcom 2007a):

> - Advertisements for HFSS products should not be shown in or around programmes specifically made for children . . . [and] dedicated children's channels.
> - Advertisements for HFSS products should not be shown in or around programmes of particular appeal to children.
> - The use of celebrities and licensed characters, promotional offers and nutritional and health claims in advertisements for HFSS products in advertisements targeted at primary school children is prevented.
> - All of the measures will apply equally to programme sponsorship.
> - Ofcom argued that: 'Taken as a whole, this package of restrictions would offer significant protection to children and will have a considerable impact on the amount of HFSS advertising they will see – providing a reduction of 51% for 4–9-year-olds and 41% for 4–15-year-olds.'

Saving kids' TV

One unfortunate, and unintended consequence of this loss of revenue to ITV has been a collapse in children's programme production in the UK, which viewers' campaigning groups such as the Voice of the Listener and Viewer see as culturally disastrous. This is a difficult argument to advance against the powerful health lobby, especially as TV, too, is seen by many commentators as 'junk', rather than as a valuable part of the nation's cultural heritage. **Save Kids TV**, a group of producers, writers and activists, whose aim is to preserve the traditions of public service broadcasting for children, as well as to save their own industry, used the UN's language of rights, in an appeal to the minister responsible for Children, Schools and Families:

> [T]he demise of quality indigenous media for kids . . . It's a failure of care . . . We are failing to engage them as citizens and failing to empower them as individuals if we distance their media from their experience . . . the £35 million required to support a public service alternative for kids was a small sum compared to the overall education budget – but the money for new programmes, widely disseminated and powerfully engaging, would be extremely well spent as an educational resource. It could do more to re-connect kids to the society in which they live than a hundred government schemes and initiatives.
>
> (2009: http://www.savekidstv.org.uk/)

Public service provision is politically important not least because it can provide spaces for children themselves to engage in public debates which concern them. The BBC *Newsround* website of November 2006 had some pertinent comments from children on the question of the junk food ban:

> I think that banning the adverts is stupid. It's not going to help either because the restaurants are still open so you can still get the food. It is pointless!
>
> Nicole, 13, Nairn

> It will make a huge difference. When I see an advert for chocolate I always want it!
>
> Florence, 14, London

> I don't eat junk food anyway, but it would be nice for other kids not to.
> Jonathan, 10, Market Harborough

> I love junk food and I never see any adverts in the streets. But TV adverts do make you feel hungry.
>
> Billy, 11, Yorkshire

These comments (representative of dozens of others) illustrate children's awareness of TV's potential to influence them, their 'media literacy' – but also, for some, its perceived irrelevance to their own personal tastes: 'I don't eat junk food anyway'; 'I love junk food and never see any adverts'. Their ease in claiming this space for their comments illustrates the extent to which many children now feel at home in the online world.

Cultural identity

The political ideology behind the drive to preserve indigenous television production for children is also linked to concepts of national identity, always somewhat contested. In the UK, with its four nations/regions, its considerable multicultural ethnicities and its attraction as a place for economic and political migrants and asylum seekers, indigenous media production is seen as safeguarding children's sense of cultural belonging, as well as being a vehicle for promoting multicultural information. A conference on media and national identity, Broadcasting Britishness, was held at the Said Business School, Oxford in June 2008, where there was some doubt among some conference speakers that media made any difference at all to a sense of national identity: 'it was not the media's role to do anything' said historian Linda Colley (quoted in Baldwin 2008: 8). Evidence presented by James Thickett from the regulator Ofcom suggested otherwise. In a survey of over a thousand people aged 16 and over, nearly 80 per cent of respondents believed that television has 'an important social role to play' and this included representing different cultural groups. More than two thirds (67 per cent) believed that 'television has an important role in helping children and teenagers to understand life in the UK'.

A study carried out by colleagues and myself as part of a BBC/AHRC Knowledge Exchange Programme, with over 200 children aged 8–15 in the four nations/regions of the UK (England, Scotland, Wales and Northern Ireland)[4], reinforced Thickett's point. All of the children demanded more information about their own nation/region in the news, and complained that neither their age group nor their locales were sufficiently represented in news coverage. These 'citizens in the making' saw one of the primary functions of news as reinforcing their sense of identity. These perceptions of differing identities and regional difference, argued the children in our study, needed to be reflected in the way in which news and current affairs were reported. These children certainly saw the media as having a political function, even if they would not have expressed it in those terms.

'As important as maths or science': media literacy

The promotion of what is called 'media literacy' (a term that can be defined and interpreted in many different ways) has become part of policy discourse in many countries (see Kubey 2001). So important is 'media literacy' seen to be that the British Telecommunications regulator, Ofcom, has been given a statutory responsibility under the 2003 Communications Act to promote it. The European Commission has also established a Media Literacy Expert Group, and UNESCO has launched a new policy statement on media literacy following a high-profile meeting in Paris in 2007.

According to David Buckingham et al. (2008: 59):

> Both in the UK and internationally, media literacy has become an increasingly significant dimension of cultural policy . . . This growing interest in media literacy reflects a new emphasis in regulatory policy . . . the focus here is on empowering consumers to make informed choices and judgments about media on their own behalf . . . Media literacy is generally conceived as a partnership between government, the media industries, teachers, parents and children themselves.

Buckingham et al. quote a former minister, Culture Secretary Tessa Jowell, arguing that 'media literacy is an essential component of contemporary citizenship, that will eventually become 'as important a skill as maths or science' (Jowell 2004, cited in Buckingham et al. 2008: 59).

Buckingham et al.'s report was an appendix to The Byron Review, a major survey of 'the risks and benefits' of new media technologies, carried out on behalf of the British Government by Professor Tanya Byron, a psychologist, in 2007–8. Her report *Safer Children in a Digital World* (2008), is itself a direct policy intervention, partly in response to media 'panics' about the dangers of the Internet, such as those reported in Sue Palmer's *Toxic Childhood* (2006). Byron's review concluded with a package of recommendations to protect children and to advise parents and teachers on their appropriate use (see Box 4.2).

What is media literacy?

Despite its centrality to media policy debates around the world, there are varying and sometimes conflicting definitions of 'media literacy.' A broadly accepted definition, as stated in Ofcom's 'Report on UK Children's Media Literacy' (2008) is: 'the ability to

- access,
- understand and

Box 4.2: The Byron Review recommendations

In order to improve children's digital safety, the Review recommended:

- The creation of a new UK Council for Child Internet Safety, established by and reporting to the Prime Minister, and including representation from across Government, industry, children's charities and other key stakeholders including children, young people and parents.
- Challenging industry to take greater responsibility in supporting families through establishing transparent and independently monitored codes of practice on areas such as user-generated content; improving access to parental control software and safe search features; and better regulation of online advertising.
- Developing a comprehensive public information and awareness campaign on child Internet safety across Government and industry, and which includes an authoritative 'one stop shop' on child Internet safety.
- Setting in place sustainable education and children's service initiatives to improve the skills of children and their parents around e-safety. This includes making sure schools and teachers have the necessary support to be e-safe.
- Specific measures to support vulnerable children and young people, such as taking down illegal Internet sites that promote harmful behaviour, such as suicide, self-harm and eating disorders, while at the same time providing the right space and support where at risk people can safely talk.

- create communications
- in a variety of contexts.'

Access includes take up of media devices, volume and breadth of use. This can vary according to age, socio-economic group and gender, with younger, richer people more likely to have Internet access and boys more likely than girls – a 'digital divide'.

Understand means interest and competence in using the features available on each platform, extent and levels of concern, trust in television and online content and use of television and Internet security controls.

Create includes people's confidence in engaging with creative content and their interest in carrying out creative tasks, most notably using social networking sites.

Buckingham et al. (2008) provide a further gloss to these definitions by arguing that media literacy is also about 'addressing basic inequalities in people's access to media – not only the so-called digital divide, . . . they are also about cultural capital, about the skills and understanding that people need in order to use and interpret what they see and hear, and to create their own communications' (2008: 59).

As can be seen from these definitions, the political, or policy-oriented, definitions of 'media literacy' almost entirely concern the ability of different groups in the population to manage various forms of media technology, which have *already* been introduced to the marketplace. In a free market system, these technologies, which have a potentially transforming effect not only on people's media use, but also on their daily lives and on their sense of themselves, can be introduced without any consultation of adults, and certainly not of children; an example is the switching off of the analogue signal and its replacement by digital transmission of broadcasting – already in place in the USA and due to take place in the UK in 2010. The market introduces new media technologies, consumers who can afford them buy them, and generally the policy agenda follows this process, rather than attempting to lead it.

Thus, one (perhaps the only) defence against the unrestricted introduction of new media technologies into children's lives, and their untested impact, is the official promotion of 'media literacy'. Ofcom have stated that media literacy is a form of consumer protection against the apparently inevitable encroachment of the market. In their document on 'Strategy and priorities for the promotion of media literacy' (2004), they argue that media literate citizens 'will be able to exercise informed choices about content and services . . . and be better able to protect themselves and their families from harmful or offensive materials' (Ofcom 2004: 3). Such an approach is described as '**inoculatory**' as it assumes that by alerting ('vaccinating') children to the risks, the persuasive techniques and the deceits of mass media, children will be protected from them.

Media education

Renee Hobbs, an experienced teacher and researcher on media education in the United States, has done a great deal to translate concepts of media literacy policy into classroom practice. She argues that new technology makes the study of communications media even more urgent now than it was in the days when everyone was agonizing over television: 'More and more educators have begun to recognize that despite their students' familiarity with the Internet and other technology, young people may or may not have skills necessary to access, analyse and evaluate the abundance of information and entertainment available online' (2008: 431).

Hobbs breaks down approaches to media literacy into four main categories: information/ICT literacy: media education literacy; political critical literacy; and media management.

1. **Information/ICT Literacy** centres on non-fiction texts and skills based on the effective use of information and communication using digital technology. Originally promoted primarily by librarians and the business community, ICT literacy seems to be turning into the major definition of literacy. For instance, ICT literacy requires the ability to organize and classify digital information; the ability to judge the authority and accuracy of digital information; and the ability to generate information in different formats – e.g. graphs, presentation slides, text messages.

2. **Media education literacy**, as used by those involved in media education in schools, is much more focused on critical and social evaluation of texts and is not confined to 'new media'. Media education, as Cary Bazalgette points out in her 1988 introduction to the topic, aims to teach about 'the processes through which texts – both public and private – reach people' (1988: 2). She uses the example of the text she is writing on a computer and its fate as a published document to illustrate what she means by 'text'.

3. **Critical/political literacy** is an extension of the educational branch of media literacy; the aim of this is to 'nurture a kind of cultural criticism that will enable young people to recognize and resist the political functions of popular culture which stimulate and manufacture desires' (2008: 436).

4. **Media management** is the kind of advice given in Sue Palmer's *Toxic Childhood* (2006) about limiting children's media time, not letting children under 2 watch TV, and keeping them away from junk food advertisements; this can have a powerful influence on policy as in the case of the UK's junk food ban (2008: 234).

New definitions of media literacy are being developed as a consequence of research done in the Comparative Media Studies programme at MIT in Cambridge. An example of its main components is given in Figure 4.5.

None of this has the force of policy recommendations in the form of media regulation and legislation, but to the extent that it informs public debate about education policy, these kinds of definitions enable specific educational goals to be set by teachers and educational administrators.

Media education in schools

Media education is rather different from 'media literacy' and has its own policy

The New Media Literacies

Participatory culture shifts the focus of literacy from one of individual expression to community involvement. The new literacies almost all involve social skills developed through collaboration and networking. These skills build on the foundation of traditional literacy research skills, technical skills, and critical analysis skills taught in the classroom.

The new skills include...

Play – the capacity to experiment with one's surroundings as a form of problem-solving

Performance – the ability to adopt alternative identities for the purpose of improvisation and discovery

Simulation – the ability to interpret and construct dynamic models of real-world processes

Appropriation – the ability to meaningfully sample and remix media content

Multitasking – the ability to scan one's environment and shift focus as needed to salient details

Distributed Cognition – the ability to interact meaningfully with tools that expand mental capabilities

Collective Intelligence – the ability to pool knowledge and compare notes with others toward a common goal

Judgment – the ability to evaluate the reliability and credibility of different information sources

Transmedia Navigation – the ability to follow the flow of stories and information across multiple modalities

Networking – the ability to search for, synthesize, and disseminate information

Negotiation – the ability to travel across diverse communities, discerning and respecting multiple perspectives, and grasping and following alternative norms

Negotiation – the ability to interpret and create data representations for the purposes of expressing ideas, finding patterns, and identifying trends

from *Confronting the Challenges of Participatory Culture: Media Education for the 21st Century*,

by Henry Jenkins, with Ravi Puroshotma, Katherine Clinton, Margaret Weigel, and Alice J. Robison

Supported by
MACARTHUR
cMs
MIT Massachusetts Institute of Technology

Figure 4.5 The New Media Literacies, from Massachussetts Institute of Technology (MIT) Comparative Media Studies program http://newmedialiteracies.org/

agenda concerned with influencing school curricula. In the USA, school curricula are decided at local level and may vary from district to district and state to state. In other countries, including the UK, the school curriculum is much more centralized with Government departments dictating what should be taught and at what stage. This can be extremely frustrating for teachers trying to keep up with rapid changes in educational and leisure technology.

Media education in schools certainly requires 'participation' in the New Media Literacies definition. But it also requires popular media of every kind to be analysed systematically in terms of their representations; their technologies; their languages, codes and conventions; and their audiences. Production students need also to be able to analyse critically what *other* people's media productions are doing. Campaigns to promote media education in school have been successful in English-speaking countries including Canada, Australia and New Zealand, as well as a number of countries in Europe and Latin America – and currently, with increasing vigour, the United States. In China, Bu Wei describes a growth in critical awareness of gender stereotyping in Chinese cultural policy which has led to proposals for gender awareness training for media professionals because 'children's culture in the mass media is highly gendered and boys and girls are portrayed as "naturally" and fundamentally different' (2008: 315) Here, media literacy and media education are more than 'protecting' consumers; they are forms of social education and consciousness-raising, which have obvious political implications, particularly in centralized and politically-repressive environments.

Appreciating media arts: 'cultural capital'

While media education in many of its manifestations has a socialization agenda and to some extent an inoculatory and protective one, there are still some voices arguing that the audio-visual media produce artefacts which are worth studying in their own right. In 1999 the Film Education Working Group of the BFI, introduced a report called *Making Movies Matter* (British Film Institute 1999) thus:

> In the 20th century, human society created a new language: the moving image ... children bring into school a vast if inchoate moving image experience .... film is more than an industry, more than a collection of commodities, more than a vehicle for stars and stories: it is a language [which should be] recognized in all its diversity and multifarious influences ... we want to celebrate the brilliance of our global moving image heritage.
>
> (British Film Institute 1999: 6–7)

Conclusions: children, media and public policy

Children's relationship with the media enters public policy at a variety of levels. Conceptually, there is the notion of the 'empowered' child as citizen in the making, who through media, whether as critical consumer or as creator, gains mastery of information about his/her society. In educational policy, 'literacy' is a word now applied almost as often to electronic media as it is to reading books and it figures prominently in public policy discussions about the importance of universal access to digital technology. Media education is a potentially important tool for children to navigate the changing media world. Media education may be celebratory; it may be critical and deconstructive; it will usually involve some form of media practice in order to teach both concepts and skills, which can be very enjoyable for children. But in every case, media education relies on access by both pupils and teachers to a wide range of media material, genres, texts and programme types in the public domain. It is these materials that have provoked most concern and antagonism in the public debates about children's relationship with the media, leading to the kinds of political discussions expressed in Parliament (see above) about the 'toxic' bedroom media culture of contemporary childhood. We turn to these debates in the next chapter.

Further reading

The Byron Review and its academic Annexes will become a classic of media policy; see Byron, T. (2008) *Safer Children in a Digital World*, Report to the Department of Children, Schools and Families, [http://www.dcsf.gov.uk/byronreview/]. For a model example of how to gather and interpret useful statistics by an official body, see Ofcom (2007b) 'The future of children's broadcasting in the UK' [www.ofcom.org]. An academic book which is still one of the most useful analyses of children's media and commercialism, despite its primarily American orientation, is Steven Kline's (1993) *Out of the Garden: TV and Children's Culture in the Age of Marketing*, London: Verso.

CHILDREN AND CHILDHOOD IN MEDIA STUDIES

Recently, the introduction of more and more media technologies to children's lives, gathering pace over the last half century, has speeded up exponentially. Sonia Livingstone and Kirsten Drotner (2008) claim that 'media permeate, even control children's lives to a degree that was unknown just a generation ago . . . debates are rife over the regulation of children's media fare for this is often more volatile and versatile than the more familiar print media' (2008: 1).

This chapter examines the tradition of studying children and childhood in terms of these 'rife' debates – children's relationship with modern mass media and its 'effects'. The studies in this tradition take two main forms. First, arising from the introduction of new media, come studies and surveys to establish the *extent* of children's use of 'new' media as they are introduced. These are then followed by further studies to pursue the 'impact' of these media.

The first group of studies asks:

- how many children
- of what kind
- are watching/listening/reading
- what kinds of media
- when
- where and
- instead of what.

Implicit in these surveys (occasionally supported by qualitative research inviting children's opinions) are assumptions about what children 'like'. If very large numbers of children are attracted to a media form, or product, it suggests that they 'like' it. If children abandon some form of media consumption, it is probably because they 'do not like' it. In this case, investment may dry up for that particular form and be transferred to the new form – this has been happening since the early 2000s with television and the Internet.

The second prolific area of study of children and the media concerns the controversial topic of 'effects' – or, what *difference* does watching TV, or listening to pop music, or playing computer games, or being exposed to violence, or educational information, or Internet advertising, make to children? The 'effects tradition' in media research has been hugely prolific, attracting large amounts of public funding and resulting in thousands of studies. (For summaries, see Comstock and Paik 1994; Bushman and Huesmann 2001).

This tradition and some of its methods and implications will be discussed in more detail below. It could not have developed without the first branch of study – that is, mapping consumption. It is when policy-makers, producers, scholars and other commentators realize just how much media children are being exposed to, that concerns about impact, harm, bad examples, and, very occasionally, good examples arise.

Who is consuming what, when, how much and instead of what?

The most obvious of the measurement-of-use studies carried out for the purpose of finding out how many people are consuming media products, are the commercial measurements taken of child audience behaviour by the media industries: for television, **BARB** (Broadcasters' Audience Research Board) in the UK; **Nielsen** in America; box office analyses of young people's cinema-going habits; circulation figures for print materials; website hits. These market figures are also a valuable resource for media scholars. Organizations such as the UK regulator Ofcom produce regular updates of such 'market' figures, for instance their major survey of children and young people's media use in the UK (2007). Classic academic examples of this kind of broad survey research are Schramm et al. (1961) in the USA; Himmelweit et al. (1958) in the UK; two European wide studies, one in the late 1990s, with results published in various forms in the early 2000s (Livingstone and Bovill 1999; Livingstone 2002), and a more recent study, EU Kids Online (Hasebrink et al. 2008); regular surveys in the USA by the Kaiser Family Foundation (e.g. 2003; 2005; Moore 2006). Academic studies, unlike market research, attempt to relate media usage to broader concerns of child development, learning, social impact and citizenship.

The child audience: baseline studies

The most comprehensive study of television and children ever made in the UK and still serving as a baseline and model for subsequent studies, was 'Television and the child: an empirical study of the effect of television on the young', carried out with over 1800 children nationwide, by a team of researchers at the London School of Economics, headed by Dr Hilde Himmelweit, and published in 1958. It was the first major study to survey how television affected the pre-existing interests, attitudes and behaviour of children. Soon afterwards, a similar massive survey of American children was carried out by Schramm et al. (1961) in the USA, which came up with rather similar conclusions.

Then, as now, the introduction of 'choice', an alternative source of media, in this case commercial television, prompted concerns about the 'impact' of this on the young. An update of the study, with a similarly large, representative sample, was carried out by a team at the LSE in the late 1990s (Livingstone and Bovill 1999; Livingstone 2002), assessing the impact of the latest 'wave' of media technology to break over the young – in this case, the multi-channel world of digital television and the Internet. This second study – which popularized the phrase 'bedroom culture' to describe children's media-filled bedrooms – is already being overtaken by very rapid changes in children's access to 'new media', such as the social networking phenomenon, and widespread access to mobile phones, which hardly featured in the late 1990s.

The earlier researchers in the 1950s were fortunate in being able to observe comparable groups of 10–15-year-old children; children who watched television (viewers) and a socially-similar sample of children who did not have access to TV (a control group). Such socially-matched control groups of children *without* access to a medium are not easy to find nowadays, as most households with young children are early adopters of new media (Ofcom 2007). Hence it is difficult to know what the impact of *non*-access to new media is, when social class is taken into account.

Amounts of TV viewing

In 1958 children were watching TV between 11 and 13 hours a week, just under two hours a day. As now, children spent more time on TV viewing than on any other leisure activity and also as now, their main viewing fare was adult or family programming. In 2008, Ofcom's review, 'How children are consuming media today', showed that 12–15-year-olds are the highest consumers of television, watching 18.5 hours a week, compared with 15.3 hours for 5–7-year-olds. Older children's Internet use in 2008 was 14.4 hours per week, in strong contrast to the younger age groups: only 5.4 per cent of 5–7-year-olds and 8.1 per cent of

8–11-year-olds used the Internet. Two thirds of children have a mobile phone by the age of 10.

In the past, as now, viewing was often combined with other activities. Before the Internet, these activities would have been radio, music, playing with friends and toys, or homework. Now the Internet, computer games and mobile phones can be added to this list. For example, Ofcom's most recent figures (2008) show that 75 per cent of 12–15-year-olds are multi-taskers (but only 29 per cent of 5–7-year-olds are).

'New' media in the USA: the Kaiser Foundation studies

The Kaiser Family Foundation in the US provides regular surveys of children's and young people's media use which have helped to map changes over time. The 'Zero To Six' study (2003) found that, in families with children aged 6 months to 3 years, the children 'almost universally' had a TV in their home, 80 per cent had computers, and nearly half had videogame consoles. For children aged 3 and younger, reading and being read to, and listening to music were engaged in more frequently than electronic media – a surely reassuring statistic for cultural pessimists. In 2005 Kaiser produced another report, 'Generation M: Media in the Lives of 8–18-year-olds', based on questionnaire research with 2032 children and young people. Despite the enormous changes in the amount of media available to young people, and the amount of time they spent with these various media, the Kaiser report's summary findings were not so different from those of Hilde Himmelweit 50 years earlier. The report concluded:

> Contrary to some expectations, the study does not find evidence for the theory that use of computers or video games displaces time spent with television . . . those young people who spend the most time using computers or playing video games also spend more time watching TV and listening to music . . . . television clearly remains the dominant medium in young people's lives by far, with music nipping at its heels, at least where older teens are concerned.
>
> (2005: 39)

So we have generations of children in developed countries such as the US and Europe whose media and leisure habits are more extensively monitored and measured than those of any other generation have ever been. The usefulness of this information to commercial companies is obvious: but these kinds of trends can also be interpreted culturally, as indicators of the quality, whether improving or declining, of children's lives.

The debate about children and media effects: a short history

John Springhall argues in *Youth, Popular Culture and Moral Panics: Penny Gaffs to Gangsta Rap* (1998: 7):

> Whenever the introduction of a new mass medium is defined as a threat to the young, we can expect a campaign by adults to regulate, ban or censor, followed by a lessening of interest until the appearance of a new medium reopens public debate. Each new panic develops as if it were the first time . . . and yet the debates are strikingly similar.

Kirsten Drotner (1992) suggested that these 'panics' could be because, since the mid-nineteenth century, the young have possessed a cultural power in the world of commercial leisure which threatens traditional power relations between youth and age. In Springhall's words, 'media panics can help to re-establish a generational status quo' (p. 7).

Steven Starker (1989) in a very useful historical review called *Evil Influences: Crusades Against the Mass Media*, produced a short summary of what he calls 'Enunciations of Evil – a Sampler'. These were examples of how each new communications technology, as it was introduced, was viewed with suspicion by those who were proficient in the currently accepted communications technology. The new medium was invariably attacked by the current 'experts' for its dangerous influence on the young and vulnerable (1989: 5–14). See Box 5.1.

Box 5.1: Mass media – The case history of a 'public health menace'

'Each new technology creates an environment that is regarded as corrupt and degrading. Yet the new one turns its predecessor into an art form.' Marshall McLuhan, *Understanding Media*, 1964

The written word

'this discovery of yours will create forgetfulness in the learners' souls, because they will not use their memories' Plato: 429–347 BC Athens

Printing (and schooling)

'I thank God there are no free schools or printing, . . . for learning has brought disobedience and heresy and sects into the world and printing has divulged them and libels against the best Government. God keep us from both.' Sir William Berkeley, Governor of Virginia, 1671

The press (and public)

'That awful power, the public opinion of this nation, is formed and molded by a horde of ignorant, self-complacent simpletons who failed at ditching and shoe-making and fetched up in journalism on the way to the poorhouse.' Mark Twain (Samuel Clemens), 1873

The novel

'Girls already have ten times too much excitability for their strength. Yet every page of every novel redoubles both their nervousness and their weakness.' O. S. Fowler, 1875

The telegraph

'Through the medium of the press and telegraph are made the sorrows of individuals everywhere . . . these local sorrows and local horrors become daily occasions of nervous disorders.' Neurologist George M. Beard, 1881

Moving pictures

'The movies are so occupied with crime and sex stuff and are so saturating the minds of children the world over with social sewage that they have bcome a menace to the mental and moral life of the coming generation.' *The Christian Century*, 1930

Radio

'I should like to postpone my children's knowledge of how to rob a bank, scuttle a ship, shoot a sherriff . . . and the horrors of the drug habit for a few more years at least.' Arthur Mann, 'The Children's Hour of Crime', 1933

Comics

'The comic books . . . seem to me to be not only trash, but the lowest, most despicable and most harmful form of trash . . . they are the marijuana of the nursery; the bane of the bassinet; the horror of the house; the curse of the kids and a threat to the future.' John Mason Brown in *The Saturday Review of Literature*, 1948

Television

'Seeing constant brutality, viciousness and unsocial acts, results in hardness, intense selfishness . . . on the native temperament of the child.'

Psychiatrist Edward Podolsky, Senate Subcommittee on Juvenile Delinquency, 1954

Computer games

'I think there are strong possibilities that the video games contribute to the problem of violence in society . . . Wherever computer centres have been established . . . bright young men . . . work until they nearly drop . . . their rumpled clothes, their unwashed faces, their uncombed hair all testify that they are oblivious to the world in which they move . . . These are computer bums . . . an international phenomenon.' J. Weizenbaum, 1976
(Adapted from Steven Starker, 1989)

Neil Selwyn (2003) reported further complaints about the corrupting effects of gaming: 'I have seen reports from all over the country of young people becoming so addicted to these machines that they resort to theft, blackmail and vice to obtain money to safisfy their addiction' (George Foulkes MP, Hansard 1981: 287, quoted in Selwyn 2003).

Starker suggests that this persistent anxiety over new media forms has its origins in a Puritanical 'single-factor' view of evil – a 'Satan figure' which can account, in a simple and simplistic way, for the evils that we see in human society. Today, he argues, this single-factor is 'the media'.

The effects research tradition

In the mid-twentieth century, the domination of television as the major medium consumed by the populace, especially vulnerable children, led to more public concern than all other media put together. The 1972 Surgeon General's report in the USA ran to five volumes, concerned particularly with the impact of television violence and its effects on children. Dafna Lemish (2007: 69) summarizes the position:

There are two particular sets of questions that have dominated studies of children and the effects of television. First does television reinforce existing behavioural tendencies and/or create new ones? Second what are the immediate and long/term effects? Each set of questions . . . has significance in regard to the methodology to be applied in order to pursue them.

Lemish's book on children and television addresses the dominance of the **effects research tradition** in television studies particularly. Many of her topics are concerned with some form of 'effect' – whether on behaviour, on learning, on 'individual development' or on 'the social construction of reality'. As she points out, finding appropriate research methods to establish the relationship between television exposure and children's behaviours is crucial, and far from easy. Methods have included experiments; longitudinal comparisons of children's behaviour and TV consumption over time; large-scale questionnaire surveys; and small-scale qualitative studies in which children discuss their views, or perform tasks.

Research methodologies

Experiments have been one of the most durable forms of trying to demonstrate direct effects of media on behaviour. Examples of experiments, in which children are exposed to aggressive television, and then given the opportunity afterwards to behave aggressively, include those conducted by Liebert and Baron (1972) and Bandura, Ross and Ross (1961; 1963), of which more below. Longitudinal studies, evaluating children's consumption of media correlated with various measures of aggression over a period of years have also been carried out (e.g. Huesman et al. 2003); there have been 'field experiments', such as Williams (1986) in which children's behaviour was measured before and after the introduction of television in a Canadian town which had just received a TV signal. This was compared with two other towns that already had TV. This 'naturally occurring' study found that aggression levels, particularly among boys, rose in the town with no TV after the medium had been introduced. All these, and more, studies found some relationships between regular exposure to television and aggressive behaviour, particularly in boys. According to Wimmer and Dominick in their account of these research methods (2006) most of these studies' findings were 'weak' in that the numerical relationships between the various TV measures and the aggressive behaviour measures were rarely strongly statistically significant (2006: Chapter 18, 5).

   The immense number of these studies, all of them attempting to strengthen findings which have already been published, but are never better than 'weak', suggests a powerful cultural need on the part of adult society to get to grips with the feeling that we are losing control of our young to the power of the media, whether to 'reinforce the generational status quo' as Drotner would have it, or to find Puritanical scapegoat type 'folk-devils' as Starker and Springhall would suggest.

The 'legendary' evidence for 'effects': the Bobo doll experiment

Possible evidence for this deep psychological need on the part of adult society can be found in looking at a particularly famous experiment on the effects of visual media which has almost become folkloric in its own right: the '**Bobo doll**' experiment, otherwise known as Bandura et al. (1963)

Albert Bandura was an exponent of a psychological theory of behaviour known as **social modelling,** that is, a view that children learn how to behave by copying other people, especially people who might be important to them, such as parents. He and his colleagues produced a number of other papers outlining the theory, but it is the Bobo doll that has passed into legend. (A Bobo doll is a large blow-up doll on a solid base, which wobbles when hit, and then returns to the upright. The number of times children attacked this doll after seeing it being hit on film was used as a measure of aggression in Bandura's experiments.)

I became interested in the status of this 1963 experiment because I had noticed, in marking undergraduate exam papers and essays on media effects 40 years later, that, even in students who appeared not to have read anything else, the Bobo doll experiment was one that everyone was able to describe. Badly-read students are not alone in finding this study extraordinarily salient. In 2009, a Google search revealed 181,000 references to the Bandura Bobo doll experiment, of which 561 were specific, recent academic citations (accessed 25 March 2009). This study has provided a model which is simple, powerful, easily understood and reinforces long-standing folk-psychology assumptions about the impact of the media which go back at least as far as Plato.

So what is the source of its power? And what exactly did it say? One reason it has stood the test of the time is its clarity. It is a classic experimental design.

The 'Bobo doll' experiment: research question

Its basic research question was: to what extent is aggression on film copied by children? It had a number of hypotheses including:

1. Children would copy aggressive behaviour performed by a model.
2. The more 'unreal' the model, the less likelihood of imitation.
3. Male subjects would be more imitative of aggression than females.

The study was carried out with 48 boys and 48 girls, aged between 3 and 5 in Stanford University Nursery School, tested individually. These children were divided into four experimental groups:

1. In the first group children saw 'real life aggression' against a Bobo doll (an

inflatable doll that falls over if hit with a mallet, and then bounces back); this was carried out by a real male or female 'model'.

2. In the second group children saw the same behaviour by real people filmed – a 'realistic' filmed model of aggression.

3. The third group of children saw the same behaviour by a cartoon 'cat' – a less 'realistic' model of aggression.

4. The fourth group provided a control condition in which the children saw no modelling of any kind.

Children in all four groups were later given the opportunity to carry out the same behaviour with a similar Bobo doll and the number of times they enacted imitative aggressive behaviour (attacking; uttering cries of 'hit him' or 'kick him'; sitting on the doll or pretending to shoot it) was measured. Then the numbers of aggressive acts for both boys and girls in each group were averaged to produce scores, which were then compared.

Hypothesis 1: Did children copy aggressive models?

The scores of every group were compared with every other group and the study found no differences between the groups who'd seen film, cartoon and live models when they were compared with each other. But all three of the 'model' groups had significantly higher aggression scores than the control group, who had not seen any modelling. It looks as if the hypothesis that children copy aggressive behaviour is significantly proved. However, from looking more closely at the other results of the experiment, it is not at all clear that seeing *filmed* aggression, whether 'real' or cartoon, is the biggest problem.

Hypothesis 2: Do 'real life' models have more effect than filmed ones?

Both boys and girls were more aggressive after watching real life models than after watching filmed models, so this hypothesis was supported. However there were some interesting variations in the impact of 'real life' models. First their effect was very much *greater* than filmed models, which is surely worth reporting in terms of trying to explain the origins of aggressive behaviour in children. Real people apparently have more influence than films. Secondly, there was a gender effect of real life models. Both sexes were more aggressive after seeing a person of the same sex modelling aggressive behaviour. Seeing a real life female model was the only condition in which girls were slightly more aggressive than boys. Boys, too, had higher aggression scores after seeing a filmed female model.

Hypothesis 3: Boys would be more aggressive than girls

Boys were much more aggressive than girls in most cases, particularly so after watching a real life male model (38.4 acts). But there was one comparison where this was not the case. When a female model performed the aggression, girls were more aggressive than boys (19.2 acts from girls, versus 18.4 acts from boys). As hypothesized, both groups were more aggressive after watching real life models than after watching filmed models, but strikingly, when boys saw a female model on film, they were more aggressive afterwards than when they had seen a male model. This would suggest that female models have a greater impact than male, or cartoon models, on both sexes (possibly because with such young children, it is primarily female authority figures who are in charge of them?). This gender-related finding would seem worthy of discussion, but it is not a finding widely reported in the many citations of this experiment.

Non-imitative aggression

A striking finding from this experiment which was not widely reported was the incidence of 'non-imitative aggression'. These were aggressive acts carried out by the children which could not be attributed to the social modelling they saw in the experiment (it could have been due to social modelling outside, of course). *Non*-imitative aggression was higher for both boys and girls than imitative aggression: in other words, children, as observed outside the experimental situation, were more aggressive *without* seeing any experimental modelling. This was particularly evident from the control group scores for children who had seen no modelled examples at all, but had the highest incidence of non-imitative aggression.

A closer look at the scores in this famous experiment thus raises serious doubts about the impact of screen violence compared to other influences. Given that the levels of *non-imitative* aggression across the board were much higher in both sexes than imitative aggression, it would seem that the impact of experimental 'imitation' was actually relatively low. It raises the question, therefore, as to whether there was some secondary source of aggressive behaviour by children in this situation which was not being measured. It certainly does not provide evidence that the most significant influence on children's aggressive behaviour is screen violence. Yet this is what several generations of my students, and countless other scholars and commentators, have believed and reported.

Many media researchers (e.g. Buckingham 1996; Barker and Petley 1997) are generally sceptical of experimental research to establish media effects – and some of their reservations can be justified. Experiments are artificial; they do not measure long-term influence; they tend to be carried out on very unrepresentative groups of children. There are also serious ethical questions about researchers encouraging very young children to behave aggressively. But even within the paradigm and framework of the experiment, there are results here which do not support the widely-accepted interpretation of this experiment that seeing filmed aggression is a primary source of young children's aggressive behaviour. Yet, as mentioned, this study has generated thousands of citations, and it continues to underpin debate about media-related violence in the young in the medical and psychological community (see Rich 2008) and in the media at large.

In raising questions over the uncritical way in which this research has been so widely reported, I am not defending explicit and gruesome violence in entertainment material offered to children. Indeed, as someone who hates watching even mild threat on the screen, I would be only too happy for someone to come up with some really conclusive evidence about the harmful effects of violence that would convince the movie industry to get rid of it. But this kind of clinching evidence has not been produced. And even if it were produced, it seems to me that two much more powerful factors than concern for children would prevent any major change in media content taking place: first, violence in screen media, now including video games (see Chapter 10) is profitable; and secondly, organized violence is a respectable tool of law enforcement and of government policy in most nations of the world. In the 2000s, warfare has been embraced as enthusiastically as ever by governments, (including those of the US and UK) and it is also very profitable for the armaments and related industries.

What we have with the Bobo doll experiment, and others like it, therefore, is certainly a 'media effect' – but not one of direct media influence on children's behaviour. It is an effect on the commentating community – whether journalists or academics – demonstrating their need for simple cause and effect evidence to support what are likely to be already-established beliefs and arguments. These beliefs and arguments, as Starker's (1989) review suggests, are historically long-standing. The 'Bobo doll' experiment and its imitators satisfy this need to a high degree, thus displacing the need to do anything to change the other more dominant factors contributing to human violence that I have mentioned.

The effects of advertising

The other main area of negative 'effects' research on children has been the impact of advertising. Given that, in most media systems, whether the press, broadcasting or the Internet, advertising is the primary means of generating income, it has been impossible for contemporary children to grow up without being exposed to a continuous stream of commercial messages from all kinds of sources. There are broader political concerns about the general commercialization of childhood and the construction of the child as a consumer, which were discussed in Chapter 4. Empirical research traditions, such as the 'effects'/social impact tradition, have sought to provide evidence of the impact of this exposure, including surveys and experiments to assess children's understanding of, and reactions to, commercials.

Researchers in this field also use experiments (see Gunter and Furnham 1998), for instance, showing children material which includes attractive representations of sweets or toys embedded in a programme segment, and a control group of children being shown the same material without the sweets and toys; then the children are given the option of choosing prizes or shown catalogues of goods represented in the films to choose from afterwards. Such studies do tend to find that a short-term exposure to an attractive representation results in children being more likely to choose sweets or toys if they've seen the film version which includes them. However, there is also evidence of campaigns that do not work with children, for instance a candy bar with a well-known baseball player on it did not sell (Schneider 1987, quoted in Gunter and Furnham 1998: 152).

As summarized by Gunter and Furnham:

- Children's advertising has an effect on the child's purchase and consumption behaviour but this is not the only effect.
- The influence of TV advertisements on children's purchase request behaviour is not greater than that of other factors.
- TV advertising increases children's purchase request behaviour.
- The amount of children's purchase requests differs according to age, socio-economic and parental factors, product category and peer influence.
- TV advertising is thus not the only influencing factor nor is it the most important.

Despite the provisional nature of the evidence of the impact of advertising on children, the belief that it does have a significant effect on children has translated into a major policy decision in the UK, with Ofcom banning 'junk food' advertising at times when children were likely to be watching (see Chapter 4). Research by Livingstone and Helsper (2006) on 'advertising literacy' suggests, rather surprisingly, that it is not the youngest children who are most susceptible to advertising, but teenagers. Factors including peer influence and more financial autonomy help to make older children more consumerist than younger ones.

Non-Western cultures

A particular problem for children in cultures where they have not been socially constructed as consumers since the nineteenth century, or even earlier – that is, children in non-Western cultures – is the sudden pervasiveness of commercial imagery showing lifestyles they can barely imagine. In a study on the impact of television advertising on children in India, Unnikrishnan and Bajpai (1996: 349) argue:

> In India, advertising on TV is today creating a set of images especially for the Indian child, . . . [that] does not sensitise children to their own or other people's realities. The affluent child might feel convinced that only his or her class of Indians really count. On the other hand, the child from a poor family class may be forced to acknowledge the lifestyles of the affluent class are the *only* legitimate ones.

In their study of over 700 Indian children aged 5 to 15 they found that most children liked advertising, and were aware of the difference between commercials and programmes, but there was much that was completely beyond their frames of reference in their own lives. For the authors, the children's responses promoted a worrying individualism, which they argue, was at odds with the traditional cultures within which the children were growing up.

Kapur (1999) points out the difficulty of leaving individual families and children to cope with this consumerist onslaught as individuals. She argues:

> Marie Winn and others propose that the family can resist capitalism by transforming itself into a private fortress [by using the off button and saying no to kids]. This is ironic at a time when capitalist expansion (the construction of children as consumers) and new technologies (the Internet) drastically challenge the public/private divide on which the family is based. . . . new technologies that blur the boundaries between the public and private domains, between home and work.
>
> (Kapur 1999: 132)

It is difficult to demur from these pessimistic accounts of the impact of commercialism on children around the world, which is becoming ever harder to avoid as public/private 'boundaries are blurred'. But, although technologies may be new, social contrasts in the worlds in which children live are not. Contrasts between affluence and poverty can be easily observed by any child on a walk through any city, town or village centre. Hence, as always, the measurement of the impact of media messages, including advertising, has to take account of other sources of information that the child already has about social and economic conditions – a point also made by a major UNESCO study on the media's social influences carried out in the late 1990s (Groebel 1998). It is the wide disparities in these conditions that constitute the real and continuing threat to the well-being of contemporary children.

Social learning and stereotyping

A major concern about the impact of television particularly, but also other mass media such as advertising, has been its impact on social perceptions: if negative or demeaning or trivialized representations of women, or of ethnic minorities (or indeed of children – although this seems not to have been of major concern to many social scientists studying these issues) are presented, will this encourage equally negative perceptions of these groups in impressionable young viewers?

Media producers have to conform to the laws of the land in not disseminating sexist, racist or inflammatory language and media broadcasting organizations have internal production codes about what they can and cannot do, or show, at different times of the day. One problem about the Internet is that such codes do not apply to it. Nation states can apply their own forms of legislation to broadcast media, but many products of digital media and the World Wide Web transcend national boundaries and national regulation.

Because television is domestic and pervasive, it is assumed that children are influenced by it on these grounds. **Cultivation theory** (Gerbner and Gross 1976; Signorielli 1990, 2001; Shanahan and Morgan 1999) argues that it is not specific content that inculcates particular attitudes in viewers, but the sheer frequency and regularity with which people are exposed to negative representations. Heavy viewers are assumed to be more prone to 'mean world' views than are light viewers. Where children are repeatedly exposed to negative images of gender or race, or where they are constantly exposed to unrealistic ideals of beauty and figure-shape, this can have a relationship with their attitudes in real life. (It's important to note the word 'relationship', not 'effect', since cultivation studies measure *correlations* between frequency of exposure to media representations, and people's attitudes, which are then assumed to be linked. But the representations do not *cause* the attitudes. Unlike experiments, cultivation studies do not seek to establish direct *effects* on behaviour, as in the Bandura examples.)

Lemish (2007) has usefully summarized the problems in a chapter on 'social constructions of reality'; the fact that many media representations (again, particularly television) have far more authoritative and frequent representations of men than of women; of white people than of black people, or people of non-white racial groups; and of attractive rather than less attractive women. The cultivation of norms assumed to follow from this predominance of biased social representation has been tested in a number of studies. Lemish describes her own study with Israeli preteens and their readings of the Spice Girls, and the different models of femininity the group represented: these discussions raised issues about what it means to be female in contemporary society, what empowerment meant ('sporty', 'posh' and so on) and the representational conflicts between images of 'virgin and whore', all of which were felt by her young female interviewees (2007: 102–10). Unrealistic images of female slenderness have also been blamed for increasing incidences of anorexia in young girls (Harrison and Cantor 1997; Harrison 2000). While expressing concern at the dominance of American, Westernized models of attractiveness and behaviour, Lemish points out that 'viewers, even the young ones, located as they are within social and ideological contexts, are selective in their viewing and creative in their interpretations of it' (2007: 143).

Cognitive effects

When a new, widely-distributed medium arrives, alongside concerns about cultural debasement, a discourse of opportunity also appears. How can film be used to educate? How can television be used for social training and information? Educational programming is produced in all countries of the world which have television; film has been used for newsreels, public information and health education and as a valuable archive resource (see for instance, the archives at the Imperial War Museum, London, [http://www.iwmcollections.org.uk/qryFilm.asp]). The Internet teems with educational sites, many of them linked to other media such as television and the press, for example, *Newsround* which has a page for teachers, [http://news.bbc.co.uk/cbbcnews/hi/teachers/default.stm] and the *Sesame Street* website, [http://www.sesamestreet.org/home]. The web has enabled academic entrepreneurs, such as Erin Reilly and Vinitha Nair to set up educational resources like Zoey's Room, which started off as an interactive technology club for girls between the ages of 10 and 14 in the state of Maine and has now expanded: 'to include more math, science and engineering in our interactive online challenges. . . . we are now able to offer the interactive technology community of Zoey's Room to girls across the nation' [http://www.zoeysroom.com/] (see Figure 5.1).

The question for educators, and also for researchers, is whether children actually are learning anything from these media, and whether the ways in which they learn are different when the medium is visual, or audiovisual, or 'interactive', from more traditional ways of learning. Some programmes are specifically designed both to research ways in which information can be presented to facilitate learning, and to investigate afterwards whether this has in fact happened. Wartella and Robb (2007) claim: 'More than 35 years of experience with preschoolers using *Sesame Street* has demonstrated that four to six year olds can learn important skills such as their numbers and letters, as well as pre-reading skills that can have a positive effect on them as they enter

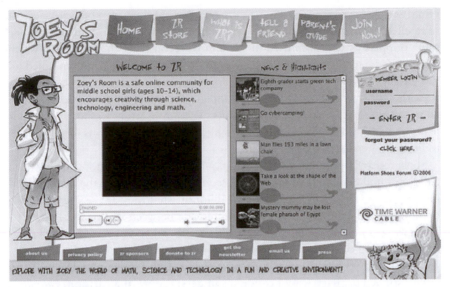

Figure 5.1 Zoey's room website, Zoey's room home page, http://www.zoeysroom.com/ Web design: Russell Sprague, artwork: Steven James Taylor

elementary school' (2007: 35). *Sesame Street,* which has been on the air since the 1960s, enabled some long-term follow-up studies with high school students which showed apparent lasting effects and higher grades among those who had watched the show as young children (Anderson et al. 2001; Huston, et al. 2001).

Formal features, reality and fantasy

Some of the most original research on children and media has been carried out by scholars who are interested in the specifics of TV (and film) as media and how children learn to 'read' audiovisual 'grammar'. This can broadly be summarized as 'formal features' research – it has links with more theoretical approaches to the study of media including semiotics and language studies. Audiovisual media, to which modern children are exposed almost as often (for some children, perhaps, more often) as they are exposed to human speech, have their own forms of expression and rules of composition, their own conventions of genre and design. How do children learn these rules and conventions?

Formal features are syntactical indicators of meaning, for example, a dissolve represents a shift in time, and also a shift in consciousness. Cuts are grammatical markers, indicating a change in perspective or point of view, or a change of scene (see Beentjes et al. 2001). Smith et al. (1985) tested children's understanding of visual formal features using puppets – they asked children aged between 4 and 7 to retell a filmed story which had several changes of shot. The children used the same puppets as had been used in the film to reconstruct the narrative. When the film had had a cut from an indoor to an outdoor shot, the children 'filled in' the missing actions by walking the puppets down the stairs or down the hall, even though they had not seen this happen. They had correctly deduced the connecting activity between the two shots. The Smith study was an example of learning which takes place without formal instruction, analogous in some ways to how children learn the rules of linguistic syntax.

Such research prompts theoretical inquiries into the relationship between children's understanding of the formal, 'constructed' nature of the medium and its genres, and the authenticity or credibility of what they are seeing. This can be summarized as understanding 'the difference between reality and fantasy' – prompting concerns about whether children are 'taken in' and 'duped' by the techniques and conventions of what they see in the media, especially the exaggerations and stylistic invention of advertising. Bob Hodge and David Tripp (1986) studied primary school children's understanding of a cartoon, *Fangface*, in terms of what the researchers called 'modality judgements' – the ability to distinguish different levels of reality from the formal features of the cartoon. The greater the degree of artifice employed, the less literally 'true' children found the material.

Messenger Davies (1997; 2008) found that children aged between 6 and 12, when asked to identify what could, or could not happen in 'real life' in a range of different programme genres (animation; news; advertising; fantasy drama; situation comedy), persistently used formal features as a way of deciding. When asked for their reasons why something could, or could not, happen in reality, they identified a large number of formal markers, including generic characteristics. 'It's comedy' so soundtrack laughter, while not being 'real', is allowed. Specific stylistic conventions, such as 'special effects', were seen as appropriate for fantasy shows, but not for news.

Interactive learning

The Internet has introduced another keyword into media educational discourse – 'interactivity'. Digital media of various kinds enable children not only to receive information 'passively' (that is, just by sitting and watching, or reading) but also to manipulate and engage with the information. Interactivity – the ability to press buttons and thereby navigate two-dimensional images and texts in a variety of formats has been promoted (particularly commercially) as a desirable educational end in itself. However, as Buckingham et al. comment:

When we look at what children are doing with this technology outside school it is clear that it is primarily a medium for popular culture . . . playing games, surfing entertainment sites on the Internet, instant messaging . . . and downloading pop music . . . by contrast what they are doing with technology in school is very limited . . . in effect the Microsoft Office curriculum.

(2008: 39)

This echoes what my colleagues and I found in our *Newsround* study about children and news, both broadcast and online, (Carter et al. 2009, see Chapter 9) in which 8–15-year-old children's most frequent use of 'interactive' technology was 'the red button' on the TV remote control; they were least likely to use interactive technology to intervene in creative ways, for instance to upload material. Interactive technology clearly has great potential – but the challenge is to enable this potential to be reached by all children who want it, not just a privileged, media-savvy few. Much of the enthusiasm for the interactive learning potential of 'new' media concerns teenagers and young adults – younger children are more restricted in their explorations of this potential, for a variety of reasons. (There is more about this in Chapter 10).

Issues of pleasure and taste

And what about 'fun', the selling point proclaimed by Nickelodeon (see Chapter 1) and the reason children most often give for enjoying media (see Palmer 1986)? There has been much less research on this question. An exception is Davies et al. (2000), at London University's Institute of Education; their study on children's media tastes argued that children's enthusiasm for 'silly', vulgar, action-packed, colourful material of the kind produced in Saturday morning children's magazines and cartoons, was a form of 'identity work' – an assertion of their own agency and an independence from the tastes of adults. In Australia Palmer (1986) explored positive socialization skills, prompted by television, with over 800 Australian primary school children, and argued that the 'fun' and 'excitement' factors of children's relationship with the medium were crucial outcomes and enabled creative peer group social interaction.

The International Central Institute of Youth and Educational Television (IZI) in Munich regularly investigates the positive benefits of entertainment media for children, using larger-scale, international audience samples. An international IZI study on what children find funny, with over 400 8–12-year-olds in Germany, USA, South Africa, UK, Ireland and Israel (Götz et al. 2005), found similarities in what children found amusing across a range of humorous programming from each country. Physical comedy such as slapstick produced universal laughter, but there were also local variations in the children's responses, arising from linguistic and cultural differences. For instance, a war film parody in a Wallace and Gromit sequence was not understood in South Africa. These findings, presented at the 2006 Prix Jeunesse, were seen as useful for children's entertainment producers, indicating that genres such as comedy need to be locally specific to be fully understood; some jokes do not travel, and this was another argument for 'indigenous', locally produced programming for children (see Chapter 4).

Another research project from IZI (Götz et al. 2005) reviewed the positive contribution of television and media to children's imagination and fantasy in four countries, the USA, Germany, Israel and Korea, with a sample of 193 8–10-year-old children. The researchers found considerable diversity of media influences in the stories and drawings children produced. These authors commented positively on the many 'missing traces of globalization and . . . the absence of violence in resolving problems' (2005: 150) in the children's fantasy stories. Their view was that media were used differentially according to children's cultural backgrounds, gender and personalities, in a constructive and imaginative way. The key methodological point here is that 'constructive and imaginative' was what the children were asked to be. One effect that we have all observed (whether as parents, teachers or researchers) is that children perform to expectations. If you expect them to be aggressive, they will be; if you expect them to be creative, likewise.

Conclusions

As can be seen from this extremely brief review of some of the hundreds of thousands of research studies carried out on the 'effects' of media on children, the findings tend to be closely dependent on the question asked in the first place. The question determines the kind of method used and the kinds of question and method used also depends on who is asking the questions. Media corporations have a vested interest in finding out whether people (including children) both use and 'like' their product, as do advertisers, so large-scale audience surveys will be commissioned, sometimes supported by focus groups. Educators want to know if children acquire (or fail to acquire) specific forms of knowledge and skill, often related to school curricula, which requires smaller-scale, qualitative, classroom-based research. Moralists and social scientists will want to know if children's attitudes and behaviour are being adversely, (or less often), positively affected by the media they consume, which tends to generate experimental methods, with all their limitations, but also with very clear-cut and hence easily-reportable findings.[1] Producers of media material will want to know if their carefully designed techniques and narratives are being appreciated.

From the point of view of what parents and children want to know, many of these studies do not specifically address their concerns. The mantra of consumer choice in a deregulated media market place would seem to leave all decisions about children's media consumption to parents, and, as they grow older, to children themselves (provided that they have been educated to be 'media literate') – and there is much research to suggest that parents and children are quite competent to do this (e.g. Marsh et al. 2005). But leaving it to the consumer begs the question of what offerings are available to choose from. The ways in which media are introduced to the market, their sources of funding, the material on offer, and the ways in which media provision is regulated, or not, are political questions.[2]

Research is particularly worthwhile when it is linked to specific, beneficial, practical outcomes, such as producing more informative and child-friendly educational material, as with the *Sesame Street* formative and evaluative studies. It is also valuable when it is educationally meaningful and is rewarding and enjoyable for children to take part in, as in some of the media education and literacy research carried out by scholars like David Buckingham and his team and the researchers at IZI. If negative effects of media consumption on children's health and behaviour can be securely established without the research itself having a negative effect, it is important for us to know this, so that public debate can be informed. But when media research influences public debate to a degree which generates unhelpful states of 'moral panic,' then we have to question whether it really contributes to the general public good and to the well-being of children. Around panicking adults is usually not a good place for children to be.

Further reading

The classic experimental study of media 'copycat' effects remains Bandura, A., Ross, D. and Ross, R. (1963) Imitation of film-mediated aggressive models, *Journal of Abnormal and Social Psychology*, 66(1): 3–11, and it should be read in the original. For further discussion of this long-standing tradition see Barker, M. and Petley, J. (eds) (1997) *Ill Effects: The Media Violence Debate*, London: Routledge, and Messenger Davies, M. (1989/2001) *Television is Good for your Kids*, London: Hilary Shipman. Excellent historical reviews of 'effects' discourse are: John Springhall's (1998) *Youth, Popular Culture and Moral Panics: Penny Gaffs to Gangsta Rap*, Basingstoke: McMillan, and Steven Starker's (1989) *Evil Influences: Crusades Against the Mass Media*, NY: Transaction. For a measured contemporary scholar's review of children's relationship with TV, see Dafna Lemish's (2007) *Children and Television: A Global Perspective*, Malden MA: Blackwell.

PART 2
CHILDREN IN MEDIA, CHILDREN'S MEDIA

'GOLDEN AGES': THE VISUAL REPRESENTATION OF CHILDHOOD

In this second section of the book, we switch direction away from historical, social scientific, political and cultural discussions of childhood and children's relationship with media, to look more closely at specific media examples. This chapter looks at ways in which children and childhood have been represented in the visual arts. Chapter 2 discussed Philippe Aries' use of medieval paintings as a source of evidence about attitudes to children and childhood in the past. From the nineteenth century onwards, with the invention of photography, and also with the development of new attitudes to children and their welfare (see Chapters 2 and 3), the ways in which children have been visually represented have proliferated exponentially. We now see images of children and childhood everywhere and the image of 'the child' has developed from its early nineteenth-century, Romantic signification of 'naturalness' and innocence, to being a symbol for practically every product a manufacturer might want to sell. As already discussed, 'the child' is also a widely-used visual signifier of the destructiveness of war and famine, and, in its delinquent form, of the breakdown of the social order (see Chapter 5).

Children and the 'golden age': making time stand still

> And then I knew, Tom, that the garden was changing all the time, because nothing stands still, except in our memory.
> (*Tom's Midnight Garden*, Philippa Pearce, [1958] 1979: 212)

Tom's Midnight Garden is a classic children's novel about the elusiveness of time and memory in a child's life, written by Philippa Pearce in 1958. The novel explores both the possibility and the impossibility of making time stand still; children grow up and grow old, but in memory, and – as in this magical 'time travel' story – in fantasy, childhood can be revisited and temporarily recaptured. Moments in childhood can also be made to 'stand still' by artistic and media representations of them, and this chapter discusses some of the ways in which portrayals of children and childhood have been captured and interpreted in contemporary media.

In *The Child in the City* (1978), Colin Ward points out the importance of remembered landscape in individuals' construction of their own childhoods. As in *Tom's Midnight Garden*, this remembered past is one explanation for the pervasiveness of the 'golden age' concept in discussing childhoods of the past (see e.g. Carpenter, 1985). The 'golden age' is what we remember of our own childhoods, whenever they were, and however mundane and even unhappy. Says Ward:

> Since childhood is one of the few absolutely universal experiences, it is not surprising that people have an inward picture, even though it may never be articulated, of an ideal childhood . . . this ideal landscape we acquired in childhood . . . a myth and idyll of the way things ought to be, the lost paradise to be regained.
>
> (1978: 2)

Ward argues that this universal memory of childhood, which even the unhappiest children share, is a form of 'myth'. Since his subject is 'the child in the city', he argues that, 'like the sentimentalised rural idyll' supposedly invented by Romantic poets such as William Wordsworth in the eighteenth century, 'there is an urban myth of paradise lost' (1978: 5).

Ward suggests that romanticized versions of childhood are more likely to be rural than urban: 'the enormous weight of literary convention, filtered through school books, pop songs and margarine adverts, postulates a childhood piping down the valleys wild, rather than roaming the city streets, still less the quiet avenues of the suburbs' (p. 5). However, mythologized versions of urban childhoods are certainly being produced currently, for example the Hovis bread advertisements (see Figure 6.1). The 2009 one shows a young boy, carrying a loaf, running through successive cityscapes from the early twentieth century, through the Great War, the suffragette rallies, the 1930s depression, the Second World War, the coronation and its street parties, the swinging sixties, the seventies with their Asian immigrants, the 1980s miners' strike, the millennium and finally up to date in the noughties. (See it on YouTube at [http://www.youtube.com/watch?v=S4tFzuFGUOI].)

Figure 6.1 Brian Mackie marches alongside 200 extras playing World War I soldiers in the 2009 Hovis TV advertisement, produced by the MCBD advertising agency. The ad is 122 seconds long, one second for every year of the product's life.

In an interview in a film on the making of this advertisement [http://www.youtube.com/watch?v=UUCuPLv6MsU], Danny Brooke Taylor, the creative director at the advertising agency, Mills, Calcraft, Briginshaw and Duffy (MCBD), called it 'an icon of who we are as a nation'. As the film shows, every image in it is intended to invoke a myth of childhood, carrying connotations of community, national cohesion and continuity. The commercial invokes an image of unchanging, sturdy childhood, whose health and energy – it is implied – come partly from eating nourishing brown bread. The same child, running through history, whether clothed in the waistcoat and boots of 1914 or the jerkin and jeans of the 1990s, illustrates the enduring values of healthy British boyhood, linking these values, of course, with the product.

Ideological connotations

Much analysis of images of children and childhood in the media operates with a basic premise: that the representation of 'the child' or children has mythological or ideological connotations beyond the actual representation of the infant in question. Images of children are used for propaganda purposes, for instance the photographs of rescued 'before' and 'after' street children (see below), which in their turn have invited academic comment and ideological deconstruction (Horn 1997; Holland 2004; 2008). Contemporary examples of propaganda childhood imagery include those of starving children in famines and wounded or bereft children in war, used particularly by charities in disaster appeals. Images of children are used in every possible configuration in advertising, including increasingly sexualized poses (see Hartley 1998; Holland 2004; 2008). And of course, most problematically of all, sexual images of real children are used in child pornography now widely circulated on the Internet.

Given this recent development, we may ask whether it is possible for any image of a child to be simply a picture of a child. Because of the image's open semiotic power – its polysemy, or ability to yield multiple meanings – it is virtually impossible to look at any image of a child without seeing something else beyond it. Patricia Holland (2004) raises concerns about a contemporary inability to find any images of childhood free of perceptual contamination:

> What sort of exploitation is involved when children, the most powerless group in society are pictured for the pleasure and delight of adults who potentially have total control of them? . . . Across the appreciation of every chubby infant falls the shadow of other pictured children – particularly those sexualised children whose images are circulated on the Internet.
>
> (2004: xii)

With photography and film, there always *is* a real child with a real life behind this image and the research my colleague Nick Mosdell and I conducted in *Consenting Children*, 2001 (like much research being conducted with children nowadays) emphasizes that this person should not be forgotten. This person has agency, and should have some control over the use of his or her representation.

Personal snapshots

As I write, I have a very cheery 'child' image in front of me – a 'child' whose permission I sought to reproduce this image (see Figure 6.2). I received it as an email attachment from my youngest daughter (now in her twenties) and I liked it, not just as a happy image of her, but also as a rare one: we have no other pictures of this, our youngest child, in the snow, so the snapshot is also a historical record. The photograph, taken by her boyfriend, shows a jokey moment, in a snowy London street, on the day of heavy snowfall of

Figure 6.2 Elinor with snowman, North London, February 2009

Photograph by Rory McQueen, family snapshot

2 February 2009. It is a record of the day in which, for the first time in over 100 years, no buses ran on London streets. This was snow of such heaviness that anyone under the age of 18 in London would never have seen such a thing before.

The picture stands next to a much older photograph of her, taken at a time before email, showing her as a dungaree-clad, boyish-looking toddler in another street, this time in Cerne Abbas, Dorset, aged 2. In this, she is obviously physically very different. As discussed in Chapter 3, the physical changes of the growth from child to adult are dramatically transforming. Photography has made the recording of these life-stage transformations a central part of our lives, in a way that was not possible in earlier periods – a central aspect of the contemporary cultural 'construction' of childhood. As Mrs Bartholomew in *Tom's Midnight Garden* said, in life, 'nothing stands still, even in memory', but in photography, things do stand still. Such images are another potent source of 'golden age', or conversely of miserable and traumatized, conceptions of 'childhood.'

Children in paintings and photographs

As discussed in Chapter 2, the relatively recent discipline of the 'history of childhood' draws many of its arguments from pictorial representations. Philippe Aries argued that medieval representations of children looking like miniature adults indicated that people in the twelfth to fifteenth centuries did not have a sense of children as being different from other people. Aries argues that, because there were no portrait images of children, this indicated that children were not seen as specific individuals with characteristics of their own. Images of children are certainly found in many forms of medieval and early Renaissance artistic representation, and it is hard to believe that some of the charming babies and toddlers seen in images of the Madonna and the Holy Family were not based on real (and one can assume from their healthy appearance, well cared-for) children. But we do not know who these children were. Their individuality does not matter.

A crucial cultural change began not only in the seventeenth century, as outlined by Aries, but even more so in the early nineteenth century, when, as part of the Romantic movement, the 'natural' and 'unspoiled' state of childhood was idealized as a privileged form of being. The importance of the individual – whether as artist, or as human person – was also foregrounded as **Enlightenment** tenets about 'The Rights of Man' spread into public discourse. Alongside the cultural idealization of childhood, throughout the nineteenth century, enlightenment theory was translated into action, in the form of the political and social movements of child welfare. These included the reform of child labour laws; improvements in health care and education, (compulsory education up to 14 was introduced in the 1870s on both sides of the Atlantic) and the 'Child Study' movement. Childhood was being 'invented'.

Children were also on the public agenda – and this political recognition of their needs, rights and problems was not unrelated to the improving status of women. As children 'became' people, so the visual representation of children began to be more individualized and specific. This process was aided by the invention of photography in the 1840s, which enabled accurate visual records of real people to be quickly, and relatively cheaply, made and kept. Unlike most portrait painting, these photographic records included images of poor people – a big step forward in the history of human visual representation.

Children as individuals: the 'Gilded Age'

Barbara Dayer Gallati (2004) discusses the period at the end of the nineteenth century known as **the Gilded Age** in the upper echelons of society in the USA; an essential ingredient in visual representations of 'the Gilded Age' was childhood.

> Family life was transformed at this time and . . . children became the centre of the family's existence. As living symbols of the family's continuation, children were seen to deserve and require special protection and education, all in preparation for their futures as inheritors and perpetuators of the family's legacy.
>
> (2004: 9–10)

Gallati examines the work of major American painters, including John Singer Sargent and Mary Cassatt, who demonstrate, she argues, 'the impact of childhood's newly attained cultural status' (p. 10). As noted, painting was not an art form that generally portrayed poor children; artists like Sargent relied for their income on fees from wealthy families. Gallati points out, 'few artists truthfully depicted the impoverished youngsters who were highly visible on the urban streets of Europe and the United States . . . . [nor] the result of philanthropic endeavors aimed at reducing the hardships experienced by children' (p. 10). This was more likely to happen through photography.

The crucial point about the representation of children in these paintings was that the reality of childhood and children began to be publicly *noticed*. The children in the Gilded Age paintings are certainly prosperous, but they are also recognizably children: they are sulky, sprawled, individuated, bored, intent on various activities; being bathed; fed; transported; both ignored and scrutinized by the adults in the scene. The increasing freedom of North American women to have professional lives in the nineteenth century further contributed to the new, realistic visibility of children. Mary Cassatt's series of paintings of mothers and children broke away from the idealized Madonna image and showed contemporary mothers and children crumpled, busy, tired and intimate. Frequently, as in the picture in Figure 6.3, the mother's face is hidden. This is not a society portrait. What we primarily see is the shape of the relationship: the reality of the physical connection between the two.

Cassatt, a woman painter, was comfortable with recognizing and portraying the social world in which children and their mothers live, as in the painting of 'women admiring a child' (see Figure 6.4). Cassatt was also one of the first, and one of the few major painters to capture children's own private worlds when intent on a playful activity, as in the image of children on a beach seen in Figure 6.5. The absence of adults is noticeable.

Figure 6.3 Mary Stevenson Cassatt, Louise nursing her child, Image thanks to Art RenewalCenter® www.artrenewal.org

As is common with images of children, the social meanings of Sargent's painting of four young sisters shown in Figure 6.6 have been interpreted in diverse ways. According to the Museum of Fine Art's description, 'some have interpreted Sargent's strategy as a poignant comment on the fickle nature of childhood and adolescence'. The author Henry James, on the other hand, described the picture as a 'happy play-world of a family of charming children'. A purely aesthetic reading by the MFA critic ignores the girls as individuals altogether and argues that 'The painting masterfully transcends portraiture, presenting not only a likeness but also a brilliant meditation on openness and enigma, on light and shadow' (Davis et al. 2003).

The portraits reflect the shift in attitudes to childhood that occurred during

Figure 6.4 Mary Stevenson Cassatt, Women Admiring a Child, 1897 (pastel on paper) / The Detroit Institute of Arts, USA / Gift of Edward Chandler Walker/ Bridgeman Art

the Gilded Age, including, as Dayer Gallati says, the child being the focus of marketing strategies and social reform; for new labour and education laws; and the child study movement which drew on new disciplines of sociology, education, medicine and psychology to 'determine the exact nature of childhood' (Gallati 2004: 10).

Children in photographs: Barnardo

Some nineteenth-century artists such as Gustave Dore used their art to illustrate the plight of the poor, including children. But the most useful tool in highlighting social conditions and childhood's place in them in the nineteenth century, was the then new medium of photography. Photography was put to the use of the child welfare and child rescue movements in a variety of ways. Dr Thomas Barnardo used 'before' and 'after' photographs of abandoned, orphaned or neglected children to show the benefits of his children's homes. These images were controversial.

Figure 6.5 Mary Stevenson Cassatt, Children Playing on the Beach, Image thanks to Art RenewalCenter® www.artrenewal.org

In her lavishly illustrated book, *The Victorian Town Child* (1997), Pamela Horn draws freely on photographic illustration to show Victorian children in a variety of contexts, for example, the two images shown in Figure 6.7. With photography, especially early photography with its long exposure times requiring people to stand still for several minutes, we always need to bear in mind the likelihood that images are staged for a purpose, as they were by Dr Barnardo. Early photographs of children were not spontaneous snapshots of the kind we take of our own families nowadays. Many had a specific agenda – for instance, to demonstrate social conditions with a view to improving them. The pictures in Figure 6.7 are an example. They show a boy rescued by Barnardo's and his appearance after being cared for in a Barnardo's home.

Figure 6.6 The Daughters of Edward Darley Boit, 1882 by John Singer Sargent, American, 1856–1925, Oil on canvas 221.93 × 222.57 cm (87$\frac{3}{8}$ × 87$\frac{5}{8}$ in.), Museum of Fine Arts, Boston. Gift of Mary Louisa Boit, Julia Overing Boit, Jane Hubbard Boit, and Florence D. Boit in memory of their father, Edward Darley Boit

Photograph 2010, Museum of Fine Arts, Boston

'The myth of the child in popular imagery': Patricia Holland

Patricia Holland (2004; 2008) has written widely on visual images of children, both contemporary and from the recent past. Her interest began, as she describes, from a 'serendipitous' gathering of a

> large and eclectic collection of pictures of children made up of postcards and greetings cards . . . museum kitsch and all those brochures, catalogues, charity appeals and other printed material that come unsolicited through the letterbox . . . little girls in fairy tutus share cardboard boxes with

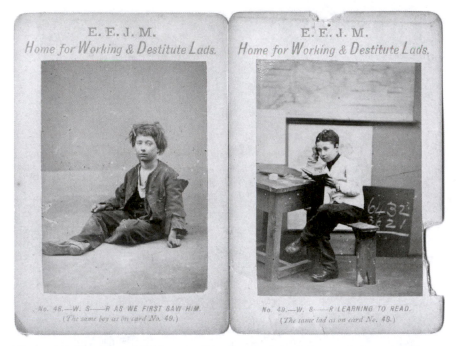

Figure 6.7 Victorian child 'rescued' by Barnardo's, © Barnardo's image library

the suffering children from international conflicts and the angry youngsters in inner city streets.

(2004: ix)

Holland's aim is to analyse the pleasure she has received from her 20-year-long 'hobby.' But she also acknowledges that she is writing within the 'context of two newish academic disciplines': the 'new' sociology of childhood which 'considers childhood . . . freed from the value-laden, instrumental preoccupations of developmental and educational approaches; and a burgeoning literature on visual culture which . . . celebrates the proliferation of popular visual forms' (p. x). She is not interested in works of art, like the paintings of Sargent or Cassatt, but in 'everyday' images such as, for instance, the 2001 H&M catalogue, full of children 'bursting with health and energy . . . and [wearing] clothes that are warm, hardwearing, good quality and stylish' (p. x).

In a later article (2008) Holland breaks down her collection of random images and concepts of childhood into more specific categories. First, there are those representations arising from 'an intense discourse of outrage in the popular press'. Second there is 'the expansion of consumer culture and the increase of advertising imagery'. Third, she draws attention to specific academic studies of specific aspects of childhood and youth such as Angela McRobbie's work on girlhood and media (1990) and Christina Hardyment's history of childcare literature ([1983] 2008). Fourth, she draws attention to what she calls institutional imagery – the visual records from schools, nurseries, clinics and hospitals. These include 'the child who is beyond such social controls – the twin images of waifs and hooligans' (p. 39). Fifth, there are what she calls images of the 'other': children who can be characterized as 'exotic, alien, poor' from the third world, and so on. Finally, sixth, there are images of children in the past, which could belong to all of these other categories too.

Holland argues that 'This popular imagery of childhood is part of adult culture not children's culture ... it is *about* them not *for* them' (2008: 37, original emphasis). Now that children have greater access to photographic technology of their own, through mobile phones and digital media, this is less the case. Whether it is a child taking the photograph of another child, or an adult creating the image, though, the subject of the picture remains to some extent 'othered', frozen in a particular moment. Holland calls our contemporary concerns about the sub-texts of even the most innocent-seeming and sunny images of childhood, a 'strange new mood' (2004: xiv). 'There seems to be a *need* to violate innocence ... childhood has become an overt focus for challenging taboos' (xiii, original emphasis) She discusses family imagery; advertising imagery; celebrity imagery; institutional images such as children in schools; and dangerous, sexualized imagery, including pornography on the Internet – raising particularly the issue of gender and girls' sexualization. The central questions, she argues, are: 'What is [the image] for? Who is invited to look at it? What has been made of it?' (p. 191).

She might also ask who are the agents or parties involved: who is the subject, and who is the image-maker and to what extent do they control the ways in which the image invites spectators, in what ways it is used, and to what extent? After all, there is always a real child, and a real photographer or painter, involved in the transaction of making an image. Painters such as Sargent did use real child models – but painters could also use imaginary and fantasy images of children; photography never can. This is a major difference between modern electronic visual representations of childhood and earlier ones: in photographs the person in the picture is always a real child at a real moment in a real life. For Holland this raises troubling questions of adult exploitation. Can any picture of a child nowadays truly be harmless and 'unshadowed'?

Children in film

These troubling questions become even more acute when considering the use of children in film – the child and the *moving* image. In film and television, children are not just the subject of a relatively instantaneous single snapshot, but may be required to spend weeks and months working on the movie, surrounded by adults and being required to undertake a variety of perhaps very unchildlike behaviours both behind and in front of the camera. (See the special issue of *Screen*, 2005.)

Children's agency: child performers

A crucial distinction here is between children *in* film, and film *for* children. This distinction has been most usefully unpacked by Cary Bazalgette and Terry Staples (1995: 94–5):

> The differences between the family film (essentially American) and what we shall call the children's film (essentially, but no longer exclusively, European) began then and begin now with casting . . . the child actors in family films had to offer not only national and ethnic identification to the child audience, but sexual appeal to the adult audience as well.[1]

By contrast the children's film movement in Europe (and more recently in a number of middle Eastern countries) has always held that the child protagonists in a children's film should not be

> desirable moppets . . . Children's films can be defined as offering mainly or entirely a child's point of view. They deal with the interests, fears, misapprehensions and concerns of children in their own terms. They foreground the problems of coping with adults or coping without them.
>
> (1995: 96)

Children in film: *City of God* and *Slumdog Millionaire*

Many films featuring children are not 'children's films' in the sense that they 'foreground [children's] problems of coping with adults or coping without them'. Indeed, they are often given ratings which prevent children seeing them and this raises questions about what purpose the child or children serve in the film, and whether these purposes are in the interests of children themselves. One way that some directors have found of avoiding the 'cute kid/moppets' problem is to use real children, not actors, as in the Brazilian film *City of God*

(*Cidade de Deus*, 2002). Here real children from the city (a slum in Rio de Janeiro) were used as the film's main performers, and ethical issues about the relationship of the real to the representational and about the proper treatment of children, were inevitably raised. The children 'performing' in *City of God* really did live in dangerous slums (not the actual city, which was 'too dangerous': [http://www.imdb.com/title/tt0317248/trivia]), and some really were involved in gangs. The children in the Oscar-winning *Slumdog Millionaire*, 2008, were also 'real' children, who lived in Indian shanty towns and returned to them after the Oscar presentations.

The film-makers in both these cases argued that their film was an act of 'rescue' (perhaps comparable to the child rescue movement of the nineteenth century); taking part in the film was a way of helping the child participants escape the violence and poverty of the slums. But this does not seem to have been the case with all the participants, including the young stars of *Slumdog*, who returned to their original neighbourhoods, and at the time of writing, still have not benefited from the advantages promised by the film-makers – schooling, rehousing and so on. The mimetic relationship with reality required in a film can also be problematic with young child performers who are often asked not to act, but to 'really' cry, or 'stare' or 'scream'. There is a scene in *City of God*, described in the 'Trivia' (*sic*) page about the movie on IMDB [http://www.imdb.com/title/tt0317248/trivia], in which a very small child is apparently shot in the foot by an older boy, and he has to 'really' cry. The acting coach made him cry by threatening him with the dentist. Another boy was told to bully a fellow actor for 15 days, which resulted in the victim threatening to leave the shoot altogether. This relation between the real and the representational could be seen as particularly problematic with this film, given that these children were required to act out sadistic and brutal behaviour virtually all the way through, and given that they were not professional actors but were the 'real' children who 'really' lived in this dangerous environment.

City of God is about as far from being a 'children's film' as it is possible to be and as such provides a useful guide to what actually *is* a 'children's film' by the Bazalgette and Staples criteria. Unlike a true 'children's film', *City of God* is not a place where children have moral agency, where the child is the 'good guy' and the adult is the 'bad guy' and where the adults are a problem for the children, rather than the other way round. It is *about* children, but not for them; the youngest children in the film would not be allowed to see it because its representation of the world these children inhabit is deemed to be harmful to other children. This is the paradox of the use of children in adult-rated films, a paradox which led one of the children we interviewed for our *Consenting Children* study, a 10-year-old girl, to assert: 'children shouldn't be used in films that children can't see' (Messenger Davies and Mosdell 2001: 1).

Consenting Children (Messenger Davies and Mosdell 2001) was a research study and report carried out for the Broadcasting Standards Commission in response to public complaints about the use, and perceived 'exploitation', of real children in adult factual programming on television. Examples were children being made to compete in a staring competition to win a prize for their parents, after which the 'loser' broke down and cried; and children's distress being exposed on camera in a *Panorama* (BBC) documentary about adoption.

Consenting Children raised a number of issues. First was the issue of the use of children and the 'eavesdropping' on, and recording of, their lives for the purposes of entertainment on television, for selling newspapers, or for artistic display and publicity – and the extent to which these children are enabled to understand, and consent, to what is happening to them. Secondly, the report was written at a time when there was a very real fear of children being harmed, specifically (but not only) through sexual abuse. The Tierney Gearon case discussed in the report, in which an art photographer's pictures of her naked children resulted in her gallery being reported to the police, contributed to this fearful atmosphere. (See the report from the Daily Telegraph, 16 March, 2001 [http://www.telegraph.co.uk/news/uknews/1326642/Gallery-not-charged-over-naked-children.html].) Cases like this help to create an environment in which parents allowing their children to play naked in the garden or beach, and to take photographs of them while they do so, may be induced to feel a sense of shame which could communicate itself in damaging ways to children. Parents would certainly feel threatened by the prospect of film-developers reporting them to the police. However, the issue of children's consent to the circulation of images depicting them is also raised, and not entirely answered, by this case. Even if Gearon's children had been happy to have their mother's pictures of them on show in a gallery, the images' subsequent reproduction in the media was beyond the children's control or consent.[2]

In our final recommendations, we proposed that news editors, picture editors and documentary makers do not routinely use images of children to illustrate difficult or emotive issues; where this is done, guidelines about not exploiting sickness and distress should be followed. Children themselves should also be consulted and quoted in stories concerning them (with full consent and, where possible, parental permission). We also recommended that media assumptions about children wanting to appear on television, and having the necessary confidence to do so, should be re-examined. From our findings, parents were more enthusiastic about seeing children on television than children themselves were. This reinforces the importance of children's consent to appear in the media being sought independently of that of their parents.

Conclusions: the real and the represented

In this chapter, I have addressed issues arising from visual representations of children by focusing particularly on the reality of the child behind the image. This links to the political questions of children's agency, raised by the 'new sociology of childhood' and the children's rights agenda (see Chapters 3 and 4). Images, whether still or moving, have been the subject of a great deal of sophisticated analysis, whether semiotic, psychoanalytic or aesthetic, in Media Studies. But from the point of view of the person in the picture, ultimately, media representations are just that: representations. Images of childhood, including verbal accounts such as the *Daily Mirror*'s scornful report about teenage drug addicts in 1985 – 'junk kids littering a junk world' – quoted by Holland (2004: 134) are one thing; what is actually going on in the lives of real children is something else. Already, despite the shock-horror existence of the *Mirror*'s 'junk kids' in 1985, the 1980s are now beginning to be constructed nostalgically in that time-honoured discourse of childhood, as a 'golden age': an innocent time before the toxicity of the screen-addicted world of children in the 2000s. In 1985, you could still buy a pint for under £1, children could still play in the street, no one had heard of the Internet and its lurking paedophiles, and my young daughter walked around in dungarees not sexualized tank tops. Media representations, especially powerful images, whether painted, photographic, or moving, freeze particular social and historical moments, and as time passes they acquire the mellowing patina of nostalgia. But underneath them, life goes on and children grow up, and grow older.

I realized this particularly clearly when I was working for *Mother & Baby* and *Parents* magazines in the 1970s and 80s, a time when my own children were young. The magazines represented many realistic aspects of childhood and child-rearing; they gave sensible, frank advice. Unlike the idealized representations of childhood in the Romantic era and the privileged realism of the lives of wealthy families in the Gilded era, they did not pull punches about the facts of life, sex and reproduction, and they covered a variety of social problems, including child abuse, family break-up and poverty. They published well-crafted, realistic images of recognizable children of all types and classes, and their families.

But I knew, as I lived alongside my own growing children, that these journalistic versions of childhood and parenthood, no matter how frank and realistic, were both curtailed and idealized. They had to fit the space, the formats and the monthly deadlines of the magazines and they had to be primarily encouraging and helpful, not pessimistic and destructive, to the parents who bought them. They also had to serve the interests of the advertisers, whose products, illustrated by attractive, healthy babies, toddlers and parents, kept the magazines financially afloat. Life, as I and my family and friends were living it, was something else – not completely divorced from the representations in the magazine, but much fuller, busier, messier, more complex and of course, much more inescapable. Images could be discarded; babies couldn't. The images stayed the same; but as the snapshot earlier in this chapter shows, the babies didn't.

In the Museum of Fine Arts in Boston, John Singer Sargent's picture of the children of Edward Darley Boit hangs by itself on one wall. On either side of it, at each corner of the wall, is a huge piece of ceramic ware – the actual vases represented in the painting. It is as if the vases have stepped out of the frame, bringing the past to life. But the children, whose presence in the painting is as vivid, indeed more vivid, than that of the vases, of course, can never step out of the frame. They are frozen in that long-ago moment in time when Sargent painted them.

Paintings like these, family snapshots, advertisements in *Parents* magazine in the 1980s, all force us to face the one unmistakeable, unavoidable and poignant fact about childhood: the fact so imaginatively represented in *Tom's Midnight Garden*. It is a fact which gives rise to countless cultural manifestations, 'Golden Age' reminiscences and a huge body of literature; a fact which is not a social construction, and which is not culturally relative. Children grow up. And in the case of the Boit children in Sargent's picture, the youngest of whom, 4-year-old Julia, died, aged 92, in 1969, they have long since not only grown up, they have grown old, and died. The idea of the Golden Age helps us to keep this difficult fact at bay.

Further reading

The ways in which children are *represented* in media invite useful scholarship from other disciplines, for example, art history – see Barbara Dayer Gallati's (2004) *Children of the Gilded Era: Portraits by Sargent, Renoir, Cassatt and Their Contemporaries*, London, New York: Merrell. The range of childhood visual representations made possible by photography, advertising, merchandising and other media is perceptively discussed by Patricia Holland (2004) in *Picturing Childhood: The Myth of the Child in Popular Imagery*, London, New York: I.B. Tauris. For the rights and voices of children themselves, and the degree of control they are allowed to exert over the ways in which the media represent them, see Messenger Davies, M. and Mosdell, N. (2001) *Consenting Children? The Use of Children in Non-fiction Television Programmes*, London: Broadcasting Standards Commission, online at [http://cmr.ulster.ac.uk/pdf/policy/consenting_children.pdf] and Messenger Davies, M. and Mosdell, N. (2005) 'The representation of children in the media: aspects of agency and literacy', in J. Goddard, S. McNamee, A. James and A. James (eds) *The Politics of Childhood: International Perspectives, Contemporary Developments*, Manchester: Palgrave/Macmillan, 208–25.

CHILDREN'S UNOFFICIAL CULTURE: GAMES, TRADITIONS AND TALES

'Babies do not want to hear about babies; they like to be told of giants and castles of somewhat which can stretch and stimulate their little minds.'
Samuel Johnson to Mrs Thrale, *Anecdotes of Samuel Johnson*, 1786, quoted in Opie and Opie (eds), *The Classic Fairy Tales* ([1974] 1992: 8)

It is grown people who make the nursery stories; all children do, is jealously to preserve the text.
Robert Louis Stevenson, quoted in Opie and Opie as above, frontispiece

The 'archaeology' of children's culture

In moving on to forms of media directly addressed *to* children, and/or which children have enjoyed (even when not addressed to them), we begin with the earliest known stories and cultural forms, such as folk and fairy tales and oral traditions. These stories and games predate contemporary commercial media, and even bypass the privileged cultural medium of print. Ideas, imagery, plots and characters drawn from these ancient forms are still current in contemporary media – such as the wizards, spells, elves, riddles, robes and creatures in the Harry Potter series, whose filmic imagery would be quite recognizable to medieval children. Cultural products handed on primarily in oral forms – such as playground games, nursery rhymes, jokes and riddles – are important from the point of view of another key perspective discussed throughout this book: they demonstrate children's agency, observable in even the most desperate conditions, for example among street children. Children's oral culture remains a product of their own imaginations and inventiveness, not those of global corporations. Playground games and rhymes may be inspired by published media forms such as TV shows, books or films, but where they originate and how they are circulated is always somewhat mysterious.

Children's games: the tribe

As Heller (2008: 272) reminds us, 'toys and games have an important function in teaching and consolidating social rules and norms'. One of the most important ways in which children learn social rules and norms is by making up their own. Despite the fact that many children in developed societies occupy what has been called a 'bedroom culture', children everywhere do still manage to get together and organize themselves for the purpose of play and other activities (some nefarious), without the intervention of adults, in school or other playgrounds, on beaches and open spaces, and, when allowed, in the street. A useful website listing some of the playground games that were still current in 2007 is 'Kids Games' at http://www.gameskidsplay.net/default.htm in which over 200 skipping games, ball games, chasing games, circle games and various rules for deciding who is 'it', are listed.

I interviewed children in North East London in 2008, and collected several new rhymes and clapping games that my own now grown-up children, and I myself, had not known in childhood. Some of the old rule-governed games and 'dips' (for choosing teams) from our day, such as 'ippy, dippy dation, my operation', are still in use. A group of 11–12-year-old girls and boys from diverse backgrounds at the Chicken Shed Children's Theatre in North East London produced 57 different games and activities. Half were sports, the other half were all playground games; some I had heard of, but with different names, such as 'Block home', which my children called 'Blocky', and some I had never heard of, such as '40–40' and 'stuck in the mud'.

Considering the richness and entertainment value of children's playground games, they have been surprisingly neglected by scholars of children's culture, perhaps because it is rather difficult to accommodate this robust genre into a model of childhood which portrays children as passive, unhealthy, oppressed victims of contemporary 'toxic' (to use Sue Palmer's, 2006, word) culture. A research project has recently started at London University's Institute of Education, investigating this unauthorized world, and relating it to social networking on the Internet: 'Children's Playground Games and Songs in the New Media Age' (AHRC 'Beyond Text' programme, see Rebekah Willett's work at [www.ioe.ac.uk/study/LKLB_56.html]). There obviously is some continuity between traditional, informal, child-generated play and Internet social networking. But there are also ways in which children's playground games do not easily fit into the contemporary view of the child as innately 'media-savvy' and only capable of being amused by electronic equipment.

'The people in the playground': Iona and Peter Opie

The pioneers of study into children's traditional playground culture were a married couple, Iona and Peter Opie. They were based in Hampshire, but had Scottish origins. As is the case with so many researchers on children and their culture, they were inspired to begin their researches by the birth of their own child in 1944 and they became collectors of rare and early children's books. Their first book: *The Oxford Book of Nursery Rhymes* ([1951] 1997), has become the basis of many other collections. Their later books include: *The Lore and Language of Schoolchildren*, ([1959] 1986); *Children's Games in Street and Playground*, ([1969] 1988); *The People in the Playground* (Opie 1992). They also produced *The Classic Fairytales* ([1974] 1992), a collection of the first versions of fairy stories to be published in English. These were not the first versions ever published, nor were they necessarily the earliest or most 'authentic' versions of the stories themselves. But from the versions published in the Opies' collection, we can see which variants of these stories were the first to become 'authorized' for English-speaking audiences. Some are quite unfamiliar; some have become the standard versions. This illustrates the most important point that the Opies wanted to make: that history is in the moment, and that the analysis of a culture and its past needs to include what has survived into the present and is still with us, often unnoticed. Much evidence for children's lives and culture, they argue, is right under our noses – not buried in archives, nor in church paintings.

They criticized the approach of early folklorists, who looked on data as 'archaeological remains, rather than living organisms which are constantly evolving' ([1969] 1988: viii).

> [I]t is remarkable how much guesswork has been expended on classical medieval and Tudor pastimes, simply because the learned commentators in the 18th and 19th centuries, closeted in their studies, lacked knowledge of the games that their own children were playing in the sunshine outside their windows.
>
> ([1969] 1988: viii–ix)

Although they were not conventional academic scholars and were never attached to a university, the Opies' approach is similar to the New Sociology of Childhood position which emphasizes children's autonomy and agency. In the preamble to their study of children's playground games they pointed out: 'Children are people going about their own business within their own society, and are fully capable of occupying themselves under the jurisdiction of their own code' (p. v). The Opies' focus on the first *published* versions of fairytales, as distinct from other supposedly more 'authentic' transcripts of oral versions, emphasizes the relativism of cultural values – another tenet of contemporary sociology.

The Opies' methods: mapping the outdoor world

The Opies studied the games that children, aged about 6–12, play of their own accord. This age group is the period of life when children are most likely to form autonomous groups away from adult supervision, out of doors and out of adult sight. The Opies' initial studies in the 1950s mapped a world which now barely exists in twenty-first-century industrialized societies: a world in which autonomous groups of children, playing and planning, were a much more common sight in the streets of cities, and also in the open countryside, than they are today (see for example Colin Ward's 1978 book, *The Child in the City*). The Opies' update of the lore and language of schoolchildren in 1969 noted some of these changes but still portrayed a world in which children were seen as an accepted part of the public sphere. They surveyed an extraordinary number: 10,000 children in England, Scotland and the Eastern part of Wales, mostly in urban settings. As a result of these researches, which included surveying historical collections both in the UK and the USA,[1] they were able to proclaim: 'There is no town or city known to us where street games do not flourish.' As in the case of other folklorists and historians, the Opies were motivated by a desire to preserve and record things that appeared to be rapidly changing and disappearing. However, as we shall see, they have not disappeared.

Children's playground culture is extensive and diverse. *The Lore* has chapters on: fun (jokes, tongue twisters, satirical rhymes, 'spookies'); riddles; topical rhymes (featuring World War 2, Mickey Mouse, Shirley Temple and Davy Crockett among others – new topical rhymes can travel astonishingly fast across the world); parody and impropriety (with many rhymes about 'bums' and 'arses' and a great deal of toilet humour); nicknames and epithets; pranks and 'codes of oral legislation'. In this chapter, codes of 'affirmation' such as 'cross my heart and hope to die', and codes of 'claiming precedence' such as 'bags I', show first, how rule-governed the unofficial world of childhood can be, and secondly, how universal these methods of establishing rules seem to be.

In their introduction to the second edition of *The Lore and Language*, in the much more media-saturated world of 1986, the Opies noted: 'Folk heroes have displaced one another; Davy Crockett has been ousted by Kermit the Frog and E.T., Diana Dors by Madonna' (1986: x). (Interestingly these 1980s 'folk heroes'

Figure 7.1 Children playing in street, New York, credit: Library of Congress, Prints & Photographs Division, [LC-DIG-ggbain-03233]

are still recognizably current in 2009–10.) Writing at the same time as Neil Postman was lamenting the disappearance of childhood brought about by television, the Opies point out, as he did – but with very different conclusions – that: 'The schoolchild jokers of today are as unconcernedly flippant about glue sniffing and drug addiction as their predecessors were about violent death' (p. x). They argue that 'children continue to regulate their own society . . . with much the same code of law and style of humour as they did thirty – or a hundred – years ago' (p. x). Jokes about housewives having affairs with the milkman also appear to be durable, as in this rhyme I collected from two 11-year-old girls in Hertfordshire in 2008:

Milkman, Milkman, do your duty
here comes Mrs Macarooty
she can do the pom, poms- pom, pom.
She can do the splits
Ooooooooooooh
But most of all she likes to kiss
K. I. S. S.
'there are actions too; when it says pom poms you throw your right hand in the air, then your left.'[2]

One reason why there have not been extensive follow-ups to the Opies' kind of fieldwork is the much greater restriction there now is on researchers having access to children without parental or teacher permission and supervision. It is rather sad that the website 'Kids' Games' states on its Games Submittal section: 'I'm sorry, but due to the volume of submissions, and the guidelines of the new Children's Online Privacy Protection Act (which we support!), I am no longer accepting new game submissions.'

Oral traditions in storytelling: folk and fairytales

Folk and fairytales are somewhat different from children's own games, songs and riddles in that they are usually invented and handed on by adults. However, they have something in common with children's playground culture in that their origins are mysterious and their authors are multiple and anonymous. The same kinds of stories also turn up, with local variations, all over the world, and at different periods of history – which suggest common preoccupations for the people who produced and transmitted them.

Folk and fairytales are still enormously popular in various contemporary forms. Pantomimes based on fairytales have become a staple tradition of children's Christmas celebrations in the UK and Ireland, which shows no sign of dying out. The Disney versions of various fairytales also remain popular, as do regular new picture book collections. It is striking, though, that panto and film mainly draw on the same few European stories: Cinderella, Beauty and the Beast, The Sleeping Beauty, Snow White and the Seven Dwarfs and Jack and the Beanstalk. An exception is the popularity of Aladdin (15 pantomime productions in 2008) – a story that comes from the Arabian 'A Thousand and One Nights'.

Origins of fairytales

All fairytales and folk myths are the literature of preliterate societies, and, as Angela Carter in her Virago collection of feminist tales, points out, 'you will find very few actual fairies within the [following] pages' (1990: ix). Marina Warner, another feminist commentator on fairy tales, notes in *From the Beast to the Blonde* (1995) that part of the literary 'invention of childhood' was the collection and publication of stories that had been traditionally handed down orally, usually by women – 'old wives' tales'. But why did women bother to do this? What was their purpose?

One purpose, obviously, as with more recent forms of literary and audiovisual storytelling, is entertainment – to while away the long dark winter evenings, and to keep bored and frazzled children occupied. But the fact that these stories were 'part of the literary invention of childhood' also suggests that they were seen as valuable tools for socialization: their goal was to pass on lessons about 'the problems of living', in De Fleur and Ball Rokeach's (1988) phrase, to future generations. Fairytales, with their monsters, witches, shape-shifting beasts and animals, injustices, strange landscapes and grisly outcomes, have provoked criticism as inappropriate media for socialization. In the past this tended to be because of their violence and cruelty; more recently they have provoked indignation on feminist grounds for their supposedly unrealistic 'happy endings', with pretty girls being passively rescued by handsome princes, instead of having independent careers (see Davis 2006 on some of the unfairly maligned Disney heroines). Scholars have interpreted them differently too.

The nature of fairytales: Maria Tatar

In her study of the tales collected by the Grimm brothers in the nineteenth century, Maria Tatar points out the common themes of many fairy stories. Citing Tolstoy's comment that 'every unhappy family is unhappy in its own way', she points out that actually: 'in fairy tales unhappy families are all very much alike. Nearly every sibling is a rival and at least one parent is an ogre . . . ultimately the hero's parents, his progenitors and guardians – are directly implicated in the misfortunes that besiege him' (2003: 59–60). Tatar argues that we cannot infer from these tales that children in the past – or in other cultures – have always grown up in abusive families:

> The popularity of the theme of abandoned children stems from psychic sources, from childhood daydreams and fantasies about grudges and reprisals against parents . . . Fantasy more than fact seems to serve as the basis for that vast class of fairy tales in which the central figure is a victimised hero. Such tales can be found all over the world.
>
> (p. 60)

In invoking psychic 'uses', her arguments link with those of psychoanalytic writers such as Bruno Bettelheim (of which more below) – although Tatar herself is a professor of Germanic Languages and Literature, not, as Bettelheim was, a child psychotherapist.

Folklore collectors: the Brothers Grimm

We owe our contemporary knowledge of anonymous orally-transmitted tales to a number of nineteenth- and early twentieth-century researchers, including two brothers, Jakob and Wilhelm Grimm, whose names have become synonymous with fairy tales. They were nineteenth-century folklorists, operating in Germany during the Romantic era – a cultural period in Europe which exalted the power of individual emotion and imagination. The beginning of the nineteenth century also saw a revival of nationalism with many European countries using national myths and folkloric legends to bolster their sense of national identity. As discussed in Chapters 2 and 3, ideas about the essential innocence and superior moral insight of children were linked to these developments. The Grimm versions of fairy tales are often seen as more authentic than earlier collections, such as those of the French Charles Perrault in the seventeenth century, because the brothers claimed to have transcribed the stories exactly as the original tellers told them.

However, this begs the question of what, in an oral tradition of storytelling, with no named authors, counts as 'authentic'. Who is to say what the authorized version should truly be? Maria Tatar (2003) points out that the Grimms, far from producing authentic versions of the tales, 'rewrote them so extensively and went so far in the direction of eliminating off colour episodes that they can be credited with sanitizing folk tales and thereby paving the way for the process that made them acceptable children's literature in all cultures' (p. 24). For example, the Grimm brothers altered earlier versions of Snow White, where it was the mother who tormented Snow White, and substituted a stepmother, possibly because Romantic and Victorian ideas about the family and motherhood had become idealized in the 'purer' and more a-sexual world of nineteenth-century middle-class society.

Tatar points out that the Grimm versions of the tales still have elements of 'unsuitability' for children (a criticism frequently made in the twentieth century); some are, indeed, quite shocking to contemporary tastes, featuring savage violence: cannibalism, incest and routine dismemberment, in which even the Virgin Mary takes part (see the story, 'Mary's Child'). Maria Tatar describes a story showing how 'children played butcher with each other' and everyone gets killed, which, she says, Wilhelm Grimm thought was 'perfectly acceptable' as a children's story (p. 181). According to Tatar, the story apparently taught him an important lesson of caution and restraint. The Grimms' *Nursery and Household Tales*, first published in 1812 and in English in 1823, have been bestsellers ever since; despite the violence, the title indicates that the book was clearly aimed at children and continues to be so.

Authored fairytales

In the late seventeenth and eighteenth centuries, traditional tales were collected and turned into literary versions by named authors; there were the French Madame D'Aulnoy's *Collection of Novels and Tales*, published in English in 1721 and Frenchman Charles Perrault's collections, published in English in

1729. Andrew Lang, a Scot, published collections of British folk tales in 1889. These collections proved so popular that many established adult writers began to produce their own – thus giving rise to original fairytales with named literary authors, a new departure. Hans Andersen, in Denmark, whose collection was first published in English in 1846, wrote wholly original tales, which many people would be surprised to learn did not come from an oral tradition, but simply from his own extremely fertile and rather depressive imagination (see the sad endings, for example, of 'The Little Mermaid' – changed to a happy one in the 1989 Disney version – and 'The Little Matchgirl').

Such was the popularity of the fairytale form in the nineteenth century that established writers began to use it: there was John Ruskin's 'The King of the Golden River' in 1851 and William Makepeace Thackeray's 'The Rose and the Ring' in 1855, which had elements of spoof – assuming, therefore, that children and other readers would be very familiar with the standard ingredients of fairytale. Charles Dickens – a big fan of fairytales, who had been 'in love with Little Red Riding Hood' when he was a child – also wrote an entertaining fairytale, 'The Magic Fishbone', in 1868.

All this initiated a cult for editions of fairytales for every generation that has never disappeared. Artists have been drawn to them, and variants created in order to update them and make them fashionable to a contemporary audience. These variants give us insights into changing historical tastes and fashions. In Perrault's seventeenth-century version of Cinderella, the eldest 'ugly' sister says she'll wear her red velvet suit with French trimming, and ruffles. Such updates have inspired many artists, once the tales began to be widely published. See for example, the illustration by Walter Crane, of Beauty reviving the dying beast, 1870, for the book *Goody Two Shoes* (reproduced in Opies' *The Classic Fairy Tales*, 1974; Figure 7.2). Beauty in this illustration is not wearing clothes contemporary to Crane's late nineteenth century, but something more akin to the Perraultian eighteenth-century fashions. Thus fairy tales and their adaptations incorporate different and sometimes anachronistic cultural connotations for each generation. 'Authenticity' – it is clear – is not a consideration in any of these reworkings, any more than it is in contemporary pantomimes; this is in the nature of fairytales and of the oral tradition.

Much earlier collections of tales had appeared in other parts of the world – the Pentamarone, collected by Giambattista Basile in Italy, published between 1634 and 1636. And earlier than that – in the eleventh century, the Indian Somadeva collected hundreds of Indian stories, in the Katha Sarit Sagara (Ocean of Streams of Story). Hindu collections include the Panchatantra, dating back to the fifth century, and of course there are Irish, Welsh and Scottish tales, all of considerable age, which were collected in the nineteenth century again, e.g. in Andrew Lang's collections.

Figure 7.2 Beauty and the Beast by Walter Crane. Cover image from the book *The Classic Fairy Tales* by Iona and Peter Opie, published by Oxford University Press, 1974.

Structuralist approaches: Vladimir Propp

> Folklore is part of the religious ceremonial practice – religious magic practice and the acts by which primitive man believed he could influence nature and defend himself from it.
>
> (Vladimir Propp, *The Morphology of the Folk Tale* [1928] 1968)

Vladimir Propp, a Russian scholar, developed a Morphology of the Folktale – a structural analysis of the elements, roles and functions of traditional tales, based on readings of hundreds of stories from the Russian collections made by Finnish folklorist, Antti Aarne. Propp argued that the structures which he had uncovered of Russian folk tales were universal. Propp outlined seven different character functions in the stories he analysed:

1. The Villain
2. The Donor or Provider
3. The Helper
4. The Princess (and her Father)
5. The Despatcher
6. The Hero
7. The False Hero

The other basis of Propp's analysis was narrative form. The list below outlines the basic recurring narrative events that he claimed turn up in all folk tales – and in other kinds of narrative too:

1. One or more absents himself/herself from home
2. An interdiction
3. They violate the interdiction
4. Villain reconnaissance
5. Villain receives information about the victim
6. Deceit of hero
7. Hero submits to deceit
8. The villain causes harm to member of family
9. Hero is approached – with request or demand

. . . final sequences of the story:

26. The task is resolved
27. The hero is recognized
28. The false hero or villain is exposed
29. The hero is given a new appearance
30. The villain is punished
31. The hero is married and ascends the throne

Why are these formulaic stories, with the same plots, scenarios, characters and functions repeated over and over again, seen as appropriate for children? One reason, obviously, is that in an oral tradition, formulas make stories easier to remember. But there have been a number of other interpretations of these stories, which suggest deeper functions and meanings.

Feminist approaches

Marina Warner, a twentieth-century feminist historian, with a particular interest in mythic figures and the ways in which they have been re-invented through history (e.g. The Virgin Mary), argues that fairytales like Cinderella embody misogynist elements in society and particularly bear witness against women – the absent mother, the harsh and hurtful stepmother, the cruel sisters. Warner's book focuses on the social context of the production of the tales; she points out that many of them are not just metaphorical but represent a literal truth about the way lives were in the past: mothers did die, stepmothers did take over. Warner stresses the rather negative image that women have in stories, reflecting the relationships in households in which young wives were often at the mercy of jealous mothers-in-law (a position that still obtains today for some young wives in traditional cultures).

In contrast, novelist and professor of children's literature, Alison Lurie, emphasizes the frequency of powerful women in traditional stories. In the chapter 'Folktale liberation' in her book *Don't Tell the Grownups* (1990), she points out: 'In the Grimms' original Children's and Household tales, 1812 (the German version), there are sixty-one women and girl characters as against only 21 men and boys: and these men are usually dwarfs not humans' (Lurie 1990: 19).

Lurie's own edited collection of traditional tales, *Clever Gretchen*, (1980) brings together a number of stories in all of which there is a powerful female protagonist who gets the better of her various adversaries – jealous stepmothers; envious sisters; giants; dwarves, beasts and general misfortune. Angela Carter, the novelist, also edited a collection of fairy tales for Virago, the feminist publishing house. Carter's collection of stories, taken from many different cultures all over the world, also emphasizes women's power and strength, as well as their occasional un-sisterly behaviour and collusion with powerful males. Carter presents the tales 'as a reminder of how wise, clever, perceptive, occasionally lyrical, eccentric and sometimes downright crazy our great-grandmothers were, and their great-grandmothers; of the contributions to literature of Mother Goose and her goslings' (1990: xxii).

Carter's and Lurie's feminism is thus more celebratory than Warner's. They obviously love these stories and have found them inspirational in their own creative work. They argue that the tales can be used to provide strong role models for girls, indicating yet again the adaptability of traditional stories, not only for children, but also for academic analysis, and for adult creative writers.

Psychological approaches: Bruno Bettelheim

Bruno Bettelheim is one of the most famous and persuasive of fairytale commentators. His book *The Uses of Enchantment: The Meaning and Importance of Fairytales* (1976), is a very accessible analysis of some of the most popular tales, and it has been widely read and cited. In my research with children's TV drama producers (2001; 1997), Bettelheim was invoked again and again by creative producers and writers seeking to explain the power of fantasy fiction for their child audiences. Bettelheim, born in 1903, committed suicide in 1990; he was a psychoanalyst who had been imprisoned in the Dachau and Buchenwald concentration camps during the Second World War. He kept himself sane by writing and mental problem-solving and went to America after the war. He devoted his life to helping very disturbed children and adolescents and after his death, there has been some controversy both about his therapeutic methods and the authenticity of his qualifications. Nevertheless, *The Uses of Enchantment* remains one of the most persuasive and authoritative books on the relevance of fairy tales for children and childhood.[3]

Life divined from the inside

Bettelheim wrote about fairytales as necessary for psychological health, drawing on a Freudian psychoanalytic perspective. He called them 'life divined from the inside', (1976: 25–6). He reminds us that 'throughout most of man's history, a child's intellectual life, apart from . . . the family, depended on mythical and religious stories, and on fairytales' (p. 24). Bettelheim points out that 'in a fairy tale, internal processes are externalized and become comprehensible, as *represented* by the figures of the story and its events' (p. 25, my emphasis). He distinguishes fairytales from myths, which teach lessons about the right and wrong way to behave, according to a society's values. Bettelheim argues: 'Far from making rather impossible demands to emulate great heroes, as myths often do, the fairytale reassures: it gives hope for the future and holds out the promise of a happy ending.' Fairytales are especially tailored for children. Myths are not:

> [F]airy stories do not pretend to describe the world as it is, nor do they advise one what they ought to do . . . The fairytale is therapeutic because the patient finds his *own* solutions, through contemplating what the story seems to imply about him and his inner conflicts at this moment in his life.
>
> (p. 25, original emphasis)

Bettelheim stresses that lack of realism is a vital ingredient of the true fairytale. The fact that stories take place long ago and far away, in places with no obvious name, about characters with no real identity or history, recounting events that are impossible in the everyday world, 'makes it obvious that the fairytales' concern is not useful information about the external world, but the inner processes taking place in an individual' (1976: 25). By 'realism' Bettelheim means the surface realism located in external, contemporary verisimilitude (for example, the kinds of fashionable costume details added by Perrault).

But, of course, there is a deeper psychological realism, a distinction between 'truth' and 'accuracy': which Alison Lurie proposes in her book, *Don't Tell the Grownups* (1990). She describes a gift she received when she was 5 – a book written by 'a high-minded, progressive author', Lucy Sprague Mitchell, which was about 'real people'. It had stories with titles such as 'This is the Grocery Man', and 'How Spot found a Home'. In the introduction to her book, Sprague Mitchell attacked fairytales: 'Does not Cinderella interject a social and economic situation which is both confusing and vicious . . . Does not Jack and the Beanstalk delay a child's rationalizing of the world, and leave him . . . without the beginnings of scientific standards?' (cited in Lurie, 1990: 17). As Lurie points out, it was Mitchell's contemporary stories that were, in fact, unrealistic:

> The simple pleasant adult society they had prepared us for, did not exist. As we had suspected, the fairy tales had been right all along. The world was full of hostile stupid giants and perilous castles and people who abandoned their children in the nearest forest. To succeed in this world you needed some special skill or patronage, plus remarkable luck and it didn't hurt to be very good looking . . . kindness to those in trouble was also advisable – you never knew who might be useful to you later on.
>
> (pp. 17–18)

'The uses of enchantment'

In a chapter on 'The child's need for magic', Bettelheim takes a similar perspective to more recent developmental psychologists about the 'primitive' perspective of the young child's thinking processes. He argues that the child's thinking (pre 7 years old or so) is animistic – the child thinks the sun is alive as 'primitive' peoples do. Animals are alive and can be guides; rivers and stones can talk. Stories answer the questions: 'Who am I? How ought I to deal with life's problems?' Bettelheim contrasts fairy stories with religious texts such as the Bible. Religious texts, he says, didn't offer solutions to the problems posed by the dark side of our personalities. As the story of Cain and Abel shows, there is no sympathy in the Bible for the agonies of sibling rivalry. Cain kills Abel and is forever 'marked' and outcast. Cinderella, on the other hand, illustrates these agonies more sympathetically, and provides a happy resolution to them.

Not all scholars would go all the way with Bettelheim's Freudian analysis of fairytales, but many readers and literary educators have found it helpful and a stimulus to further critical thinking, especially in understanding the enduring power they continue to have for children. Mary Hilton, a lecturer in primary language and literature, talks about 'the deep play of narrative fantasy' (1996: 41):

[C]hildren like adults need to fantasize, to dream. Popular fictions seem often shamelessly to address and repeat the dream themes which allow the pleasure of organizing growing sexual identity with its intense anxieties and repressed material. Children's continued repetition of highly gendered play narratives from Power Rangers to Barbie are perhaps a way of repeating to themselves fantasies of potent desire . . . we often find evidence of children doing totally different things with toys and narratives.

These repressed fantasies, according to psychoanalytic theory, are girls' intense identification with their mothers, which is not broken as they become women. In contrast, says Hilton, there is a breaking of this identification in boys as they become adolescents and become markedly physically different from their mothers (suggesting again the relationship between biological development and cultural motifs). Adolescent boys now identify with warrior/heroes and, Hilton points out, the villains in their favoured fantasy stories are often 'feminized', with soft voices. The feminine is rejected. Bettelheim sees fairytales as offering ways out of these repetitive patterns, though. His view of fairytale heroes and heroines is that they are androgynous and offer ways for the child of either sex to come to terms with their fears and fantasies and to recognize their ability to overcome them. Thus psychoanalysis offers somewhat contrasting approaches to the interpretation of fairytale texts.

Adapting fairytales: from ninth-century China to twentieth-century Disney

Fairytales are told and retold in many forms and in many countries. For some contemporary children, fairytales are known primarily through the versions produced by the Disney studios, but the Disney versions, too, are capable of considerable variations in reception and interpretation (see Wasko et al., 2001, a cross cultural study with hundreds of young people from 53 countries around the world). The first full-length animated film feature was a fairytale: *Snow White and the Seven Dwarfs*, produced by Disney in 1937. Despite some industry scepticism that a 'cartoon' could attract a feature-film audience, the film was a huge hit, and has become a classic, the first of a long line of Disney fairytale adaptations. Amy Davis points out in her study of Disney female characters, *Good Girls and Wicked Witches* (2006), that, despite criticisms of sentimentality and distortion of the 'original' (whatever the original is supposed to be), the Disney versions have succeeded in capturing the timeless qualities of fairytales, which enable them to be made continuingly meaningful for successive generations: 'they must, in some way, still hold relevance for modern audiences' (2006: 19).

Two case studies: Cinderella and Beauty and the Beast

The most famous and widely-told fairytale of all is Cinderella – or Aschenputtel, in the Grimm version. The first edition of Cinderella in English was Robert Samber's translation of Perrault's version of the tale, which introduced the glass slipper, published in London in 1729, in *Histories or Tales of Past Times*. This is the version that appears in the Opies' collection of classic fairytales: it was translated from the *Histoires ou Contes du Temps passe* by Charles Perrault, published in Paris in 1697.

The earliest version of Cinderella is Chinese, written down around 850 AD. It is the story of Yeh-hsien and follows the familiar pattern of a mother dying, a wicked stepmother preferring her own daughter and mistreating the heroine. Yeh-hsien's 'godmother', or special helper, is a golden fish (in other stories, as in Aschenputtel, it is a tree, in Rashin Coatie, a Scots version from the sixteenth century, it is a little red calf). All represent the dead mother watching over the daughter. The stepmother kills the fish, eats it and hides the bones under the dunghill. But an enchanter tells Yeh-hsien where to find the bones and she hides them in her room and prays to them whenever she wants something. There is a big festival, she cannot go, but she does go – and when her sister recognizes her, runs away, losing her golden slipper as she runs. The local warlord claims he will marry the person it fits, and Yeh-hsien becomes his 'chief wife'. The stepmother and sister are stoned to death.

We can see that certain symbols remain constant through these different versions of the tale. Marina Warner points out that tiny bound feet were valued in China, and the erotic symbolism of the foot entering the shoe was noted by Bruno Bettelheim. In the Grimm version, the sisters hack their toes off to make the shoe fit – an indication of their falseness. The hacking off of the toes (and the subsequent scene when birds peck out the sisters' eyes) are now usually left out of modern versions of the story; they certainly do not appear in the Disney version. Perrault's version has Cinderella forgiving her sisters and inviting them to live in the palace with her, which Bruno Bettelheim does not approve of. For him, the violent defeat of envious, savage people in fairytales represents symbolically a psychological victory for the child over their worst emotions and impulses. As such, these violent and conclusive denouements must remain in order to reassure the child that destructive emotions can be overcome.

The Perrault version of 1723 has been around in the English-speaking world longer than the Grimm version. The issue of 'authenticity', so central to debates about the nationalistic elements of traditional tales – whose country's version is the 'purest' – is raised here: it is also an issue in some scholars' dismissal of the Disney versions. For many scholars, including Bettelheim, the Grimm version is seen as more authentically the product of the peasant oral tradition, yet its publication in 1812 came long after the Perrault version. It is the Perrault version that most pantomimes, picture books (and the Disney film) are based on. Aschenputtel/Cinderella in the Grimm version is far more active and ingenious in evading the prince than she is in Perrault's more ladylike account. This can be seen as a feminist point, though it is unlikely that the Grimms intended it as one. It is probable that Aschenputtel owes her feistiness to an anonymous peasant grandmother, rather than to a courtly male author, and in this sense, we can accept Aschenputtel as genuinely 'authentic.'

Bruno Bettelheim argues that Cinderella, in whatever incarnation, is basically a story about sibling rivalry. For a Freudian, the origins of sibling rivalry are often oedipal – the brother or sister is a rival for the affection of the parent of the opposite sex. Bettelheim argues that this is an emotion which arouses shame – so that the child feels their degradation is deserved – they deserve to be cast down among the ashes and cinders. Ashes and cinders are symbols of mourning, but also of degradation and dirt – and the child associates anxieties about dirt with anxieties about toilet training.

Although we may not agree with a straight Freudian interpretation of the recurring symbols in these variants of the story, they do provide striking imagery for animated versions, which the Disney movies have exploited to the full: striking clocks, transformed pumpkins and mice as footmen, as well as the Disney-esque troops of helpful birds and animals, symbolizing the heroine's sympathy with the natural world, are brilliantly served by animation. Film translates symbol into motion – and filmic techniques, such as light and shadow, musical motifs, and differences in graphic style, create new symbols to illustrate Cinderella's goodness, her stepmother's envy and cruelty, and the spirit of the dead mother. These techniques can certainly be described as a contemporary form of 'authenticity' in the re-telling of the tale. The symbolic re-interpretation of enduring themes is how the transmission of fairytales has always worked.

Beauty and the Beast

Bettelheim makes a similar psychoanalytic argument for Beauty and the Beast, a variant on the Greek myth of Cupid and Psyche. The first English translation of Beauty and the Beast was from Madame le Prince de Beaumont, in 1761 – a French version, which makes the setting of the 1996 Oscar-nominated Disney film, in eighteenth-century France, appear historically authentic. Beauty and the Beast, says Bettelheim, posits the immature view that we have a dual existence as animal and as mind and that they are separate. These must be unified to complete human fulfilment. According to a Freudian interpretation, this is the humanization and socialization of the id by the superego. The offspring of this union is Pleasure or Joy.

Beauty and the Beast has been interpreted as one of a number of stories warning about the risks of curiosity – such stories being particularly directed at girls and women (as in the case of Bluebeard). Once again Maria Tatar provides a corrective to overly moralistic or conspiratorial interpretations of fairy tales. She asserts 'if there is a secret message planted in fairy tales it is inscribed in plain sight, right on the surface of each tale's events' (2003, p. 177). She argues that the collectors have overlaid the original 'moral' of the story with a secondary morality, e.g. Bluebeard isn't about the 'crime' of the wife's curiosity (like Eve and the apple in the Garden of Eden), as patriarchal collectors suggest. It's really about the crimes of passion of Bluebeard himself. Beauty and the Beast, she argues, is about the link between sexuality and bestiality.

However, from the perspective of what these tales suggest to children, perhaps wondering about their own sexuality and sexual development, Bettelheim's more compassionate interpretation of Beauty and the Beast acknowledges the fact that adolescence *is* a difficult and 'beastly' time; that male sexuality, and sexuality in general, may appear 'beastly'. But, says Bettelheim, through love and loyalty, the beast turns out to be 'life's most charming companion' (1976: 291). In the 1996 Disney version, one of the most imaginative and sophisticated Disney renderings of a fairytale, many female viewers have pointed out that the Beast is actually more attractive – or becomes so in the course of the movie, as we increasingly take Belle's perspective – than the pretty young man he turns into at the end. This young man to us, the viewers, is a stranger. The Beast, through the course of the film's narrative, is a person we have learned to identify with and 'love': a classic example, in fact, of the empathetic process which both Bettelheim and Mary Hilton describe as the psychic power of the fairytale.

Conclusion: permitting variations

So there are a variety of interpretations, historical, ideological, psychological and artistic and some of them are contradictory. Bettelheim is positive about the beneficial effects of fairytales. Others, such as Marina Warner, or Jack Zipes (1986), are less enthusiastic. Notable in these discussions is the extent to which these powerful fables *permit* scholars and commentators, as well as readers, hearers and viewers, to engage with strong emotions about, for example, the roles of women in society, or the right relations between men and women, or the powerful and the dispossessed. The costumes and trappings may vary, but the basic scenarios still function as sites for addressing universal themes. The basis of these tales – both the narrative events, as Propp describes them, and also the basic emotional conflicts – reversal of fortune, sibling rivalry, the unrecognized virtue being rewarded, the hero or heroine earning their rewards through bravery, kindness and wit – turn up in many other children's narratives, the subject of the next chapter: children's literary fiction and its screen adaptations.

Further reading

A must is *Nursery and Household Tales*, collected by Jacob and Wilhelm Grimm, translated Margaret Stern ([1948] 1972), London: Routledge and Kegan Paul. Classic scholarly interpretations of oral and folk culture are *The Uses of Enchantment: The Meaning and Importance of Fairy Tales*, by Bruno Bettelheim, (1976) London: Thames and Hudson; Maria Tatar's ([1987] 2003) *The Hard Facts of the Grimms' Fairy Tales*, Princeton, NJ: Princeton University Press, and the works of the Opies, for example: Opie, I. and Opie, P. (eds [1969] 1988), *Children's Games in Street and Playground*, Oxford: OUP. For further insights into the case (and rather sad life) of Hans Andersen, see Alison Lurie's sympathetic chapter on him in *Boys and Girls Forever* (2002).

8 CHILDREN'S LITERATURE: ON PAGE AND SCREEN

The previous chapter discussed 'unofficial' children's culture – stories, rhymes, games and jokes that originate and circulate among children themselves. The chapter also discussed fairytales and folk tales which, even when they were collected or adapted by named authors, originated in anonymous ones. When we talk about children's literature, in the form of printed books or comics aimed at children, we are moving on from discussion of a childhood culture which is unofficial, to cultural products for children which are deliberately intended for children, and marketed to them as such. This category includes the favoured form which, according to Neil Postman (see Chapter 2), helped to 'invent' childhood – the printed book.

However, children's literature cannot now be kept aloof from other media enjoyed by children. This chapter will also look at screen adaptations of children's books, and at some of the ways in which storytelling formats are converging through new technology. New ways of reading are producing new ways of writing. For instance, Henry Jenkins in his chapter 'Media literacy and the Harry Potter Wars' (Jenkins 2006) argues:

> [S]torytellers now think about storytelling in terms of creating openings for consumer participation . . . [creating] an interplay between the top-down force of corporate convergence and the bottom-up force of grass-roots convergence that is driving many of the changes we are observing in the media landscape.
>
> (2006: 175)

Jenkins points out that books such as the Potter series are not just about reading, but also about writing; he describes how 13-year-old Heather Lawver launched a school-based newspaper, *The Daily Prophet*, based on the newspaper in the Rowling series, which now has 'a staff of 102 children from all over the world'. Sophisticated fan fiction and artwork based on the series can also be found at [fictionalley.org].

Nevertheless, children's literature has sometimes suffered the same critical neglect of its content as applies to other children's media. Peter Hunt argues:

> Children's literature (as a concept) has had to fight against the academic hegemony of 'Eng Lit' to gain any recognition . . . The conventional literary system is . . . very like the traditional family: adult male literature dominates, women's literature is secondary . . . while children's literature is not only at the bottom of the heap but (worse) is very much the province of women.
>
> (1992: 2)

However, there are several indicators that Hunt's rather tongue-in-cheek remarks are exaggerated. There has been a Children's Literature Association in the USA since the 1970s, (see [http://www.childlitassn.org/]) with its own journal, *Children's Literature*, and its own quarterly, the *Children's Literature Association Quarterly* [www.childlitassn.org/chla_quarterly_journal.html]. There is a Children's Laureate in the UK (until 2009 poet and critic, Michael Rosen, currently picture book writer and critic, Anthony Browne). In Ireland, a new group bringing together scholars from Northern Ireland and the Republic of Ireland, and including scholars from Germany, Spain, France and Holland, has recently been formed, the Irish Society for the Study of Children's Literature. And although women such as Louisa May Alcott, (*Little Women*), L. M. Montgomery (*Anne of Green Gables*) and Frances Hodgson Burnett (*The Secret Garden*), have been responsible for some of the most enduring classics of the genre, men, too have produced many children's classics. Hunt himself points out that 'serious' adult writers such as Leo Tolstoy, Graham Greene, Thomas Hardy and Mark Twain wrote for children. Currently, Philip Pullman, Michael Morpurgo, Anthony Horowitz and Eoin Colfer are producing exciting, bestselling children's fiction. In virtually all of these cases, there is a symbiotic relationship between these stories and screen culture, with TV and film adaptations and merchandizing spin-offs being integral to their widespread cultural circulation.

Alongside serious academic interest in children's literature is another set of discourses almost completely divorced from it: the discourses described in Chapter 5 about the effects of popular culture and 'mass' (as distinct from 'literary') culture on contemporary children. When concerns are expressed about the degradation of children's culture, children's books are usually exempted (see, for example, Sue Palmer's *Toxic Childhood*, 2006). And yet literature, too, as Peter Hunt reminds us (1994) includes many down-market categories. The end of the nineteenth century, as well as being a 'Golden Age' of classic literature (of which more below) and a time when children's needs and rights were entering the public domain, also saw the burgeoning of genre fiction such as school stories, and the rise of the comic book and comic strip – categories still popular today.

The 'Golden Age' of children's literature

The nineteenth century initiated a period which has been described by Humphrey Carpenter (1985) as the beginning of a Golden Age in children's literature – a time when books especially written for children became a lucrative market, and produced many examples of what we now think of as 'classics', as well as a lot of pot-boiling and moralistic stories which have disappeared without trace. This period coincided with, and was linked to, the change in the public perception of childhood noted in earlier chapters. As Carpenter put it (1985: 10), 'by the second half of the 19th century, the child had become an important figure in the English literary imagination.' The nineteenth and early twentieth centuries also accelerated another important childhood construct: the child as consumer. In *The Commodification of Childhood* (2004), Daniel Thomas Cook quotes a clothing and 'dry goods' industry magazine, *Infants Department*: 'infant welfare is a sound business venture which pays handsome dividends . . . more than a good deed, it's good business' (2004: 69).

Writing for children was also becoming 'good business'. As both Peter Hunt (1994) and Carpenter describe in their historical account of the development of children's literature, many professional writers began to see – as people working for children still do[1] – that writing for children, with the child's point of view as the main driving force of the narrative, opened up new creative possibilities, and new readerships among the newly-literate child populations arising from universal education.

From an artistic point of view, a child readership permits elements not possible in adults' stories: fantasy; adventure; the breaking of boundaries; the discovery of the unknown, all permit narrative possibilities that are less likely for stories with adult characters, who have already made the discoveries that still constitute mystery and adventure for children. Books for children, even in their earliest days, were also a source of spin-off merchandizing. Peter Hunt (1994: 29) tells of the beginnings of commercial publishing for children in the 1740s – *A Little Pretty Pocket Book*, produced by John Newbery, which was a commercial 'mixed media text' – an early example of 'intertextuality'. The book included a 'letter to read' from Jack the Giant Killer, and a give away ball for a boy and pincushion for a girl.

The arrival of the author

However, some new elements *were* introduced into children's culture by children's literary books, the first being the named professional author. Another element that becomes important with the arrival of published literature, as distinct from traditional tales, is realism – stories about real, contemporary children, not fantasies about 'long ago and far away'. With the advent of the author, and the rise of a literate child readership, who could be assumed to want to see reflections of their own lives in their entertainment, more specific and up to date information was introduced into stories for children. This nowadays creates problems of datedness (for instance Edith Nesbit's 'beastly' slang) and of political incorrectness (for example, Helen Bannerman's *Little Black Sambo*, published in 1899). One generation's realism becomes the next generation's embarrassing lack of coolness and cultural insensitivity. But some storytelling elements are durable. Authors who manage to combine these elements with entertaining and recognizable contemporary childhood experiences, in the right tone of voice, produce the classics.[2]

Realism in terms of children roaming the streets and fields and having autonomous adventures, is less convincing for our contemporary children living in an indoors 'bedroom culture' (Livingstone 2002) than it would have been for nineteenth- and early twentieth-century children. Hence, fantasy has once again become a dominant genre in children's storytelling – including literature, TV and film. In fact, as Nicholas Tucker points out, there has always been an irony in stories for children which promote adventurous independence, to child audiences who are sitting safely at home reading a book: 'The paradox of trying to advocate such do-it-yourself adventures through the agency of private reading, an activity involving little more physical effort from a child than sitting in a chair, can be a hard one for an author to outface.' He calls this 'compensatory fantasy' from authors who were probably quite bookish as children themselves (1992: 158–9). Hence the same criticism that has been made of children watching TV – that it keeps them sitting still, contributing to obesity, and to a lack of engagement with the real world – has also been applied to reading.[3]

What is a children's book?

So what is a children's book? How do we identify a story intended for children, rather than for other audiences? In 1984 (republished 1993) Jacqueline Rose wrote a much-cited book on 'the impossibility of children's fiction' in which she argued that the story of Peter Pan (James Barrie's 1904 boy who never grew up) 'is a front . . . for what is most unsettling and uncertain about the relationship between adult and child. It shows innocence not as a property of childhood but as a portion of adult desire' (1984, 1993: xii). Rose was writing at a time of great public scandals about child sexual abuse – scandals which have recurred frequently since, especially in the context of child pornography on the Internet. As Rose argues, the issue of childhood 'innocence', its existence, or not, and its loss, is constantly present in any discussions of children's culture. It underlies our ideas about what is, or is not, culturally, ideologically and even aesthetically 'suitable' for the young.

Despite its proclaimed 'impossibility', children's literature within the publishing industry, within libraries, and within children's own homes and schools, has certainly established a recognizable institutional identity, distinct from other forms of literature. It has its own authors, who – with some exceptions – tend not to write for adults; it has its specialist publishers such as Walker Books and Puffin. It also has certain generic characteristics which distinguish it from adult literature.

In teaching about children's literature, and especially in considering adaptations of children's books for television and film, with their relatively strict, age-related guidelines of suitability (pre-watershed; PG; 12A; 15 and so on), I have found that a number of generic characteristics seem to be constant for children's storytelling – a storytelling space which I have described (borrowing Gillian Cross's term in her *Demon Headmaster* books) as 'crazyspace'. This space is not like the space of adult fiction, nor, despite recognizably realistic elements, such as modern slang, schools, pop music and so on, is it 'real'. It is a space where children, not adults, have agency, and it thus contains numerous possibilities of what Alison Lurie (1990), writing about children's fiction, has called 'subversion.' This subversion often takes childish, 'silly' forms, which mask its political implications and make it invisible to adults. (See Gillian Cross's *The Demon Headmaster Takes Over*, 1997; also Messenger Davies 2001a; 2005a; 2005b.) For children it is a space that belongs to them; it is a space that has been cultivated by public service broadcasting and by the public library system – adult-founded, and funded, institutions.

The characteristics of children's fiction

Obviously, children's fiction is specifically directed at a child readership – that is at people broadly under the age of 16. But it will be identifiable as 'children's' in a number of specific ways.

First, it is likely to have a child or children as its main protagonists. There are exceptions to this, as to every, rule. Particularly in fantasy stories, the main protagonists can be creatures (*The Borrowers*), toys (*The Mouse and his Child*; *Pinocchio*; *The Velveteen Rabbit*; *Winnie-the-Pooh*), or animals (*The Wind in the Willows*). However, these protagonists will be child-like in significant ways, the most important being that they conform to the fairytale trope of being at the mercy of bigger, older and more powerful beings. This is the universal condition of childhood.

The second characteristic is that – unlike in real life – the child protagonists almost invariably prevail against the more powerful beings creating the narrative problems for them. As Eileen Colwell memorably said: 'What hope does a band of desperate men have against four children?' (quoted in Hunt, 1994: 117).

Third, child protagonists prevail because children hold the moral high ground. In a true children's story, the adult characters are not the heroes, and they either misunderstand what is going on, or are positively malign. Otherwise, as in the case of E. Nesbit's kindly adult helpers, they are merely a supporting cast. Generally, the child protagonists in this genre overcome the disadvantages posed in the narrative and they defeat or escape the malevolent elders, which is far from the case in real life – hence 'the impossibility' identified by Rose.

There is an alternative category of adult protagonist who turns out to be a positive agent of the child's development, rather than creating obstacles to it. In Jacqueline Wilson's admittedly tough world, for example, children are not always encouraged to mistrust and dislike adults. This follows the tradition of E. Nesbit's child characters: the Wouldbegoods, the Treasure Seekers, and the Five Children who met 'It'. Despite the fact that their behaviour is often very inconvenient for the long-suffering adults around them, these adults almost invariably turn out to be benevolent: the Old Gentleman and Perks the Porter in *The Railway Children*, the various servants, and so on.

In books for very young children, adults are almost invariably kindly and produce slap-up teas at the end of various gentle adventures – John Burningham's Mr Gumpy, of *Mr Gumpy's Outing* and *Mr Gumpy's Motor Car*, is a quintessential example. In 'real life' of course, no middle-aged gentleman would be trusted to take children and animals out in his boat or car.

Generally, following this rule, children's fiction has happy endings – but not always. Lucy Mangan, writing in the *Guardian*, 11 April 2009, about *Charlotte's Web* by E.B. White, described her childhood self's broken-hearted reaction to the death of Charlotte the spider at the end: 'I know that people in real life die. But why do they have to die in books?' This is a good question: the young Lucy, an avid reader, was well aware of the 'rules' of childhood fiction and was incensed that in this case they had been 'broken'.

As in fairytale, in children's fiction there will often be magical or mysterious powers to help the child protagonists. In realistic fiction, these magic powers include luck and coincidence, as in the denouement of E. Nesbit's *The Railway Children*, with the kindly Old Gentleman on the train helping to get the children's father released from prison.

What would seem an obvious point, but is sometimes overlooked, is that the story's language (whether on the page or in dramatic dialogue) has to be accessible and comprehensible to children – the younger the child to whom the book is addressed, the simpler and sparser the language. The brilliant Dr Seuss succeeded in writing witty, illustrated, rhyming stories, like *The Cat in the Hat*, using the basic vocabulary of reading primers. J.K. Rowling's *Harry Potter and the Philosopher's Stone* (1997), about the 11-year-old Harry, is simpler and clearer in its style than the later books (*The Goblet of Fire* onwards) where both Harry and many of his readers have become adolescents.

Children's books do not have to have words at all. The earliest books for babies and toddlers usually consist simply of pictures – although books consisting simply of pictures can also be offered to older readers, for example Raymond Briggs' stories of Father Christmas and the brilliant *The Snowman* (1978).

'Children's' as a genre is censored. Although children's stories may include romantic storylines, and will almost certainly include violent events such as battles and fights, (particularly in stories for boys) there will be constraint on specific descriptions of sex and violence, and the use of bad language, and this will be even more the case in screen versions. (See the descriptions for each category of classification for the British Board of Film Classification at [http://www.bbfc.co.uk/classification/c_ucu.php].)

A children's book will be marketed in such a way as to identify it as specifically for children. There has even been a suggestion, resisted by many authors, that children's books should have 'age labelling' on them, in keeping with the modern spirit of niche marketing. For books, child-related identifications can include special graphics, tie-ins with toys, computer games, promotions of various kinds, including child-oriented promotions in libraries and to schools.

Although they may be resisted for books, age restrictions and labelling apply to screen versions of children's stories. The early Harry Potter films were classified as PG (Parental Guidance and hence allowable for young children) but the fourth, *The Goblet of Fire*, was given a 12A, 'suitable for 12 years and over'. The 2009 *Harry Potter and the Half Blood Prince* was also 12A. There has been some Internet discussion that the final film(s) *The Deathly Hallows*, could be rated 18.

Children's books are also often chosen as set texts for study in school.

We can see from this list of characteristics that a particular construction of 'the child' emerges: the child is a person with agency, with superior moral insight to adults (a Romantic concept); a child is likely to be a victim of unjust forces but through his/her essential childlike moral force, he/she will in some way prevail over them; a child needs to be protected from 'adult' corruption in the form of explicit representations of sexual behaviour and too much violence and obscene language, and also from the painful knowledge that people die and things do not always turn out right; a child needs to be addressed in specific kinds of language, usually simpler than that addressed to adults, and with clear narrative structures and outcomes (which, for many adult readers, makes children's literature extremely attractive as a literary form); a child has a capacity for fantasy, playfulness, fun, naughtiness and 'silliness' ('crazyspaces') that – unfortunately – seem to be denied to us by writers, with one or two honourable exceptions, when we become adults. There is 'usefulness' in children's literature; in general it aims to help, or at least not to permanently downcast, its readers. The child reader has to be offered some kind of hopeful incentive by the benevolent adult writer to persist, even if it is a struggle, in the steep 'developmental climb' that constitutes growing up.

Adapting children's literature for the screen

The issue of adaptation and translation from the literary text to the screen raises a number of questions about what is meant by contemporary 'childhood' and what is 'suitable' for children of different ages. This is in the context of the highly commercialized and expensive modes of production characteristic of film and TV, for which targeting age-related audiences very precisely is seen as economically essential. Adaptation means not only translating from one medium to another, as in the case of books to film or television; it also means making stories from the past, or from other cultures, relevant to child readers and viewers.

Adaptation is an integral part of literary culture for children nowadays, because one of the ways in which children are first introduced to literary texts is through screen versions of them. There is evidence that children can be brought to read the original texts having been exposed to the screen versions, a process which librarians and teachers tend to approve of (see Home 1993). Screen adaptations have turned out to be one powerful way to keep the classical literary canon in the forefront of children's cultural consumption.

In discussing the question of adaptation I want to talk about two examples of children's literature, one from 'the Golden Age,' the other which is the most successful children's literary text (in commercial terms) ever and which for this reason may find it difficult ever to earn the label 'Golden Age'. The first example is Frances Hodgson Burnett's *The Secret Garden*, which was not very successful when it was first published in 1911, but has become a literary 'sleeper' – a book which has never been out of print, which has been published in many editions and has been adapted into film (three times), television (three times), audio-text and a stage musical. The second example is the Harry Potter series by J.K. (Joanne) Rowling – seven books, the first published in 1997, the last in 2007, and so far, six films with two more to come; the film of the last book, *The Deathly Hallows*, will be in two parts.

'Golden Age' survivals: *The Secret Garden*

The Secret Garden has never been out of print since it was first published in 1911. One reason it has not dated, is because it successfully manages to combine the realism required of modern children's fiction with universal 'fairytale' themes. Alison Lurie (1990) says that Mrs Burnett is remembered now, when other writers like Elizabeth Ward and Mrs Eden Southworth are forgotten, because:

> At least twice in more than half a century of constant and often exhausting commercial productivity, she happened to tell one of those stories that express concealed fantasies and longings; stories that are the externalized dreams of a whole society and pass beyond ordinary commercial success to become part of popular culture.
>
> (1990: 136)

These two stories were *Little Lord Fauntleroy* (1886) and *The Secret Garden*.

I have written more extensively about *The Secret Garden* elsewhere (see Messenger Davies 2006a; 2002; 2001b), so will refer to it more briefly here. It serves to illustrate some issues about the way in which children's literature is treated when it makes the crossover from the literary text into a commercial audiovisual product, such as film or television.

Issues in adapting classics: the case of *The Secret Garden*

1. Classic books are useful for adaptation, because they are out of copyright thus saving money, and development time.
2. An argument for adapting classic books is that children 'should' have access to high quality children's literature – to 'good writing', and the best authors, above all the products of the Golden Age. In *The Hill and Beyond: Children's Television Drama, An Encyclopaedia* (2003), Alistair McGown and Mark Docherty list all those fictional texts that have been adapted by British children's television alone, whether by BBC or commercial channels between 1950 and 2000. There are nearly 100 of them (and these exclude transatlantic and European versions, of which there also scores).

3. Local specificity is an issue; this works on domestic television, less so on the big screen. Adaptations for Hollywood mean that local characteristics of stories can be lost, and more general, fantastic, universal (that is, recognizable to an American audience) ingredients have to be introduced, as happened with the 1993 Warner Bros production of *The Secret Garden*, compared with the 1975 BBC version.

4. There are issues of datedness and changing values for social acceptability. An example in *The Secret Garden* is its discussion of 'natives' – the inhabitants of India, where Mary Lennox's story begins. There is also the question of servants and how they are treated. Adapters cannot totally alienate or confuse a modern audience of children, with very different social value systems. The task in translating nineteenth-century respect for the social role of dukes, for instance, is to make the behaviour of the main characters sympathetic and identifiable to a modern audience, who may not know the book, or the period of history.[4]

The Secret Garden endures, and has been popular for adaptations into different media, because of the opportunities it offers for dramatic characterization – its physical, and especially, psychological realism. The theme of children who are damaged by being 'spoilt', as well as neglected, still has resonance with later generations of children and parents. The importance of the lost garden and the children's relationship with the natural world echoes current environmental concerns. The regenerating garden, and the big, gloomy house, also offer plenty of scope for art designers and directors. The use of accurate contemporary regional dialect was an important ingredient in the original book – again, this is still appealing for contemporary audiences, more prominent in the locally-produced BBC version (1975) than in any of the Hollywood versions. Losing the dialect scenes obliterates an important ideological aspect of the story. Learning to 'talk Yorkshire' represented the damaged upper-class children's regeneration and incorporation into the healthier way of life represented by regional working-class culture. This prefigured concerns of later writers about class and region. In a 2007 exhibition at the British Library 'The writer in the garden', it was pointed out – correctly – that *The Secret Garden* has much in common with D.H. Lawrence's later novel, *Lady Chatterley's Lover* (1921).

Adaptation: Harry Potter

One set of children's literary texts which has brought together all these concerns, and in many ways has blown apart – or as Jack Zipes put it, 'blurred the focus' of (2002: 171) – the distinctions between them, is the Harry Potter series by J.K. Rowling.[5] The Potter books have been damned by literary critics on many grounds, including being 'formulaic and sexist' (Zipes 2002: 171) and particularly in being so massively commercially successful that Joanne Rowling, their author, is now one of the richest women in the world, richer even than Queen Elizabeth II. Zipes asks: 'How is it possible to evaluate a work of literature like a Harry Potter novel when it is so dependent on the market conditions of the culture industry?' (pp. 171–2).

Other critics have fewer problems with 'evaluation'. Rowling has been praised for her 'brilliant' literary strengths by author, critic and authority on children's literature Alison Lurie:

> Rowling is clearly on the side of children . . . Her heroes' secret power . . . can also be seen as a metaphor for the special powers of childhood: imagination, creativity and especially humour – as well as being exciting, her books are often very funny . . . hers, like Baum's [Frank Baum, author of *The Wizard of Oz*], is a fully imagined world to which she has a deep ongoing commitment.
>
> (2002: 113–14)

A.O. Scott, writing in *Slate*, directly contradicts Zipes on the issue of quality:

> [I]t's evident that J.K. Rowling is a formidably talented – and, more important, a rigorously competent – novelist, much better at the rudiments of effective fiction writing than any six American novelists under 50. She's meticulous in her plotting, economical in her descriptions, and exact in her portraiture. There's no reason why solid storytelling, brisk prose, and vivid characters should appeal exclusively, or primarily, to children, though children are less likely to submit to being bored, pandered to, preached at, or intimidated.
>
> (Scott 1999)

Rowling has been praised above all, for encouraging children – especially boys – to read: to consume fiction in numbers previously only found in the mass television audiences of the 1960s–1990s. To the extent that the critical, academic and journalistic commentaries on Harry Potter far transcend traditional literary-criticism boundaries, my point is made. The phenomenon is much more than simply the product of cultural industry marketing (although the marketers have found plenty to say about it – see Stephen Brown's witty analysis of Harry Potter's 'brand magic', 2005). There have been religious, sociological, psychological and medical commentaries – as well as theological debates both for and against (stories about magic are seen as highly suspect among some Christian groups). The fact remains that these are children's books and they have been claimed, read, loved and adapted for their own imaginative purposes by millions of children throughout the world – see [fictionalley.org]. See also the international study on the sources of children's fantasy and daydreaming reported in *Media and the Make-believe Worlds of Children* by Maya Götz, Dafna Lemish, Amy Aidman and Hyesung Moon, 2005. Children's culture, adopted by children for themselves, remains hard to confine within disciplinary, commercial and other adult-constructed boundaries.

Dustin Kidd (2007) praises the fact that 'the books have changed the publishing industry in important ways. For instance as a result of the Potter novels, a new list of children's bestsellers was formed' (2007: 85). Stephen Brown (2005) interprets this differently. He suggests that the invention of a new category – children's bestsellers – was an example of what Peter Hunt complained about – the failure by adult literary culture to take children's literature seriously.

> Beset by complaints that the Potter-led list was preventing the appearance of old-time literati like John Updike, Philip Roth and Saul Bellow, *The New York Times* [best-seller list] took decisive action. On 23rd June 2000, when the publication of *Goblet* (*Harry Potter and the Goblet of Fire*) would have given Rowling four of the list's top five places, she disappeared from it completely, only to reappear on a special children's bestsellers' list.
>
> (Brown 2005: 119)

In describing the *New York Times*'s attempt to airbrush Harry Potter out of its prestigious list, Brown argued that Rowling was the victim of intellectual snobbery. This, he proposed, was the old accusation of 'intellectuals' longstanding prejudice against children's literature' (p. 219), as also noted by Peter Hunt. Definitions also come into play: whether the Harry Potter books are, indeed, 'literature', or simply – as A.S. Byatt contemptuously put it (quoted in Brown, 2005: 218), 'a secondary, secondary world . . . for people whose imaginative lives are confined to TV cartoons'.

Nevertheless, the NYT best seller list has always traditionally included both kinds of literature, adults' and children's. It appears that it was a children's book (or a series of children's books) that led to the newspaper altering its criteria. This is a clear example of the way in which the Harry Potter phenomenon exposed the ambivalence of the distinction between 'mass culture' and 'literature.' The interesting question, in comparing the series with a constantly-reinterpreted classic such as the 100-year-old *Secret Garden*, is whether the Harry Potter series will appeal to future generations of children, and whether the films, too – as in the case of the 1939 classic *The Wizard of Oz*, with Judy Garland – will have an enduring shelf-life.

Growing up on film

In the *Radio Times* of 4–10 October 2008 (2008: 37), Andrew Collins, in an article entitled 'The trouble with Harry', identified some problematic aspects in the relationship between the Harry Potter books and their screen versions and with their readerships and audiences. Writing about *Harry Potter and the Goblet of Fire*, the fourth in the series of seven books, Collins draws attention to the generational and biological changes that have overtaken both the book's readers, and particularly the star of the movie, Daniel Radcliffe. Radcliffe was 11 when he was cast in the first film, *The Philosopher's Stone* (2001), and he will be 21 when the final part of the franchise, *The Deathly Hallows*, arrives in cinemas in May 2011: 'Radcliffe is growing up much faster than his broomstick-riding counterpart', says Collins.

As Collins points out, the (in)genius of the Potter literary saga is that the first book was aimed at children broadly the same age, or younger, than its protagonist: 11. In the first book, Harry starts the equivalent of secondary school, at Hogwarts, and in each succeeding book, he enters the next school year – just as many of his readers were likely to be doing. Accordingly, with each year, and with each successive Harry Potter book, the language and the complexity of the relationships in the stories become more adult. Rowling astutely calculates that her readers are growing up along with her hero, and like him, are facing more arduous physical, hormonal, emotional and intellectual challenges as they do so. This is reflected in the increasing linguistic complexity of the books' literary styles. It was a highly successful marketing strategy.

But with the films, as Andrew Collins suggests, there is a problem, partly because they were produced later than the books. *Goblet of Fire*, screened on a mainstream broadcast channel, ITV1 at 7.10 on a Sunday evening in October 2008, when many young children were in the audience, was the fourth in the series, featuring a 14-year-old Harry (and a 16-year-old Daniel Radcliffe). As befits material written for a 14-year-old audience, the story is darker and more complex than earlier episodes. Collins points out: 'it is the first film to feature the unspeakably horrible Voldemort and the death of one character (as in the book)' and he asks: 'Come 2011, will the tone have to be even darker to keep the young adults (who were children when they saw the first film), buying tickets? In other words, will Harry Potter be too old to go and see a *Harry Potter* film?' (2008: 37).

The problems noted by Collins connect with scholars' abiding interest in how we define children and childhood. They especially address the awkward fact that children are people in the process of rapid change, one of the essential characteristics that help us to recognize 'a child'. Collins' query highlights the ever-present issue of development in discussions of children's media and culture.

What is 'too old'? Why does it matter that Daniel Radcliffe is 16 when he is supposed to be 14, and 21 when he's supposed to be 17? What is the problem of 'darkness of tone' in a film intended, as Collins argues, for 'kids'?

Conclusions: what will last and in what form?

Collins' point also raises the issue of whether literature can have any permanent value when it is too closely linked to a particular historical and social moment, and/or to a particular generation, that is, the children growing up between 1997 and 2007 when the last Potter book was published. Can these stories last as stories? Will they still have meaning and resonance when they are no longer linked to the publishing and cinematic marketing strategies aimed at a particular growing generation that has helped to make them so massively popular? Will the films become timeless classics of fantasy fiction, like *The Wizard of Oz* (1939, MGM, based on the books by Frank L. Baum), or will they seem hopelessly outdated in the future? In a converged technological world of computerized home cinemas, streaming video material on demand into our bedrooms, will the idea of 'cinema releases' or 'movie classics' still be meaningful in any way at all? Or will the Harry Potter books, even if out of print, become legends in children's playground lore? What has certainly emerged from the Potter phenomenon is the 'impossibility' of children's literature – not in the sense of the 'disappearance of childhood', but in the sense that exciting and massively popular children's storytelling cannot be contained within one format, or medium. It will often spill over into other branches of children's – and even adult – culture, and commercial markets will find ways of exploiting this overspill in the form of merchandise, toys, films, computer games and TV programmes. And then there is fan and playground culture . . .

The Potter stories were adapted into film – a medium especially suited to the spectacular special effects required by the narratives. But one of the most effective ways of merging children's storytelling formats creatively has traditionally been the despised (by critics such as A.S. Byatt) medium of television. Television as a storytelling and information medium, rather than as the destroyer of childhood, will be the subject of the next chapter.

Further reading

Peter Hunt's (1992) (ed.) *Literature for Children: Contemporary Criticism*, London: Routledge, is a good introduction to some critical issues in studying children's fiction. Alison Lurie's *Don't Tell the Grownups: Subversive Children's Literature*, London:

Bloomsbury (1990) is a refreshingly pro-child account of children's literature, from a distinguished adult novelist. She is good on fairytales too. The whole of the Harry Potter series by J.K. Rowling is a must, as is the Potter fan-fiction at [www.fictionalley.org]. One of the liveliest and most insightful texts you will read on the marketing of literature, (which, after all, is a cultural commodity too), with particular reference to Harry Potter, is Stephen Brown's (2005) *Wizard! Harry Potter's Brand Magic*, London: Cyan Press.

9 | CHILDREN'S TELEVISION

In choosing to place a chapter on television in the second half of this book, I have made an ideological decision. It is obvious to anyone who has read this far, that the medium of television turns up repeatedly in discussions about politics, history, sociology, psychology and media effects. Television in children's lives is rarely viewed as a creative medium of expression in the way that literature, music, film and storytelling are. Partly it is viewed as a kind of toxic virus responsible for killing off 'childhood' and having damaging 'effects' – from making children violent to turning them into greedy, obese consumers. Otherwise, there is a perennial concern with measuring how *much* children are watching, what they are watching, when, and instead of what. This informs both commercial and policy decisions. These concerns were addressed in Chapters 4 and 5, reviewing the traditions of research on children and media and the intersection of these with policy.

In this chapter, I want to treat television in a similar way to the one in which I have treated children's literature and fairytales in Chapters 7 and 8: as a vehicle for informing and entertaining children, via artefacts ('programmes') which deserve critical scrutiny. Although much of children's viewing, as already noted, is of adult programmes, in this chapter, I want to focus on the kinds of programmes made specifically for children: pieces of work produced by people who if they were working in other media, would be called 'artists', 'authors' or at the very least 'craftworkers'. This discussion will be placed in the context of the changes that are overtaking the medium currently, as a result of digitization, and competition from other media, including the worldwide web.

The tube of plenty: universal access

Broadcasting – television and radio – is the only creative medium ever invented for which social class has not been a barrier to access. In its early days, radio provided dedicated material for children, including drama, information and preschool broadcasts such as *Listen with Mother* (BBC). This is less the case now – despite campaigns such as Children 2000, to provide children's radio. However, radio is still an important and accessible medium in many parts of the world, including Africa. But after its introduction in the 1950s and 1960s in the USA and Europe, and later elsewhere, television quickly became the main medium of choice for children

In describing television as valuable because it is accessible, this is not to say that it always delivers superbly creative and informative material for children; it does not (see Götz et al.'s analysis below). Children are exposed to a great deal of mediocre entertainment and commercial bombardment, and much of what they watch is made for adults, not for them. It is television's accessibility, plus the size and universality, including the presumed vulnerability, especially of 'lower-class' children, of television's child audience which has led to such widespread alarm about negative social effects. If access to television were confined to a middle-class minority (as other less widely-scrutinized media such as children's film, theatre or literature tend to be), moral panics about its bad examples would not be so persistent (see Barker and Petley 1997).

The upside of this general accessibility is that, when television does deliver exceptionally creative, original, inspirational, amusing and informative material, (as it often does) the chances of children of every kind of background being able to see it are very high. This is the platform on which campaigners for children's television build their case. This was the rationale for the introduction in 1969 and (in the USA, very rare) public subsidy of one of the longest-running classics of children's television, *Sesame Street* (of which more below). The value of universal access is a principle in danger of disappearing as the free-to-air broadcast networks give way to a multiplicity of subscription digital channels around the world.

Academic discourse: 'Television after TV'

In 2004 Lynn Spigel and Jan Olssen published an edited collection entitled *Television after TV*, in which a number of scholars examined the possibility that television is 'dead'. They set out the ways in which television has reinvented itself under new technological and economic pressures – pressures which were themselves self-inflicted by the various media systems that run television – including: 'Internet convergence, changes in regulation policies and ownership rules, the advent of HDTV, technological changes in screen design, the innovation of digital television systems like TiVo (Sky Plus in the UK) and new forms of media competition' (2004: 2). In *Television after TV*, Jostein Gripsrud is sceptical of the view that time-shifting, the availability of multi-channels, and 'choice' between what in fact often consists of the same material recycled, constitutes a post-TV era. Gripsrud points out the integral relationship between TV viewing and people's daily routines, which cannot be drastically changed. This is particularly true of children's routines. He comes back to the crucial issue of function and argues: 'The reasons for variance [in the use of recording technology] . . . concern some of the primary aspects and functions of broadcast television: simultaneity, liveness and ritualization of every day life' (2004: 216). Gripsrud challenges the argument that following drama series 'live' at particular moments in the day and week, is a hopelessly outmoded way of consuming television in the era of the boxed set and TiVO/ Sky Plus.

In my conversations with children and teenagers in North East London about their media habits – young people who were fully conversant with all the possibilities of time-shifting, viewing online and boxed sets – a desire for 'liveness' was still noted. Said a 15-year-old boy: 'I watch TV when there's something on I want to see. For *Heroes*, we all [his whole family] have to be here at 10 o'clock'. The boxed set syndrome – or syndicated repeat viewings – does not work with serials, he argued. Similar ritualized viewing has been observed in other parts of the world. Strelitz and Boshoff (2008) describe teenagers' collective viewing behaviour in South Africa:

> Every evening, with the regularity of the ritual it has become, 15 to 20 of these students gather to watch their favourite programmes. The viewing sessions start at 18.30 when they watch *Isidingo*, a local African drama set on a goldmine . . . at weekends they often meet to watch South African soccer. Missing from their daily TV diet are any foreign productions.
>
> (2008: 242)

This is an echo of some of the claims made for the medium in the early days of television. In an article on 'television in the home and family' (1998) Susan Briggs described the 50th birthday celebrations of television in 1989 at the Smithsonian Institute in Washington, which 'focused, as many opinion and pressure groups have done, on the impact of television on the home' (1998: 110). She points out that television in its beginnings was advertised as a 'force for family togetherness: 'There is great happiness in the home where the family is held together by its new common bond – television', claimed one advertisement. A Los Angeles survey in 1949 even predicted that the divorce rate would fall in America, thanks to television. It would seem that, despite many more negative and unpredicted developments since then, including the prevalence of TVs in children's bedrooms, togetherness continues.

Children's television production

Children's programmes are produced and broadcast all over the world, and most countries have at least some indigenous production. However, it is much cheaper to buy in imported, mainly American programmes than it is for less affluent countries than the US to make their own. In a 24-country, five-continent-wide survey of children's television provision, with a special emphasis on representation of gender and ethnicity, Götz et al. (2008: 5) noted:

> The biggest export region of children's TV programmes is North America with 60 per cent, followed by Europe with 27.9% and Asia with 9.3% . . . Children's TV consists primarily of fictional programmes, largely cartoons, which are not produced domestically but are purchased.

According to their analysis, 77 per cent of all children's programming in the 24 countries in their survey is imported. The USA (82.7 per cent) and the UK (67.7 per cent) have the highest proportions of domestic production. Kenya (0.7) and New Zealand (0.5 per cent) have the lowest. From the point of view of their study's primary focus, the representation of gender and ethnicity, there were causes for concern. The programmes analysed included twice as many males as females (and most females were young and slim) and 72 per cent of all characters were Caucasian. Given these imbalances, there is all the more reason to examine ways in which children's television can be utilized to provide more diverse, nuanced, original, indigenous and pro-social (in the broadest sense) material: the aim of the World Summit movement, and campaigns like Save Kids TV.

Offering 'choice'

The pressure to produce 'high quality,' indigenous television programmes for children has to come from beyond children themselves and also from outside the industry, since 'high quality' (which can be defined in many ways, but they all usually involve additional expense) does not have a primarily commercial justification. It derives more from the discourse of children's rights as set out in the Children's Television Charter (see page 55). A purely free market system based only on consumer 'choice', with children hypothetically being able to 'freely opt' for expensive drama, or factual documentaries, or programming with positive representations of ethnic minority girls, cannot operate. It cannot operate because this material has to be there for children to choose in the first place and it is only in regulated broadcasting systems, supported by public funding, that a regular range of such public service broadcasting content is provided.

Regulated systems do still exist in the UK, and variably in Commonwealth countries such as Canada, New Zealand and Australia, and in a number of European countries including Scandinavia, Holland, Germany and France. The USA 1990 Children's Television Act in principle acknowledges and attempts to guarantee children's 'rights' to educational TV material, and less exposure to commercial advertising. This is thanks to decades of civic and parental lobbying (see Kunkel and Goette 1997; Kunkel and Wilcox 2001). There is also, of course, the material provided on the minority Public Broadcasting Service (PBS) – including *Sesame Street* (of which more below).

The 'canary in the coalmine'[1]: the case of the United Kingdom

The UK, while having many shortcomings in terms of the way it treats children (see the UNICEF report in Chapter 3) does have at least one claim to virtue. It is probably the only country in the world where the hypothesis that children will voluntarily watch – i.e. 'choose' – non-commercial genres over supposedly more popular material such as cartoons, has been able to be tested over a long period of time. Mixed-genre, protected daily schedules of children's programming, including drama, documentary, news, arts, preschool, live entertainment, comedy, magazine and animation – much of it without advertising – have been available for British children almost uninterruptedly since television began in the 1950s. For most of that time there has been competition between publicly funded (no ads) and commercial broadcasting (with ads) for the child audience, resulting in considerable diversity of schedules. It has also resulted in diversity of audience behaviour.

Until 2006 such programmes were provided by both the BBC, and the commercial broadcasters, ITV, Channel 4 and Channel 5 who had a public service obligation (greatly reduced by deregulatory legislation first in 1990 and more so in 2003) to produce news, documentary, religious and, prior to 2003, children's programming. Now, the BBC is the main provider of children's material, certainly in terms of original production, and has restricted its target audience to the under 12s since 2006. The commercial companies have ceased to commission new children's production, with some limited exceptions such as Channel 5's preschool offering, Milk Shake. (For the history of children's programming in the UK see Blumler 1992; Home 1993; Messenger Davies and Corbett 1997; Buckingham et al. 1999. For an impassioned international defence of it, see Palmer 1994).

Choosing diversity

Table 9.1 shows 10 sample weeks over a period of time from 1990 to 1995, which my colleagues and I drew up for our report to the BBC on children and television drama in 1997 (Messenger Davies et al. 1997). This list of the programmes reaching number one in children's top tens for ratings in these selected weeks indicates how availability of diverse genres relates to diversity of choice.

   If we look at the 'all-programme' top-rated shows for the child audience, we see only two titles: *Neighbours*, the Australian soap opera, and *Gladiators*. If we look at the parallel children's programme list, (the same child audience) we see much greater diversity of genre choices. *How To* (ITV) was a factual, magazine programme, giving information on how to make and do things; *Blue Peter* (factual, live magazine, BBC) is still running. *Byker Grove*, a pre-teen and teen soap, set in a youth club in the North East of England (BBC), *The Tomorrow People*, a sci-fi series (ITV) and *Children's Ward* (ITV) set in a hospital, were all original home-produced dramas, no longer in production. In the 1990s, all these

Table 9.1 Top rated programmes watched by children, 1990–1995

Period (week ending)	Top rated (adults)	Rating (% of child audience)	Top rated (children's)	Rating
12.11.95	*Neighbours*	26.9	**How 2**	**18.1**
25.6.95	*Neighbours*	20.9	*Aladdin*	12.2
13.11.94	*Gladiators*	36.1	**Byker Grove**	**21.1**
12.6.94	*Neighbours*	26.8	*Where's Wally?*	16.7
21.11.93	*Gladiators*	40.2	*Tiny Toons*	24.4
13.6.93	*Neighbours*	27.7	*Ducktales*	16.9
22.11.92	*Neighbours*	39.2	**The Tomorrow People**	**25.6**
7.6.92	*Neighbours*	28.9	*Ninja Turtles*	17.0
24.11.91	*Neighbours*	38.1	**Blue Peter**	**22.4**
9.6.91	*Neighbours*	31.4	*Defenders of the Earth*	18.0
25.11.90	*Neighbours*	39.1	**Children's Ward**	**26.1**

Source: Messenger Davies, O'Malley and Corbett 1997.

programmes had ratings which compared well with the adult/family show *Neighbours*. The other five top children's titles in this list are diverse cartoons, including the classic *Ninja Turtles* and *Where's Wally?* This table shows that if children's viewing choices were reliant only on a 'family' type schedule, their choices would be narrow. When children have their own schedule, their choices are more generically diverse and the material they choose is also more demanding. These choices competed well in ratings terms with 'family' programming. It is interesting to note seasonal fluctuations too; in the summer, child audience sizes are smaller.

This situation has completely changed. In the UK, there are currently 31 different channels for children, not including the BBC1 after-school schedule. Apart from *Lizzie Maguire* and *Hannah Montana* on Disney – glossy American sitcom-type high-school teen shows, with artificial laughter tracks, aimed particularly at girls – there is no live action drama. There is no news or factual programming in the early afternoon, although the CBBC channel has *Newsround* and *Xchange* later on.

If children's television is 'the canary in the coalmine', warning of the absence – or demise – of public service values in broadcasting generally, then we could argue that British children's television – praised by Edward Palmer in 1994 and by Sachiko Kodaira in 2005 as an example for the rest of the world – could be the canary's canary.

Children's genres

So, if original children's production were to cease altogether, what would be lost? Traditionally, there are five main genres in children's programming, as defined by the audience ratings organization, BARB: 1. Drama; 2. Cartoons/Animation; 3. Factual; 4. Light Entertainment/Quizzes; 5. Preschool. These arbitrary labels cover a multitude of sub-genres; animation can be dramatic (as in the case of *Fairytales of the World* or *The Animated Shakespeare*). Drama includes family comedy such as *My Parents are Aliens*. The BBC's offering, *Horrible Histories*, based on Terry Deary's books, is dramatized versions of real, but caricatured, historical events and facts – '51 historical facts in each episode', according to the blurb. With its clever spoofs of adult shows like *Wife Swap*, in which a seventeenth-century Puritan couple, Mr and Mrs Miserable, swap spouses with a Cavalier couple, Mr and Mrs Merry, it is very funny and has all-ages appeal. 'Preschool' includes examples of all the other four genres, adapted for the very young.

These five genres are discussed in turn.

1 Drama

The two genres most in decline in the new multi-channel world of children's viewing are original drama, particularly serious drama aimed at older (12+) children, and factual programming. In their collection, *The Hill and Beyond: Children's Television Drama, An Encyclopaedia* (2003), Alistair McGown and Mark Docherty assert: 'The last three decades of the 20th century have witnessed the maturity of the subgenre [drama] and the delivery of ever more complex and contentious programming, true to its audience' (2003: iii). Table 9.1 gives an indication of the kind of drama they were talking about.[2]

Of the three 1990s drama programmes in Table 9.1, two (*Byker Grove* and *Children's Ward*) were long running series, with soap-like continuing and developing characters and storylines, relying on a continuing relationship with the child audience as it, too, grew up. Some of these storylines were controversial, as with a gay relationship in *Byker Grove* in 1995, and regular treatment of death, sickness, delinquency and bereavement in *Children's Ward*. The third 1990s drama, *The Tomorrow People*, was a science fiction series about a group of young people with special powers who banded together to save the world from evil – this, at least, is a theme that can be revisited, since it does not rely on contemporary realism.[3] Live action drama does not sell abroad very effectively, because it tends to be locally specific, but it has a better chance if it exists in the hybrid form of fantasy/reality, as in the case of *The Tomorrow People*, and the BBC's (2009) drama offering, *MI High*.

It is instructive to compare *MI High*, a clever and entertaining show, aimed at the under-12s, to the hit series of the mid-late 1990s, *The Demon Headmaster* (DH), aimed at a child audience up to 15, to which it owes a great deal. Both series share the classic children's fiction formula, expressed succinctly by Eileen Colwell: 'what hope have a band of desperate men against four children?' (quoted in Hunt 1994: 117). In *MI High*'s first episode, the villain is an 'alien' taking over the Prime Minister (thus also owing much to *Dr Who*, and *Star Trek*). In the more realistic DH stories, the Demon Headmaster (whose powers and motives are never explained) is an educationist: first a headteacher, then the head of a research station and finally a scientist in a university, who has not 'been taken over'. He is just, in the words of one of the child interviewees in my BBC drama study (Messenger Davies, 2001a): 'a normal person who hypnotises people and has normal evil thoughts; he's just a normal person underneath' (2001: 219).

In the Demon Headmaster stories, there is no need to account for dictatorial behaviour by 'alien take-overs'. As my interviewees knew, 'headmasters could kill. Some headmasters do' (2001: 220). The DH represents the hegemony of scientific 'progress', unregulated by ethical considerations. The children oppose this morally, practically and intellectually (Dinah, the chief child protagonist, has a very high IQ). They did not require magical transformations to become junior Superheroes as happens in *MI High*. They used children's weaponry, such as 'gunge', jokes, and computer games. They were not super-heroes, nor wizards; the only power they had was an ability (never explained, but certainly feasible in naturalistic terms) to resist hypnotism. The collaboration of the children is contrasted with the brutal individualism of the head and childhood's combined reason and rightness prevail.

The disappearance of challenging drama for older children is illustrative of a troubling policy change in British children's broadcasting. The many problems identified for British children in the UNICEF and Children's Society reports of 2006 and 2008 (see Chapter 3) would suggest that children approaching and living through adolescence are more than ever in need of cultural spaces where their lives can be realistically and sympathetically examined and where young people can be represented as active moral and political agents.[4] Realistic drama's ability to reflect teenage children's lives was also evidenced in the long-running popularity of the school series, *Grange Hill*, which ran from 1978 to 2008. Similarly thoughtful (but more short-lived) series, frankly addressing teen problems both at home and school were produced in the 1980s and 90s in Canada – *Degrassi Junior High* – and in the USA – *My So-called Life*.

Grange Hill was eventually cancelled, apparently due to declining audience figures, amid controversy. Its final audience was 500,000 – a far cry from the millions it had enjoyed in the 1980s. However, the BBC's major teen investment, the online website *Blast* [http://www.bbc.co.uk/blast/], where money for young people's services has been diverted, has far fewer regular hits than half a million on its expensive website (McFarlane et al. 2009). The economics, as well as the politics, of the decision to attract teenagers with online material rather than with broadcast material seem questionable in this case.

2 Cartoons

Cartoons – or animation – are another 'canary in the coalmine' phenomenon. The increasing proportions of animation in children's schedules has been seen as an indicator of declining programme quality and genuine choice – and a major contributor to the decline in indigenous production (Blumler 1991; Messenger Davies and Corbett 1997; Ofcom 2007). At every stage, the increase in animation was seen as a warning sign of the decline of original, high-quality programming and the 'invasion' of 'alien' (primarily American), commercial products (see Kodaira 2005).

The figures are indisputable, but the genre of animation (if indeed it is a genre) has been perhaps unfairly impugned and its malign place in the ecology of children's entertainment greatly over-simplified. In the first place, it encompasses a very wide range of genres and techniques, and in the second place, it overlaps with other genres, particularly preschool television. The problem with animation is its sheer quantity compared with other genres; the fact that it is primarily imported in bulk (see Götz et al. 2008) to pad out children's schedules; and the fact that much of it is formulaic and simplistic and occasionally (but not as often as claimed) violent. But where animation output is 'diluted' in Mallory Wober's (1986) term by other genres and cultural experiences, and where it includes masterpieces of the form such as *The Simpsons*, the products of the Ardman studios, old favourites like *Scooby Doo*, exuberant characters such as *Spongebob Squarepants* and exotic adventure stories such *BenTen*, the loss of animation from children's viewing would be an event to be deplored as much as any other loss. There seems little chance of such a loss happening, however.

3 Factual programming and news

Recently, scholars in several countries of the world have started to examine children's relationship with news media within a framework of concern about children's rights: seeing children as 'citizens in the making' who, even though they do not yet have the vote, are economically active, or soon will be. As discussed in Chapters 3 and 4, children under 18 are already affected by social and political actions and, well before they are eligible to vote, are sometimes direct actors in the public sphere, whether – at one extreme – as child soldiers in conflicts, or at the other, as child carers and rescuers of people in trouble. An important space for their public, citizenship role to be represented is in news and factual material in the media.

Children and news

In 2002, the UNESCO International Clearing House on Children and Violence on the Screen at Nordicom, produced a report on *Children in the News*, a summary of research in Asia, the USA, Egypt, Brazil and several European countries including Sweden, Greece, Portugal and the UK. Diverse research methods had been used, including content analysis of the ways in which children and young people were depicted in the news, and studies testing their understanding and recall of the news.

In general, the picture of children's representation in news material in the UNESCO study, whether press or broadcast (online was not widely discussed), conforms to findings that colleagues at Cardiff, Bournemouth and Nottingham Universities and myself have found in our own recent research on children and news (Carter and Messenger Davies 2005; Carter 2007; Messenger Davies 2006b, 2007; Mendes et al. 2009). Wherever children appear in adult news, they are represented as problems. This will be either as potential criminals – as one child in our study put it: 'Children are shown as a responsibility in adult news . . . something which commits teenage crimes and eats unhealthily. THIS IS NOT RIGHT' (Girl, 12). Or it will be as unheard victims – a boy pointed out: 'It is usually sick children or children in poverty that are shown in children's news, like the two seriously injured Iraqi children that were saved in Kuwait' (Boy, 12). Secondly, even where stories concern them, child participants are rarely consulted or quoted. Thirdly, there is very little news provision directed specifically at them, which explains what is going on in the world in terms which are both meaningful, and which ultimately offer what Dutch researchers Nikken and van der Molen (2008) call 'consolation'.

Some exceptions to this are the news programmes in France, Germany, Israel, Sweden and the UK discussed in Messenger Davies, (2007), on their coverage of the Iraq war. In the USA – where the rest of the world is entitled to hope that future citizens are being educated about their global role – there is no regular news coverage for children. The PBS channels, broadcasting from different stations, with different schedules around the country, have a full schedule for children from early in the morning until 5.30 pm, but programmes are aimed mainly at younger children and do not include news. PBS did have an election special on 4 November 2008, the day of the presidential election. Their website at www.pbskidsgo.org has a site called Newsflash Five, off air during the summer so not offering daily live news. Ellen Seiter and Megan Pincus in an article for *Televizion* (2004) described how American parents were advised to provide their children with 'a protective silence' about the Iraq war. Seiter and Pincus's research indicated that children's views about military action 'almost resembled comics, and many of their questions went unanswered' (2004: 34).

Young 'citizen-journalists'

Children are now being seen as participants in a new era of 'citizen journalism' in which 'ordinary people' are able to contribute to and even create the news through mobile technology and the Internet.[5] This possibility was one of the questions behind our study on the BBC's *Newsround*, the longest-running children's news programme in the world, starting in 1972 (Carter et al. 2009). This research, jointly funded by the BBC and AHRC (Arts and Humanities Research Council) (see [http://www.bbc.co.uk/blogs/knowledgeexchange/cardifftwo.pdf]), produced some provocative findings. The study consulted 220 children aged 8 to 15 in the four nation/regions of the UK about what they thought news was, what kinds of news they liked, where they found it, their views about broadcast versus online material, and how they thought *Newsround* could be improved. It was obvious that these children were both interested in, and knowledgeable about, news and current affairs and expressed a strong sense of potential citizenship. In interviews and video diaries, all the children expressed entitlement to be heard:

> I think that even though we can't vote, kids our age have important things to say, for example we have things to say about education and how it can be improved, transport, how it could be cheaper or free for us, and we do have opinions on the government and how they could change or improve services for young people.
>
> (Karishma, Bournemouth, 13 years)

In Wales, Scotland and Northern Ireland, pleas for acknowledging regional difference and identity were strong: 'It's [*Newsround*] not always local enough, because it's fine with gender and age, but we are a small country and we don't get paid much attention to' (Eliza, Portrush, Northern Ireland, 10 years).

There was particular concern among older children in our sample (11 and over) that *Newsround*, following BBC policy of targeting under 12s, did not address children in their age group. 'They cover many interesting stories, but not for our age group because none of my friends watch it and neither do I' (Girl, Cardiff 15 years). Once again, the lack of a 'space' in broadcast schedules where early adolescence and its concerns can be addressed, and see itself represented, is identified as lacking.

Television as favourite source of news

A number of findings indicated policy directions for producers, which may go against current trends of putting information and educational material online, rather than broadcasting it. First, when asked what their 'favourite source of news' was, the overwhelming majority of children in our study said 'television' (two thirds of the sample). Only 6.9 per cent said the Internet. Secondly, children in our sample did not see 'interactivity' as a means of acquiring information and education. Their primary use of interactive technology was for games, or using the 'red button' on the TV remote control. Their least frequent usage of interactive technology was to 'interact' or upload material.

With children under 12, there is likely to be a parental veto on uploading information and becoming 'citizen journalists'. There is also considerable variability in technical competence. There is wider evidence of journalistic activity among children and young people, for example Children's Express in the UK; the Youth Media for Europe network at [www.youthmediaforeurope.com];

and The Children and Broadcasting Foundation in Africa. However, these opportunities are primarily for teenagers aged 14 and over. 'Citizen journalism', particularly for younger children, cannot replace the kind of contextualization and information given in children's news programmes like *Newsround*, the Dutch *Jeugdjournaal*, with its strategies of 'consolation' and the now-cancelled *First Edition* (Channel 4, UK) in which children were able to interview politicians and experts about major international and national issues of the day. These opportunities would appear to be particularly necessary for those rising voters, the young teenage audience – and also for aspiring young journalists.

4 Light entertainment and children's tastes

But citizenship does not just consist in access to factual information and the capacity to intervene in public affairs. There has always been a strand in children's 'rights' discourse claiming the importance of 'fun'. In March 2009, the head of children's programming at CBBC, Anne Gilchrist wrote a letter to the press defending the 'childishness' of children's programming after it had been criticized by a columnist:

> Some adults don't like children's television – to them, it's shouty and the humour is childish. But if you're nine, shouty means excited and engaged, and childish is . . . well, it's what they're about.
>
> (Anne Gilchrist, Controller, CBBC London W12,
> *Observer*, 29 March 2009)

It can be difficult to defend children's television in terms of the 'shouty' material it produces and also its 'childish' humour. But in some research on children's tastes, entitled 'In the worst possible taste', a team of researchers at the Institute of Education, London University, produced such a defence (Davies et al. 2000): 'It seems to be assumed that left to their own devices children will choose to watch material that is not only morally damaging, but also inherently lacking in cultural value . . . [but] Children and good taste are . . . fundamentally incompatible' (2000: 5–6). They point out that children's tastes are distinctive, and don't map neatly onto generic labels; children enjoy the kinds of 'adult' programming that are less popular with adults such as *Gladiators*. Their own comedy programming such as *Chucklevision*, full of slapstick humour, 'makes Mr Bean look like Jane Austen' say the researchers (p. 17). Davies et al. discuss the aesthetics of children's TV choices as peculiar to children – they call it a form of 'identity work', in which TV programmes they enjoy are used by young viewers as a way of differentiating themselves from 'uncool' and 'boring' characteristics, such as material 'enjoyed by your granny' or 'unfunny' programmes.

Davies et al. argue that children's tastes have an element of subversion (c.f. Alison Lurie on children's literature; see Chapter 8): 'a celebration of ' "childish things" that self-consciously challenge or mock adult norms of respectability, restraint and "good taste" ' (p. 22). They conclude by making the political point made at various points in this book: 'these programmes speak to their sense of their own powerlessness' (p. 23). Children are always going to be at the mercy of adults – but in children's fiction and drama, as distinct from adult fiction and drama, the tables are turned. And seeing adults in humiliating situations and generally make fools of themselves is a joy, as an international study on children and humour, conducted by IZI, found out (Götz et al. 2005). There were some cultural variations in what children found funny, but across all six nations (South Africa; the USA; the UK; Ireland; Germany; Israel) in the study, the humorous material that produced the highest amusement 'scores' was a reality TV show in which adults fell over (see Götz et al. 2006).

Figure 9.1 The value of humour: children laughing (Millstrand School, Northern Ireland, 2006).

Photograph: Rowan Morrey, CMR

David Kleeman (2006: 26) puts the serious case for humour, in terms of children's psychological and even physical well-being:

> [T]he rewards of amusing children far outweigh the challenges. Physio-logically (in the release of endorphins), psychologically (in the development of coping and social strategies and self esteem) and educationally (in fostering flexibility and creativity), laughter is quite simply good for kids.

Kleeman deplores the Parents Television Council's list of behaviours deemed inappropriate for young people's entertainment, including 'drooling, flatulence, burping, disobedience, negative portrayal of parents and more'. He comments: '[the absence of all] this might create a tasteful show, but surely it would also be flavourless' (p. 26).

5 Preschool television

Both nationally in the UK (with the 'triumph' of CBeebies – Barwise 2004) and internationally, (with appealing shows like the Canadian *Arthur*) preschool television seems to be a less threatened branch of children's TV production, not least because of its commercial potential in developing spin-off merchandising (see Steemers 2004). In a paper to a conference at the University of Westminster in September 2009, Jeanette Steemers posed the question about what makes a preschool programme worth investing in (see Box 9.1).

Box 9.1: What do licensing executives want?

- 3D rather than 2D animation – this is more 'toyetic', i.e. can more easily be translated into spin-off toys
- Animation and costumed characters rather than live action
- Teams of characters/friends (this provides 'collectability')
- Detailed backgrounds and worlds (play sets to buy)
- Props (vehicles, pets, accessories)
- Distinctive not generic characters
- Sufficient episodes to sustain awareness and longevity
- Domestic free to air broadcast (CBeebies, Milkshake on C5)
- Classic or educational properties that resonate with parents
- Online applications to extend and sustain the brand

This is asking a very great deal. One producer at the conference remarked: 'if we knew the formula we'd all be living in the Bahamas by now'. Nevertheless some preschool productions have found the formula. Commercially-successful 'toyetic' international exports, with their own 'worlds' of profitable merchandising, play sets, props and costumes include: *Bob the Builder, Postman Pat, Chuggington, Tractor Tom and Thomas the Tank Engine.*

The other criterion for selling, particularly to the American preschool market, is educational content. At the conference, Mary Ann Dudko, a media educational adviser, outlined the specific and prescriptive requirements for producers hoping to sell programme ideas in the US.

- There must be curriculum goals.
- The educational content must be organically placed within the stories. (This plays a significant role – it is the cost of entry for producers hoping to sell a programme idea to the US preschool television market.)

Other factors include:

- developmental appropriateness;
- humour, fun, play value;
- content covering all aspects of child development and early learning;
- formative and summative research to determine whether the goals continue to be met;
- a website with age-appropriate educational activities and content;
- related educational outreach materials.

These do not apply to material for older children (over 6).

The surreal worlds of preschool television

Obviously the creation of 'worlds' generates commercial as well as educational opportunities. But the idea of a special, protected, privileged space is also a powerful metaphorical one in children's entertainment and this is particularly so for preschool television. Iconic shows have locations: Sesame Street; Mr Rogers' Neighborhood; Teletubbyland; The Night Garden; Balamory. The idea of a special 'space' in the broadcast schedules with its own design, personnel and logos is also powerfully appealing for children's sense of cultural ownership.

Teletubbies

One of the most successful preschool television series ever devised was *Teletubbies*, produced by Ragdoll Productions, headed by Anne Wood. *Teletubbies* became the BBC's 'flagship' preschool show, replacing *Play Days* in 1997 and was the biggest marketing, and indeed, cultural, phenomenon in British preschool TV ever. Produced between 1997 and 2001, it had a format which

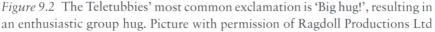

Figure 9.2 The Teletubbies' most common exclamation is 'Big hug!', resulting in an enthusiastic group hug. Picture with permission of Ragdoll Productions Ltd

enabled it to be repeated with material that could be recycled and packaged, and sold on commercially: unlike its studio-bound predecessors, *Play School* and *Playdays*, it was not tied to a particular time and place in the schedules.

The show was controversial for a number of reasons, including being aimed at a very young age group – under 3s – and it was also criticized for not using proper language, since the Teletubbies spoke in a kind of special babytalk. There is in fact a great deal of correctly spoken language in the programme, much of it spoken by children's voiceovers to filmed inserts, showing small children playing, working and socializing. Using children, rather than adults, to commentate and explain to the child audience was a significant, radical departure in preschool TV. At the London World Summit on Children and Television in 1998, a Norwegian delegate attacked the show for being an extended toy advertisement. But, as Steemers points out, without merchandising, children's television production would be likely to cease altogether.

Jonathan Bignell (2005) uses *Teletubbies* to explore further the concept of 'space'. He argues that 'television is a key boundary space that negotiates understandings of adulthood and childhood, self and other, now and then, here and there' (2005: 374). As he points out, with television screens inside the Teletubbies' stomachs, TV is 'literally embedded in the characters' (2005: 374). Bignell has concerns about the relationship between 'real' and 'represented' children in *Teletubbies*, and describes the show's aesthetic as 'dissolving distinctions between the alien and familiar' – a place 'where anything strange might happen' (p. 376). This is actually true of a very great deal of preschool television, not just *Teletubbies*. In fact it could be described as its defining characteristic.

Little Airplane Productions: a 'real space'

Little Airplane is one of the most successful of the new breed of independent producers of children's material, with production offices both in New York and London. Their series, featuring little birds and other creatures, *3rd and Bird*, was commissioned and co-produced by CBeebies in the UK. Interestingly, despite its programming relying almost exclusively on virtual computer technology to produce their animated stories, the company places considerable emphasis on the location and origin of its programme material in an *actual* physical space.

On a web page entitled 'Our Home' [http://www.littleairplane.com/our-home/default.aspx], the website proclaims: '300 year old elements adorn our beautiful studio, located in the heart of New York's historic, South Street Seaport . . . we create every aspect of our shows in house at Little Airplane, from concept to final delivery'. Studio tours are part of the service the company offers to regular groups of visiting children (and visiting researchers), and the producers run workshops there for aspiring children's TV creatives.

Photographs of the 'Great Room' where production staff hold meetings, and of musicians playing in an eighteenth-century room adapted as a recording studio, also adorn the site (see Figures 9.3 to 9.5). The company's founder, Josh Selig, originally worked for *Sesame Street*; the website tells us that his film *The Time Out Chair* (2003) 'has been recently acquired by the Museum of Modern Art in New York'.

In stressing its relationship with high art and culture, a handcrafted approach to creativity, and the eighteenth-century elegance of its production surroundings, the company continues a tradition of emphasizing the creative aesthetic and dedicated artistry of people serving the young child audience: these are

Figure 9.3 300-year-old elements adorn the beautiful studio located in the heart of New York's historic South Street Seaport. Picture with permission of Little Airplane Productions, Inc.

quality products, not mere 'trashy cartoons'. Quality incorporates an acknowledgement of the specialness of the audience: 'Little Airplane productions is committed to celebrating young children and treating them with dignity. We consider it both a great privilege and a great responsibility to represent and serve such a distinguished audience' says the home page [www.littleairplane.com].

Sesame Street

The programme that could be described as the founding father/mother of this spirit in international preschool television, carefully researched and

Figure 9.4 Every morning at 9:45, the 77 member team gathers as a group in The Great Room. Picture with permission of Little Airplane Productions, Inc.

Figure 9.5 Each week, a full orchestra performs award winning music in the music recording studio. Here, the '3rd & Bird!' band performs a song from an upcoming episode. Picture with permission of Little Airplane Productions, Inc.

devised to be both educational and entertaining, is *Sesame Street*, launched on the American Public Broadcasting System (PBS), from the Children's Television Workshop (now Sesame Workshop) in 1969. Charlotte Cole and her co-researchers at Sesame Workshop, Beth Richman and Susan McCann Brown, call it the 'single largest informal educator of young children in the world' (2001: 147). It has more than 120 million viewers in more than 130 countries.

It has been adapted into 19 different international versions, each with its own characters, sets and curricula. Each local production 'has the same essence as the series produced in the United States, in a context that reflects local values and educational priorities' (2001: 147). This cultural specificity is at the heart of the co-productions' success, according to the authors. In 2007, *Sesame Street*'s inclusive message was brought to a part of the UK where inclusivity has long been lacking – a place where sectarian division produced 30 years of conflict and violence – **The Troubles** – broadly between 1969 and 1999, Northern Ireland.

A special screening of a film called *The World According to Sesame Street* at the Cinemagic Film Festival in Belfast in 2007 launched the local co-production between the BBC and Sesame Workshop, *Sesame Tree*, aimed at increasing understanding in young and divided (by sectarianism) Northern Irish children. The producers emphasized the workshop's and its team of Muppets' efforts in

Figure 9.6 A muppet with children in India, picture with permission of Sesame Workshop

'tackling the world's most challenging issues facing 3- to 5-year-olds, including HIV/AIDS in South Africa and post conflict resolution in a divided Kosovo'. Sesame Workshop is thus operating in areas with delicate political and social implications – and thus, as with the more overtly educational aspects of factual programming like *Newsround* and *Jeugdjournaal*, it has a civic agenda.

I interviewed Charlotte Cole, head of research at Sesame Workshop, in 2008, about the programme's – and the Workshop's – philosophy:

> Sesame is about diversity and inclusion: handicap; special needs. Everyone can see themselves on screen . . . We don't want to be perceived as American cultural imperialists or social engineers. We provide a framework that has worked in different places . . . In Northern Ireland, Sesame Tree is linked to the new statutory curriculum with mutual responsibility and understanding as components. Our philosophy is to give a positive image on screen of diverse backgrounds.
>
> (2008, personal interview)

Figure 9.7 Sesame Street's international cast of characters, picture with permission of Sesame Workshop

Figure 9.8 Sesame Tree characters, Northern Ireland, picture with permission of Sesame Workshop

The ways in which Sesame Workshop is diversifying in the 'post-TV' era shows the company's initiative in exploiting new media. Recent research, *Pockets of Potential* (Shuler 2009), is subtitled: 'using mobile technologies to explore children's learning'. It reports on 25 different handheld technologies – in other words, mobile phones – in the US and elsewhere to 'encourage "anytime, any-where" learning', to 'reach underserved children' and to 'enable a personalized learning experience' (2009: 3). But, said Charlotte Cole in my interview with her, 'television is still king'.

Surreal improvisation – another 'Golden Age'?

The contrast between the elaborate technologies of the new world of preschool television and its early days could not be more marked, but the content shows strong elements of continuity. Bignell's description of *Teletubbies*' aesthetics as 'surreal' sums up preschool television generally. Surrealism is certainly permit-ted by CGI animation, and the kinds of clever claymation used by Ardman

(*Shaun the Sheep*). But it can also be permitted by very simple low-tech production values, as in the simple drawings of *Ivor the Engine* (1959; 1975–7). The creator of Ivor, the late Oliver Postgate, in an article just before he died ([2003] 2008), passionately defended preschool television along these lines:

> When Peter Firmin and I made our first film series, about a Welsh railway engine who wanted to sing in the choir, we received about £10 a minute for the finished films . . . we had to rely on the basic handwriting of animation, laboriously pushing along cardboard characters with a pin. We were thrown back on the real staple of television: telling and showing a good story, carefully thought out. I must have produced some of the clumsiest animation ever to disgrace the television screen, but it didn't matter.
>
> (Postgate [2003] 2008)

Conclusion: creating and charting spaces

Karen Lury in her introduction to *Screen*'s special issue on 'the child in film and television', vol 46 (3) 2005, argues that crucial to all understandings of screen provision for children is the concept of space, both physical and metaphorical. Children's television is important because it is a space for and about children, institutional, metaphorical and generic. Broadcast schedules are spaces that are confined and mapped, with specific time slots and 'addresses' on the programme guide, and thus relatively straightforward to navigate. Programmes are meeting points.

One problem with the Internet, which is proposed as taking over from television as a more liberating space for children, is that it is not so easily navigable in this way. Cyberspace even changes as we look at it. To borrow the favourite metaphor for danger to children from fairytale, the Internet has elements of the uncharted forest. Users do not always know which way to turn, and there may be wolves, beasts, and other dangers, such as cyber-bullies, lurking there, as well as the problematic fact that the landscape keeps changing; a pathway that led to a clearing yesterday is gone today. Social networks have spaces and rules of course, but research shows that networks are primarily used by older children. There is also the problem of surreptitious surveillance of children, as we will discuss in the next chapter. Media for children have to do what children's television has done: provide means for them to find their way around, to feel that the space is theirs and that it is both adventurous and safe. We will see to what extent 'new media' provide this in the next chapter.

Further reading

For critical discussion of children's television programmes, see David Buckingham's edited collection (2002) *Small Screens: Television for Children*, Leicester: Continuum/ Leicester University, and his and Cary Bazalgette's collection (eds) (1995) *In Front of the Children*, London: BFI. For children's responses to entertainment see Götz, M. et al. (2005) 'Is that funny anywhere else?' An international comparison of humour in children's programmes, *Televizion*, 19/2006/E,[http://www.bronline.de/jugend/izi/english/ publication/televizion/19_2006_E/19_2006_ E.htm]. See also Messenger Davies (2001a) *'Dear BBC': Children, Television Storytelling and the Public Sphere*, Cambridge: CUP.

10 | DIGITAL – 'NEW' MEDIA

'The kids are in a different world than the one we grew up in. They're first language users of new media technology. For us it's a second language – and it's much harder to understand it. For them it's easy.'

This was my brother describing the media environment his children, aged 16, 14 and 12, live in, compared even to the relatively recent media environment his nephews and nieces – my children – grew up in. For my children, television was the dominant medium, with computer games (primitive ones like Pacman) and Game Boys beginning to come into vogue, and the local video store a convenient way of catching up with movies missed in the cinema. There was no Internet at home or at work and the only person to have a computer was me – an Amstrad, running on software (Quill) which is now completely obsolete.

As teenagers, the most sophisticated technology my children acquired was the harbinger of the oncoming, convergent and, especially, mobile media world, Sony Walkmans. On these they could hear both live radio (then, and still, an important if critically neglected medium for children) and cassette recordings. The audio cassette was a major part of their cultural lives, enabling them to record their own musical and other compositions, and – especially – to make compilations of tracks for special occasions to give as gifts – a process now re-invented as 'mashing' and 'remixing' using downloads from the Internet. Piles of their cassettes, alongside huge stacks of videotapes, now lie unused and un-needed, since most of the music on these obsolete tapes can now be downloaded from the Internet, stored on an iPod or MP3 player, and carried around.

The media world my children's young cousins now occupy is different again. For them, digital media are the primary shapers of the media environment in which they live. 'They don't watch television', claimed their father, although they do. However, their television watching, viewed on a Sky satellite package, can be digitally controlled in a number of ways – most usefully through the Sky Plus/TiVo technology, which means, in theory, that their television viewing of any particular programme is no longer tied to a particular time of day (but see again, Chapter 9).

It is the Internet that has made the most difference, permitting them to use email; play online games; do research for homework; join social network groups (although, in common with many, their parents restrict their access to these in a variety of ways) and to navigate various websites, some of them linked to television programmes. One of the biggest changes – one very convenient to their parents, and which I wish we'd had when my older children were teenagers – is their ownership of mobile phones (the youngest of our children did have one as a teenager). In common with over 80 per cent of their age group (12–15, Ofcom 2008), my nephews and niece each have a phone, which enables their parents to keep in constant touch with them and allows the youngest child, a girl, a degree of social freedom.

The pace of change has caught the industry itself by surprise, with an unprecedented rate of collapse among media businesses, partly brought about by the credit crunch of 2008–9 but also by the rapid migration of advertising following consumer/readers, to the worldwide web and away from traditional media, including television, and print media such as newspapers. In a period of economic crisis, it can be disturbing for our familiar media landscapes to be drastically changing too. At such a time, we can expect our conceptions of 'the child' to be under scrutiny and reconstruction.

Constructing the child 'new media' user

The swiftness of many of the changes in the development of 'new' digital technology in people's lives has a tendency to outpace the rate of academic research on the phenomenon. Nevertheless, the old debates continue: the American Academy of Child and Adolescent Psychiatry has an information sheet for parents on its website headed: 'Children and Video Games: Playing with Violence' [http://www.aacap.org/cs/root/facts_for_families/children_ and_ video_games_playing_with_violence], accessed 28 May 2009). Once again, a new communications technology is presented to parents as a potential threat to children, rather than as an opportunity.

Neil Selwyn (2003) itemizes the ways in which 'new' technology has gener-ated a new set of discourses about the construction of childhood. He analysed seven print sources including the UK Parliamentary record, Hansard 1981–2001,

The London Times index of news stories (1980–2000), BBC News online archives (1997–2001), Adflip online database of ads and commercial marketing (1980–2000) and Educational Computing and Technology magazine, (1982–2001). From these sources, he identified six ways of defining children in terms of their relationship with computers:

1. The 'natural' child computer user – 'the naturally adept user of technology . . . with an *innate* [his italics] capability'. Typical terms used by BBC News (2000) were 'natural born net babes' and 'net savvy young' (Selwyn 2003: 358).
2. The 'successful child' computer user – a development of the 'natural child' but this time, characterizing children as 'exceptional' – 'all kids are inventors', as one ad put it. This emphasizes the 'transformative potential' of the computer in promoting learning, maths and so on (p. 358).
3. The 'adult' child computer user; one who teaches teachers, as in the example of John Battle MP, quoted from Hansard (1997: 1187, cited in Selwyn 2003): 'teachers will be learning from pupils for once'.
4. The 'dangerous' child computer user: 'a child who is actively and aggressively using ICT at the ultimate risk of harming both themselves and others' (p. 362) and 'watching computer porn' (Evans MP, Hansard 1993: 581, cited in Selwyn 2003).
5. The 'victimized' computer user: the 'innocent child user' who is inadvertently exposed to a 'tide of indescribable filth on his computer' (*Daily Mail*, 15 September, 1995).
6. The 'needy' child computer user: this discourse focuses on children's lack of skills and the need to educate them, and also to 'train them as future workers' (Selwyn 2003: 366).

Selwyn concludes that these are all different ways of 'selling' media technology to the adult population; the child computer user is used as a political and commercial selling point, to support what he calls the 'real winners' of the information age, 'the technocracy within government and business' (p. 375).

What is striking about Selwyn's analysis is how early and long ago these discourses began – back in the 1980s – yet we are still calling these media 'new media' and governments and other bodies are still commissioning major studies like the Byron review (2008), and the Kaiser Foundation surveys (2006; 2008) to evaluate their 'impact'. This suggests that the questions Selwyn poses are still unanswered, and may in fact never be answered.

The social and historical context of 'new' media

In *Young People and New Media* (2002), Sonia Livingstone compares the impact of IT with social pressures at the time of the introduction of printing in the fifteenth and sixteenth centuries. The first book was produced in Europe in 1450 and fifty years later about 20 million books, representing 10–15,000 different texts had been printed. She suggests that this earlier explosion of communications technology was not only technology-driven but also the result of political and socio-economic conditions which were 'oppressive and intolerable'. During the current information explosion, she argues that online communities are a way of dealing with life challenges, such as 'divorce, lack of consensual family values' and so on (2002: 241). The social contacts and activities offered by new media are 'an escape ... a realm of advice, images of diverse life strategies, a sphere for considering and contesting alternative viewpoints' (p. 241). Although children in developed societies now are not in the same oppressive and intolerable conditions as were children in the fifteenth and sixteenth centuries, Livingstone's case is that communications media are seen to provide an outlet and escape from some of life's difficulties, now, as then.

Implications for policy: Digital Britain

The points made by both Selwyn and Livingstone are echoed in 'Digital Britain', a major policy document by Stephen Carter on behalf of the UK Department of Culture Media and Sport (DCMS) in 2009. (See [http://www.culture.gov.uk/what_we_do/broadcasting/5944.aspx].) Carter echoes Livingstone in seeing the arrival of digital culture as a revolutionary moment, but he is more optimistic about its impact on society generally than Livingstone is. And where Selwyn is sceptical about the ways in which the child computer user is used as 'a political and commercial selling point', Carter, from inside the 'technocracy' of Government, enthuses about the 'quiet revolution' and its importance to 'the wider economy'. His report states:

> Around the world digital and broadband technologies are reshaping our Communications, Entertainment, Information and Knowledge industries, the wider economy, and the way of life for all of us. We are at a point of transformation ... A successful Britain must be a *Digital Britain*. Digital technology has led to a quiet revolution over the past decade in our lives at work, at home and at leisure ...; hundreds of television and radio channels; user-generated content; instant connectedness with virtual communities of interest and friendship; and keeping extended family networks in touch with images as well as words.
>
> (2009: 3, original emphasis)

David Buckingham's (2009) concern is with the impact of technology on educational policy. He agrees with Neil Selwyn in being sceptical about this process and argues:

> The current push to insert computers in classrooms is principally driven by commercial companies seeking new and predictable markets for their products; and by governments that are apparently desperate to solve what they regard as the problems of public education. Both typically espouse a form of technological determinism and a belief in the all conquering power of technology ... This has led to a neglect of basic educational issues not only about *how we teach* with technology but also about *what children need to know* about it.
>
> (2009: 36, original emphasis)

Buckingham argues that most uses of technology in schools are 'narrow, unimaginative and instrumental' (2009: 37). Outside school, he points out, children are living in 'increasingly media-saturated childhoods' but children's main use of technology is for popular culture. Buckingham raises the perennial concerns of media educators. Technology is not just about acquiring a new set of skills. As with other media, 'the Internet raises challenging questions in representation – bias, authority and ideology' (2009: 37).

Transatlantic perspectives

The more cautious and sceptical attitudes of British and European commentators to the Utopian prospects of new technology for children contrast with some of the best-known transatlantic commentators on the subject. Henry Jenkins, until recently working in the MIT Comparative Media Studies program, and now at USC, has been a particularly eloquent enthusiast for the educationally liberating powers of the Internet. In *Convergence Culture* (2006: 3) he argues:

> [This] circulation of media content across different media systems, competing media economies and national borders, depends heavily on consumers' active participation ... convergence represents a cultural shift as consumers are encouraged to seek out new information and make connections among dispersed media content.

Jenkins and his MIT colleagues (2007) itemize specific new media literacies arising from these participatory experiences. These include 'appropriation', (that is, borrowing and reworking existing materials); multi-tasking, collective intelligence, judgment, networking and negotiation. Buckingham et al. (2008) point out a number of challenges in Jenkins et al.'s positive and optimistic analysis, including 'the ethics challenge'. How are young people representing themselves through all the material that they upload onto their blogs, websites and social network pages – and what might happen as a result of these representations? There are unanswered questions here, but also well-grounded concerns about Internet 'stalkers' and potential grooming of unsuspecting children, as well as the possibility of children and young people getting into trouble for copyright infringement. Buckingham et al. (2008) also raise doubts as to how much personal material and user generated content is actually being put onto the web. They argue that the opportunity to give young people a voice 'can be overstated' (2008: 50). Apparently 'only 0.16 percent of users of YouTube actually contribute videos, while only 0.2 percent of visitors upload images to the photo sharing site Flickr' (p. 50) These are somewhat contradictory positions. If children are not uploading material as much as everybody thinks they are, then the ethical risks are also not as great as feared.

The celebratory examples Jenkins – and others at MIT – describe, mainly concern 'young people' and adults rather than children and they thus beg the question of how people are enabled to become participatory in the first place. Participation for children depends on access (parental expenditure, broadband availability) but also on a degree of literary competence, and especially, motivation. The considerable numbers of children and young people who say they do not have Internet access in major surveys such as those carried out by EU Online and Ofcom, may not all be barred simply by non-availability. Julian Sefton Green (2002) asks of children's interactive websites: 'when these kinds of texts become commonplace . . . will we really value their personalised interactivity as a distinctive pleasure? Or will they too become as repetitive and routine as the texts they have appeared to replace?' (2002: 206). The answer is – we don't know. The orthodoxy among most commentators, as Neil Selwyn's analysis suggests, is that all children are enthusiastically embracing the converged world of digital multi-media, but this may not in fact be the case.

'New media': what are they, and how are children using them?

So what is the actual position? This section sets out what we know so far about the facts and figures of (mainly Western) children and young people's Internet and digital media use as derived from the many major surveys on it that have been produced since the mid-2000s. The main concerns of these surveys are, first to find out what children are doing with websites, social network sites, games, mobile technology and so on, and then to evaluate the advantages and risks. We begin with the Internet itself.

The Internet

The term 'the Internet' encompasses a vast range of material – information, education, entertainment, multi-player gaming, pornography, fan websites, images, films, TV shows, radio programmes, social networks, archives, official information, newspapers, emailing, messaging, maps, 'wikis' and Wikipedias, all marshalled by powerful (both technically and increasingly culturally and economically) search engines, such as Google; there is also a lot of material that I, and everybody else, do not and cannot know about. Every time I go online, I happen across something I've never seen before. This is even more likely to be the case for children, despite their 'first language' ease with digital technology.

Children's access to and use of the Internet: international studies

Several attempts have been made to find out how much children have access to the Internet. In a Europe wide study, EU Kids Online (Hasebrink et al. 2008, [www.eukidsonline.net]) reporting on figures from 2006, stated that half of all children under 18 years old in the 25 countries of the European Union had used the Internet, with higher figures applying to teenagers. However, the report notes 'there are substantial differences across countries, ranging from less than a third of children in Greece and Bulgaria to over two thirds of those in Estonia and Denmark.' (2008: 5). This still leaves a considerable proportion of children, even in developed European cultures, who do not use the Internet, either because they do not have access, or because their parents do not let them, or – and the possibility has to be accepted, even for this so-called 'media-savvy' generation – because they do not want to.

Rideout et al. (2005) in a report for The Kaiser Family Foundation give data from a study of over 2, 032 8- to 18-year-olds in the USA in 2005. It found that, in the period since 1999, the proportion of children with home computers went up from 73 per cent to 86 per cent and, as the report put it, home Internet access 'rocketed' from 47 per cent to 85 per cent, with many families having two or more computers. This study indicates the difficulty for researchers in keeping pace with the 'digital revolution'. The report discusses the 'popularization of DVD players' and suggests that 'as families added DVD players to their home entertainment options, they have kept their VCRs as well and in many cases the VCRs have migrated into children's bedrooms' (2005: 38). In 2009–10, the VCR has joined the audio cassette player and my Amstrad computer in the rapidly growing pile of obsolete technologies.

Uses of the Internet

According to Ofcom figures (Ofcom 2009) based on a survey with nearly 3, 700 children aged between 5 and 15 in the UK, around two thirds of children aged between 8 and 15 used the Internet in 2007. Reasons for using the net varied according to age: 39 per cent of 5–7-year-olds, 48 per cent of 8–11-year-olds and 37 per cent of 12–15-year-olds used the Internet to 'find out things'. Five- to 7-year-olds were the highest entertainment-seekers – 52 per cent used the Internet for 'fun'. A significant comparison in this survey was the 27 per cent of 12–15-year-olds who used the Internet for social contact, which hardly any of the younger age group did. This 12–15 group was also the keenest to download material from the Internet – 40 per cent of them downloaded music, film, clips from other people and TV shows. As with other kinds of media, age is an important determinant of use.

According to Ofcom, 'no sustainable business model has emerged for children's content online'. They argue that online content is seen as 'must-have' support for existing TV properties, in other words, from a commercial point of view, where children are concerned, television would appear to be still the primary medium for capturing their attention in large numbers, and this is seen as a way of leading them to the Internet.

Social networking and emailing

According to the Ofcom 2008 report, reported in 2009 the main growth in social networking in the UK is the development of social networking sites such as Bebo and MySpace, and, for younger children, Club Penguin. In this Ofcom survey more than half – 52 per cent – of 12–15-year-olds had a profile on a social networking site and 13 per cent were 'interested' in having one. This still left a third of them – 33 per cent – who 'were not interested'. For 8–11s, only 16 per cent had a space, 17 per cent were interested, and the majority – 57 per cent – were not interested. Nine per cent did not know. There were no figures for 5–7-year-olds.

The high proportion of 'not interested' in this sample raises another aspect of the term 'choice': the option of saying 'no thanks' to new technology. One problem in offering children true choice between a range of communicative experiences is the disappearance of earlier technologies such as the videotape, or the CD, or the cassette tape, or 'wet' photography. The latest communications medium to be threatened with obsolescence through 'convergence' is the printed book, with the rise of electronic readers such as Kindle and the option of downloading whole books from the Internet. The question is raised: if and when all communications technologies are 'converged' into one, what choice for the consumer will there actually be? (see also Livingstone 2009).

Social networking: risks and anxieties

According to the EU Online survey, there is evidence that social networking and sharing experiences with 'distant others' is common among children from the UK, the Netherlands, Sweden, Spain, Poland, Norway, Italy, Ireland, Iceland, Germany, France, Estonia, Denmark, Czech Republic, Belgium and Austria. In the UK section of the study, 'UK Children Go Online', a positive and high correlation was found between the number of online opportunities and the number of online risks for 12–17-year-old Internet users. The positive association between increased *opportunities* of going online, with the increased *risks* of being online, means that either way, children and young people are going to be disadvantaged. 'Increasing opportunities tends to increase risks, while decreasing risks tends to decrease opportunities. No way has yet been found, it seems, to increase opportunities while decreasing risks' (Hasebrink et al. 2008: 47). The choice of avoiding both opportunities and risks by using other kinds of technologies would not seem to be offered as an option here.

Children themselves have differing attitudes to online 'risks'. In the Ofcom (2008/9) survey, among 12–15-year-olds, girls were much more worried about safety and security issues than boys. Concerns included: 'strangers might find out information about me', or people might be 'posting photos, about me, or pretend to be me'. Thirty-two per cent of girls were worried about bullying online, compared to 21 per cent of boys. There were noticeable gender differences about anxiety in this survey: 40 per cent of boys would allow their social network profile to be seen by 'anyone', compared with only 25 per cent of girls.

Games

Much of the concern about children's relationship with 'new' digital media has centred on computer games. The American Academy of Child and Adolescent Psychiatry in an advice sheet for parents warns:

> While some games have educational content, many of the most popular games emphasize negative themes and promote:
>
>> the killing of people or animals
>> the use and abuse of drugs and alcohol
>> criminal behavior, disrespect for authority and the law
>> sexual exploitation and violence toward women

racial, sexual, and gender stereotypes
foul language, obscenities, and obscene gestures
(updated 08/06, [http://www.aacap.org/cs/root/facts_for_families/
children_and_video_games_playing_with_violence],
accessed 28 May 2009)

If we look at the titles of some of the best selling games, we can see why the Academy might be concerned:[1]

The top 10 selling Xbox 360 games.

Halo 3 (8.1 million sold)
Gears of War
Gears of War 2
Grand Theft Auto IV
Call of Duty 4: Modern Warfare
Call of Duty: World at War
Forza Motorsport 2
Fable II
Assassin's Creed
Marvel: Ultimate Alliance
Guitar Hero II (2 million in North America and Western Europe)

25 million live games downloaded up to 2007.

Nearly all of these games involve either warfare, or killing, or dangerous activities of one kind or another. I am not a videogamer, but I'm prepared to accept the enthusiasm of people I respect, who are gamers. However, in observing them, it seems to me that the physical procedures of gaming (sitting at a computer) provide a very limited range of options for action. The software may be very complex, but the driving technology is limited in what it permits the player to physically do – basically just sitting and pressing buttons, either alone, or in communication with others in the room or online. Contrastingly, in the software of the game design, button-pressing, monotonous though it is, facilitates vicarious dramatic actions: explosions, crashes, leaps, jumps, escapes, explorations, collapsing buildings and so on. As Nicholas Tucker remarked about the 'activity' of reading (see Chapter 8), gaming involves a great deal of sitting down indoors.

Online gaming

However, there are more socially interactive ways of being a gamer. 'Massively multiplayer' online games (MMOGs) or massively multiplayer online role-playing games (MMORPGs) permit the player to join forces with other players online and complete the various levels of the tasks together. Such games include the Sims Online (the Sims being a hugely popular game which has transcended some of the limitations of games' audience appeal) and World of Warcraft. Buckingham et al. (2008) cite a survey of over 30,000 MMORPG players which found that 25 per cent of them were under the age of 18 and that 80 per cent of players regularly play MMORPGs with someone they know in real life.

Gender and games

Although there has been some attempt to market games to girls, some in ways that are highly stereotyped (see, for example [http://www.girlsgogames.co.uk/?gclid=CPDSgbiu35oCFQdN5QodVEyYyg]) and some girls do play with the bestselling titles involving warfare and assassination (Cassell and Jenkins 2000; Kerr 2006; Thornham 2008) it is obvious from lists like the one above[2] that, because violent action has become such a standard ingredient of the best sellers, computer games are being marketed to and used primarily by boys. Digital and online material seems to be creating more and more opportunities for gender roles to become more stereotypically fixed, despite the best efforts of female game designers. This extends to actual, as well as virtual socializing. My 16-year-old nephew regularly goes to a small videogame store in his town, where he meets and plays with other gamers, obviously a desirable and harmless social activity. 'But', he said 'if a girl went in there, everyone would freeze.'

Gender, age, neurology and 'nature'

Gender differences have been a concern for some of the policy reviews into gaming, such as the Byron Review (2008). In a literature review for Byron on the impact of new technologies on children, Mark H. Johnson, Director, Centre for Brain and Cognitive Development Birkbeck College, London, gives an account of brain development in childhood (2008) and suggests that there may be neurological differences between boys and girls. 'Male and female adults respond differently to scenes of a sexual or violent nature. Female children may be less aroused by sexual scenes, but can show greater physiological responses to unpleasant scenes' (2008: 19).

Johnson also draws attention, again, to the contribution of age to children's responses:

> At different developmental stages, brains are likely to react differently to content on the Internet or violent games. For example, under and around 4 years, children have difficulty identifying the source of memories, and may thus confuse reality and game play. Before puberty, relatively poor

inhibitory abilities result in a lack of control over emotions and practised responses. During adolescence changes in the prefrontal cortex and reward systems of the brain lead to increased risk-taking.

(p. 19)

In contrast to the positive list of literacies itemized by Jenkins and his colleagues (Jenkins 2006; Jenkins et al. 2007) Johnson puts together a more negative list of possible effects of playing video and computer games – which, however, is highly cautious in the terms used. Phrases such as 'likely to' and 'may transfer' and 'may include' are used repeatedly, since, as Johnson points out, there is no actual concrete evidence for some of the possible dangers. Johnson accepts that 'Large amounts of time engaged in video games or on the Internet during childhood *are likely to have* both positive and negative effects on brain function and development' (p. 19, my italics). The positive effects listed include *possible* transfer of perception and cognitive skills to other computer-based tasks, which '*may be* useful in an increasingly computer-based school and employment environment' (p. 19, my italics).

Some of the negative effects listed are more general, and could equally well apply to other childhood activities such as reading, doing homework, sitting in school, watching television and films: these 'risks' arise from a 'lack of physical exercise . . . and a lack of expertise in fine motor skills relevant for whole body action (such as in sports)' (p. 19).

Johnson's conclusions are measured and, since they are based on a scientifically-detached stance towards children and young people's media use, with no particular axe to grind either for or against 'convergent culture', they are worth noting. They stand in contrast to some of the more emotive and less evidence-based arguments put forward both by 'moral panickers' and enthusiasts (including commercial promoters).

> Adolescence is a period of brain development characterized by increased risk-taking and a relative lack of inhibition. This poses potential risks on the Internet (e.g. gambling sites), but frequent technology use *may reduce* [my italics] the time available for risks of mortality in real world situations . . . Since mild arousal of the brain is attractive to many individuals, this *may potentially cause* some to seek increasingly realistic violent scenarios. However, this link is unproven.
>
> (2008: 19–20, original emphasis)

Games and education

Many researchers and game designers are exploring the possibilities of using games for educational purposes. Klopfer et al. (2009) in an extended article called 'Moving education games forward' (see [http://education.mit.edu/papers/MovingLearningGamesForward_EdArcade.pdf]), give a useful and comprehensive history of educational games development. These authors are involved in the design of educational games themselves as part of the MIT Education Arcade project. They summarize the positions of two different groups, each arguing the educational benefits of computer games. One group sees gaming as educationally valuable in its own right, as a way of developing collaborative skills, and problem solving. The other group sees games as a means to an end: a way of teaching traditional academic subjects. Klopfer et al. suggest that these positions are somewhat opposed to each other. 'If the first group embraces games and abandons school, this second group often embraces school to the detriment of anything that looks like real gaming' (2009: 2).

They make the same point made by all other scholars who study the relationship between children and their media behaviour: the point that this relationship does not exist in a vacuum. Benefits and drawbacks of the medium always interact with children's environment including family and other relationships:

> [T]echnology alone does not create or encourage good learning and creative practice. We tend to believe that the children who make the most of these technologies do so in the context of families and communities of practice (and sometimes schools) that support their efforts . . . disadvantaged children were far less likely to spend time with single applications or sites, and tended to skim surfaces rather than dive deeply.
>
> (Klopfer et al. 2009: 3)

The tension would seem to be in adapting something that is playful and self-generated (and valorized by Jenkins et al., 2007, as such) for more pragmatic purposes such as school learning (of whatever kind) and business success. Once a playful activity becomes school learning, or work, it ceases to be play; once something begins to become a duty, it is likely to be resisted. The problem with 'convergence culture' is that it converges in a very limited space – primarily a computer screen; as such it is experientially limited. Jenkins makes the same point about his son playing computer games, unlike himself who used to play out in the open air (see Cassell and Jenkins 2000)

Mobile phones

According to Ofcom (2008) two thirds of children have a mobile phone by the age of 10. Children aged 8–11 make on average 10.8 calls per week. Children aged 12–15 make 16.9 calls per week. Boys and girls make the same amount of calls per week but texting is far more popular among girls: girls aged 8–11 make 25.8

texts a week, boys make 15.8 texts a week. This goes astronomically higher for teenagers: girls aged 12–15 make 86.6 texts a week, boys make 61.7 a week. This excess of messaging has given rise to yet more causes for anxiety. A *New York Times* article of 25 May, 2009 is headed 'texting may be taking a toll'. Apparently American teenagers are now sending and receiving an average of 2, 272 text messages a month (Nielsen). 'The phenomenon is beginning to worry physicians and psychologists who say it is leading to anxiety, distraction in school, falling grades, repetitive stress injury and sleep deprivation' says the article. It's also apparently causing repetitive strain injury to their thumbs ([http://www.nytimes.com/pages/todayspaper/index.html], accessed 28 May 2009).

The mobile phone and young people's habit of texting can clearly be added to the ever-growing list of communications technologies for people to worry about. Nevertheless, as always with new media technologies, scholars can be found both to defend the technology, and to demonstrate its intellectual useful-ness. David Crystal, the linguist, says, in his 2008 book on the subject, *txtng: the gr8 db8* (that really is how the title is spelt) that he has 'never come across a topic which has attracted more adult antagonism' (2008: viii). Given the antagonism and suspicion shown towards television and computer games – and indeed towards earlier communications technology (see the Starker breakdown in Chapter 5) – this argues a very high degree of antagonism indeed towards texting. Crystal, in contrast, describes texting as 'fascinating . . . it is the latest manifestation of the human ability to be linguistically creative and to adapt language to suit the demands of diverse settings . . . we are seeing in a small way, language in evolution' (2008: 175).

David Crystal describes how mobile phones are particularly creatively used in Japan, where as well as 'planning physical encounters', text messages are also used by young people for the collaborative composition of novels. An author known as Yoshi 'had a huge success' with a text messaging novel called *Deep Love* (2008: 80). In 2004, a novel called *Outside the Fortress* by Quian Fuchang, managed to tell the story of an adulterous love affair in 4000 words, split into 60 chapters. China has a mobile literature channel. Crystal is enthusiastic about the literary ingenuity of text authors, although he acknowledges that 'SMS . . . has some weaknesses. Its brevity disallows formal patterning say of the kind we might find in a sonnet' (2008: 79). Nevertheless some of the poems he quotes are poetry by any definition. A favourite one by text poet Norman Silver (2006) goes as follows:

langwij
Is hi-ly infectious
children
the world ova

catch it
from parence
by word of mouth
the yung
r specially vulnerable
so care
shud b taken how langwij
is spread
symptoms include acute
goo-goo
and the equally serious ga-ga
if NE child
is infected with langwij
give em
3 tspoons of txt
b4 bedtime
& 1/2 a tablet of verse
after every meal

(Crystal 2008: 84–5)

The social advantages of mobile phone use also have their champions. In an article on children, youth and the mobile phone, Ling and Haddon (2008) point out that SMS messaging was invented by young people themselves; the fact that this made young people 'pioneers' was, they argue, important for their self-esteem. An analysis of Japanese youth shows 'the use of mobile communication to anticipate and to summarize physical encounters ... spontaneous, fluid nature of planning' (2008: 145). They point out with justice that 'within the social shaping of technology tradition ... SMS practices are often cited as the best and most widespread contemporary example of unanticipated innovation from users' (p. 147).

Genuine causes for concern: some common risks

A genuine and major cause for concern with children's and young people's use of 'new media' is invasion of their privacy, not only by strangers and pos-sible stalkers, but also surveillance by governmental or corporate institutions. This surveillance is something of which young people (and their parents) are often completely unaware. Christian Fuchs (2009) in a survey of 700 Austrian students who subscribed to social network sites, Facebook, MySpace and StudiVZ, an Austrian site, points out the value of the data uploaded by these young people to governments and corporations:

Electronic surveillance by nation states and corporations aims at controlling the behaviour of individuals and groups, i.e. they should be forced to behave or not behave in certain ways because they know that their appearance, movements, location, or ideas are or could be watched by electronic systems.

(Fuchs 2009: 108)

He points out that very large amounts of personal information are freely uploaded to such sites as Facebook, including pictures of the person, addresses, mobile phone numbers, political opinions and information about sexual orientation. The most alarming outcome of Fuchs's study was that a high proportion of the students (more than averagely literate and well educated) were unaware of the small print of the regulations governing the operation of these sites. Many did not know, for example that:

> By signing up to Facebook, users agree to its terms of use and thereby grant the company a license for using and selling all content that is uploaded to the platform. Facebook stores personal data and usage data. These data are also used for personalized services. Facebook automatically uses targeted advertising. Facebook is allowed to automatically collect information on users from other websites and to publish these data on the users' Facebook profiles. Facebook is allowed to share user data with its advertising clients. It may pass on data to authorities for crime prevention or law enforcement. MySpace allows targeted personalized advertising that is automatically activated. Users can opt out, but doing so is very difficult.

(p. 109)

According to the EU Online survey, 'across Europe, notwithstanding considerable cross-national variation, it appears that giving out personal information is the most common risk (approximately half of online teenagers)' (2009: 115). Other risks identified by the respondents in the 21 countries in the survey, were 'seeing pornography' (the second most common risk for one in four respondents); seeing violent or hateful content was the third most common risk (approximately one third of teens); and being bullied/harassed/stalked affected around one in five teens. Meeting an online contact offline, was 'the least common but arguably most dangerous risk', showing considerable consistency in the figures across Europe at around 9 per cent. Internet skills and Internet use both increase with age, 'Hence, older teenagers encounter more online risks than younger children' (Fuchs 2009: 115). Boys were more likely to seek out pornographic or violent content and to meet somebody as as result of online contact; girls were more likely to be offended by explicit material. There were differences between countries. The EU Online researchers conclude that as a broad generality, (i) Northern European countries tend to be 'high use, high risk'; (ii) Southern European countries tend to be 'low use, variable risk'; and (iii) Eastern European countries can be characterized as 'new use, new risk' (p. 118).

There are various contextual issues to explain the differences, including different national policies on regulation and different parental approaches. The researchers propose that the existence of a public service broadcaster 'could be a major protective factor' (p. 120).

What about the little ones? CBeebies

As can be seen from the above accounts of research, most of the inquiries into the advantages and disadvantages of new media, and their policy and commercial implications, draw on research primarily with teenagers and young adults, with direct consumer potential for advertisers. Yet much of the anxiety around violence, bad examples and sexual exploitation focuses on much younger children (as in the Byron Review). The liberatory and celebratory claims made for 'new literacies' of appropriation and collaboration are also more difficult to support when we look at the very young. Most websites, even those aimed at young children, such as the BBC's and the *Sesame Street* sites, drawing on years of experience of producing educational material for the very young, still have to rely to some extent on print literacy. Children who cannot read very well cannot take full advantage of the Internet – and accordingly may be less at risk from some of its dangers than teenagers are. They are also more likely to be protected by various parental control software.

Julian Sefton Green (2002) has examined some of what he calls www.texts, linked to popular children's TV programmes and aimed at younger children (p. 188). He identifies two key principles of these sites. First they must be interactive, or at least offered as simply problems to be solved: 'If you don't know what to do, click to find out'. Secondly, because the website has to appeal to all ages, including the very young 'it tries to avoid a reliance on print text in favour of visual cues . . . making it as intuitive as possible' (p. 189). This is quite a tall order for web designers and it seems to me that many of them have not succeeded yet.

However, I am not a young child. So I arranged to observe some young children, aged 3–4, 'interacting' with the BBC's CBeebies' site. They were in a nursery school, and acting under the supervision and observation of a nursery attendant, but operating individually and allowed to explore the site as freely as they liked. The CBeebies website is obviously tailored entirely for very young children and its great virtue, as with the CBeebies channel, is no advertising, in contrast to all other children's websites that I looked at, including those linked to TV such as Fox Kids and Cartoon Network.

A young child would need an adult's intervention to get started on their first visit to the CBeebies site, and this was the case with a couple of beginners in the nursery group I observed. Once they got the hang of it, for example, by realizing that clicking on large pink arrows makes things happen, they began to navigate without help. Obviously the instructions given by voiceovers helped, and the tone of these was kindly and clear. The fact that the instructions also appeared as written captions ought to aid print literacy, too. The site used the time-honoured technique of frequent repetition and 'try again' as used in educational children's TV. There were also recaps of stories and games. One great virtue of the Internet is that it does permit the child to revisit the same material repeatedly, in any order they like – unlike broadcast or recorded television, but in common with books. Nevertheless, it seemed to me that the site incorporated a lot of assumptions about children's capacity to work things out without an adult. If an adult were going to be on hand all the time, the question then arises – why not do something else, other than sit at a computer, with that increasingly rare quality time that adults now have with their young children?

The children playing with the CBeebies site attempted a 'cooking game' which required them to follow instructions about choosing utensils, weighing out materials, putting cakes in ovens and working out when the cakes were ready, using an onscreen timer: obviously they were applying several cognitive skills here. Two other things struck me as I watched them. First, quite adept eye-hand skills are needed to manipulate Internet material; that is, you need the ability to use the mouse and to recognize that when you move the mouse with your hand, the cursor on screen responds. One or two children were using three-dimensional cues and pointing to the screen with the other hand, while they moved the mouse, as if to make the cursor move with their hand, in real space. The tactile and the three-dimensional were still the most important cues for them. Secondly, the children collaborated with each other. A couple of children awaiting a turn advised the child sitting at the computer on what to do, and the child at the computer readily complied. Real teamwork appeared to be going on between these very young children, which was certainly a positive effect. These skills were grounded in the physical reality of the children's personal and play space within their nursery environment. They were not just linked to the virtual world of the games onscreen, although the virtual world was obviously stimulating their interactions. This illustrated the ever-present importance of context for describing and understanding children's relationship with media.

When it was breaktime, their nursery assistant told them it was time for them to put on their coats and go outside. The computer was abandoned. Off they ran, to clamber on climbing frames, ride on tricycles, kick and throw balls, dig

Figure 10.1 Pieter Bruegel the Elder, 'Children's games' 1560, Kunsthistorisches Museum, Vienna. Image thanks to Art RenewalCenter® www.artrenewal.org

in the sandpit, cluster in little groups and chatter, hold the hands of the adult supervisors, or hang about by themselves watching the others – in short doing all the things that children since recorded time have done when given the opportunity to play.

Further reading

Many of the surveys mentioned here, such as the major EU Online Survey, and other international scholarship on the subject of the Internet, are reviewed in Sonia Livingstone's book on the subject, (2009) *Children and the Internet: Great Expectations, Challenging Realities*, Cambridge: Polity Press. Henry Jenkins's (2006) *Convergence Culture: Where Old and New Media Collide*, New York and London: New York University Press, is a must for a Utopian view of the creative and educational potentials of new media for the young. The Byron review is a valuable analysis of some of the risks and advantages from a policy perspective: Byron, T. (2008) *Safer Children in a Digital World*, Report to the Department of Children, Schools and Families, [http://www.dcsf.gov.uk/byronreview/]. David Crystal's (2008) *txtng: the gr8 db8*, Oxford: Oxford University Press, is both entertaining and scholarly.

11 | SOME CONCLUSIONS

Contemporary children are among the most studied and monitored group of young people that have ever lived, thanks to the invention of modern communications technology, and to the institutionalized development of modern science and social science (two movements that developed historically in tandem – see Chapters 2 and 3). Unlike children born before mass literacy enabled ordinary people to write, and before the invention of photography, there is no shortage of evidence about contemporary children for future historians. This includes evidence supplied by children themselves, both in the form of research data, and in the form of their own self-expression, most recently on the Internet (see for example the World Wide Kids' Art Gallery at [http://www.theartgallery.com.au/kidsart.html]). Children have taken their place on the public stage – and for this we have to thank, for good or ill, developments in communications media.

But there are other contemporary children who have not benefited from mass literacy, the inventions of science, and the opportunities for self-expression offered by new technology. This is recognized by the UN Convention on the Rghts of the Child (1989), stating that children, 'by virtue of [their] physical and mental immaturity, need special safeguards and care'. These safeguards particularly apply to 'children living in exceptionally difficult conditions' such as situations of armed conflict.[1] In many countries, including developed ones such as the UK, the high ideals of the Convention are not fully met. The key point is that the Convention represents a contemporary idea of childhood which is *officially* universally accepted: childhood is seen a state of being which is both vulnerable, and has 'rights'.

Children, media and culture

The relationships between children, media and culture always need to be seen within the broader context of how children are socially, historically and officially defined at any given moment. Because times change, cultures change and media technology changes – currently, extremely rapidly – it can be tempting to say that children have irrevocably changed too. Certainly some aspects of modern children's lives in the developed world have changed, and many of these changes are both represented in, and influenced by, media and cultural products. But some aspects of children and childhood do not change, and one of the fascinating aspects of conducting research in this field is to find echoes among contemporary children of behaviours and attitudes that would have been familiar to children in medieval times, to children in Africa, Asia, Lapland and Patagonia. These characteristics include enduring features of growth and development that can be observed in children's skeletal remains from pre-historic times, as well as in contemporary children all over the world.

They also include cultural characteristics such as independent play; a fascination with stories in which children (or child 'avatars' such as small animals, elves, toys, androids) are powerful and overcome physical and moral challenges presented by an indifferent adult world; rhymes, jokes and jingles displaying a fascination with the body and the taboo; an ability to 'mash' – to incorporate images and motifs from adult contemporary culture, both popular and 'high' (a distinction to which children's tastes seem completely indifferent) into their play; differences *and* similarities between boys and girls; and – even in pre-adolescent childhood – an awareness of the transience of all these things: nostalgia, the 'good old days', the 'golden age' when 'we were young', appears even in the discourses of primary school children (see Messenger Davies 2001a).

There is a great deal of serious, challenging, even disturbing scholarship around the topic of children and childhood. Much of it is necessary, to reflect the very serious issues of health, inequality and abuse that face children in all societies to some degree. These issues are bound up with the social and political conditions of adulthood too, particularly with the needs, rights and political progress of women, who, as mothers, have historically and geographically borne the main responsibility for children's 'special safeguards and care'. Thus, children's lives and culture intersect with everybody's lives and culture.

The importance of fun

Anyone who spends time researching the topic of children's media – the stories, TV programmes, films, websites, comic books, artwork, music, theatre, games, jokes and playground codes – is likely to tell you that they are having a very enjoyable time. Despite the extent to which research with children is now hedged around with restrictions, police checks and very necessary ethical reviews, studying children and their culture is fun. Leaving a nursery school in which a 4-year-old has patiently explained to a 3-year-old why a computer 'mouse' is not the same thing as a 'mouse-mouse', or leaving a drama group in which children have uproariously sung 'My old man said follow the van', is hard to do without a broad smile on one's face.

Obviously, such experiences enable us to revisit similarly liberating moments from our own childhoods and may be, to some extent, illusory. Memories of childhood for many people may be far from happy or comfortable. But media and culture provide means for even disadvantaged children to seize moments of empowerment, enlightenment and joy from the most unpromising environments.

The adult work of providing such moments for children is one of the most important projects of any society that claims to call itself cultured.

NOTES

Chapter 1 Defining children, media and culture

1 This is William of Ockham's precept that 'All unnecessary facts in dealing with a subject should be eliminated', otherwise known as 'Ockham's razor'. William, of Ockham in Surrey, was a philosopher who died in 1347.
2 Most countries set 18, the age of legal adulthood, as the minimum age for military service, but child soldiers are used in many conflicts. The CIA site states that Burundi has used 10-year-olds in the military.

Chapter 3 The science of childhood

1 The necessity for 'love', or nurturance, as well as – or perhaps even as more important than – food, was famously demonstrated by Harry Harlow in his experiments in the 1950s (which we might consider somewhat unethically cruel today) with young monkeys. He showed that baby monkeys, given the choice between a wire model 'mother' that delivered milk and a wire 'mother' covered in soft terry towelling, preferred to interact with the soft mother, not the one with the milk (Harlow 1959).
2 For instance, the National Child Development Study, 1958, following the 17,000 children born in Britain in one week in 1958, [http://www.esds.ac.uk/longitudinal/access/ncds/l33004.asp].
3 Prout cites Ilingworth's *The Normal Child*, published in 1986, as the 'landmark paediatric text' – not least because 'it was as concerned with psychological develop-ment as it was with the physical . . . [leading to] the wave of surveys that aimed to establish patterns of growth and their correlates' (2008: 27).

Chapter 4 The politics of children and media

1 The *Guardian*, 24 February, 2009.
2 For instance, Des Freedman's authoritative book on *The Politics of Media Policy* (2008) has no index entry for children or youth.
3 About 177 million children and teenagers under 18 years old worldwide are clinically overweight or obese. The figures include 22 million overweight children under 5 years old, according to the International Obesity Task Force: 'the growing epidemic is piling pressure on many cash-strapped national health systems'. See [www.burger corp.com.au/information].
4 'What do children want from the BBC? Children's content and participatory environments in an age of citizen media, using *Newsround* as a case study', Cynthia Carter, Cardiff University; Stuart Allan, Bournemouth University, Máire Messenger Davies, University of Ulster, Kaitlynn Mendes, De Montfort University, funded by AHRC/BBC KEP programme, report at [www.bbc.co.uk/blogs/knowledgeexchange/cardifftwo.pdf].

Chapter 5 Children and childhood in Media Studies

1 It's important to note, with experimental studies, that negative or neutral findings tend not to be published: experiments that *don't* find a relationship between violence, or consumerism, and children's behaviour have less chance of being reported.
2 There has been a small-scale but occasionally effective tradition of parental civic action which has influenced the provision of media material for children. Action for Children's Television (ACT) successfully influenced the USA Children's Television Act of 1990 to reduce advertising in children's programming and to increase educational material (see Trotta 2001). Corcoran (2004) reports the effective action of a group of parents in Germany, where private broadcasters took action against the PSB children's channel, Kinderkanal, claiming unfair competition. Parental resistance prevailed. 'Soon after, Nickelodeon bowed to the inevitable and pulled out of the German market' (2004: 175). In Britain, the Voice of the Listener and Viewer and Save Kids TV to some extent provide forums for parents and children to express their views on broadcasting and media provision.

Chapter 6 'Golden ages': the visual representation of childhood

1 Bazalgette and Staples are referring to a notorious case in 1937 when Graham Greene was sued on behalf of the child star, Shirley Temple, for describing her as 'a complete totsy' in a review. Temple won the case. Unfortunately, in the present age, when sexualized and even pornographic images of children are circulated on the Internet, the point that Greene was trying to make – admittedly offensively – can seem more

justified. A similar point about the sexualization of children in mainstream culture was made in the film, *Little Miss Sunshine* (2006). People need to be more careful nowadays about how children are visually represented, not least because of the ease with which their images can be manipulated. Hence, many still images of children in controversial news stories have their faces pixilated.

2 Ofcom produced guidelines on the use of under-18s in programmes in December 2007. These guidelines made many of the same points. See [www.ofcom.org.uk].

Chapter 7 Children's unofficial culture: games, traditions and tales

1 See especially Alice B. Gomme, *Traditional Games of England, Scotland and Ireland*, 1894–8. She was the first secretary of the Folklore Society, founded 1878.

2 Other action rhymes and also a 'Chinese restaurant' rhyme similar to those sung by my children, demonstrated by I and E, include:

Double double this this double double that that double this double that double double this that (a clapping rhyme)

Dum dum day ay dum dum away awaya see see k-ay see see away awaya mumma miacka mumma miay ay mumma miacka mumma miay ay ookabocka ookabocka ookabuka splat.

(while you are saying ookabucka etc. you and whoever else is playing puts out both of their clenched fists and one of you touches each fist; whoever's fist is touched on splat has to put their hand behind their back and if they get touched again they are out.)

I went to a Chinese shop one day to buy a loaf of bread bread bread

but when the waiter asked my name this is what I said said said.

My name's Charlie

I do karate,

punch you in the body

oops I'm sorry,

please don't call my mummy,

you'll be sorry,

Chinese, Japanese, Indian chief.

3 See for example, *The Informed Heart. Autonomy in a Mass Age* by Bruno Bettelheim. Glencoe, Ill.: The Free Press, 1960.

Chapter 8 Children's literature: on page and screen

1 See the interviews with producers in *The Provision of Children's Television in the UK*, Messenger Davies and Corbett, 1997; Michael Forte, then Controller of Children's and Young People's programming at Carlton/Central, argued: 'Children's programming is very stimulating. You look at children's programmes; compared to the prime time schedule, children's is very exciting and imaginative and they're made with slender resources and new talent. You can make up ideas, and you work with new talent all the time' (interview with Michael Forte, April 1997).
   See also Alan Horrox, quoted in *Dear BBC* (Messenger Davies 2001a: 73). Both these producers worked for ITV – now no longer making children's programmes.
2 It has been interesting to note in the relatively youthful Lucy Mangan's series on building a children's library, 'The Book Corner', in the *Guardian* each Saturday (2008–2010) that around 80 per cent of the books she has mentioned as indispensable for young readers were read both by me and by my now grown-up children. See [http://m.guardian.co.uk/ms/p/gmg/op/view.m?id=88884&tid=34&cat=Family].
3 There are some recent exceptions to the current prevalence of the fantasy genre, notably the former children's laureate in the UK, Jacqueline Wilson. Her stories often deal with broken families, tug-of-love children, school bullying, difficult siblings and so on. In *Clean Break* (2005) for example, 'fat' Emily/Emerald, kind and sensible half-sister to pretty, girly Vita and neurotic little brother Maxie, has to deal with the departure of her beloved stepfather and the difficulties of living in a single parent family. The most famous of Wilson's creations (also a long-running CBBC TV series) is Tracey Beaker, who lives in a children's home.
4 See Julian Fellowes' comments on the adaptation of Mark Twain's *The Prince and the Pauper*, for BBC television in 1998 (in *Dear BBC*, Messenger Davies, 2001a).
5 *Harry Potter and the Philosopher's Stone*, 1997; *Harry Potter and the Chamber of Secrets*, 1998; *Harry Potter and the Prisoner of Azkaban*, 1999; *Harry Potter and the Goblet of Fire*, 2000; *Harry Potter and the Order of the Phoenix*, 2003; *Harry Potter and the Half Blood Prince*, 2006; *Harry Potter: The Deathly Hallows*, 2007 – all published London: Bloomsbury and by Scholastic Press in the USA.
   They have also been published in over 60 languages including Breton, Welsh and ancient Greek and have sold 300 million copies. (Source http://www.abebooks.com/docs/harry-potter/harry-potter-translations.shtml, accessed 10th May 2009).

Chapter 9 Children's television

1 In the past, canaries were taken into coalmines as an early warning for the escape of poisonous gas. If the canary died, it was time for the miners to leave.
2 The contrast between the 1990s drama scene and the present looks like a serious cultural decline. *Dr Who* producer and author, Russell T. Davies, (who began his career in children's television) drew attention to this decline in a speech to **BAFTA** in

March 2009, calling for money from the National Lottery to be put into children's television: 'They put money into rubbish films, why can't they put money into children's television?' [http://news.bbc.co.uk/1/hi/entertainment/7952655.stm].

3 The revived *Dr Who*, BBC, initially written by Russell T. Davies, has contributed to this. Always popular with children, *Dr Who* was never a children's programme, produced by children's departments or production teams – and it is not now. Its influence is obvious though.

4 *The Demon Headmaster* is not alone in this representation of children as moral and political agents: see also *The Face at the Window* (2003) and *That Summer Day* (2006); see Messenger Davies 2005a.

5 Evidence of this was seen in Iranian responses to their contested election result in June 2009, in which protesters used mobile phones, and networking sites such as Twitter, to share information locally and globally. See also the film taken by a visiting American fund manager in London of a passer-by, Ian Tomlinson, who later died, being beaten by unidentified police officers during a public protest at the G20 meeting in April 2009. YouTube: [http://www.youtube.com/watch?v=HECMVdl-9SQ& feature= channel_page].

Chapter 10 Digital – new media

1 Source: [http://enwikipedia.org/wiki/Listofbest–sellingvideogames#citenote-36]. This list was taken from Wikipedia – a source students are usually recommended to avoid. However, in this case, every game listed has its own specific reference, so further primary sources can be reached by going to this Wikipedia page. This is not always the case with Wikipedia information. Also – the games titles are all authentic – the point I wish to make.

2 There are many more games from other manufacturers, such as Nintendo and Sega, with similar titles, e.g. Sega's Mortal Kombat and Street Fighter.

Chapter 11 Some conclusions

1 From the Preamble to the UN Declaration on the Rights of the Child: entry into force, 2 September 1990 in accordance with article 49.

GLOSSARY

Attachment The process whereby new babies and their caretakers become mutually and affectionately bonded to each other: stable and consistent attachments are seen as necessary for future psychological health.

BAFTA British Academy for Film and Television Arts: the professional organization for the UK screen industry, c.f. the American Academy for Film and Television Arts, which awards the Oscars.

BARB Broadcasters' Audience Research Board, the organization in the UK measuring audience sizes and responses. 'Ratings' as these measurements are named, are so-called because they are used to calculate advertising rates for commercial broadcasts. See [http://www.barb.co.uk/].

'Bobo doll' An inflatable life-size doll which wobbles when hit, and then returns to the upright. It was used in a famous 1963 experiment by Albert Bandura (see Chapter 5).

'Canary in the coalmine' In the past, canaries were taken into coalmines as an early warning for the escape of poisonous gas. If the canary died, it was time for the miners to leave.

Behaviourism A psychological theory of the mid-twentieth century, claiming that all human behaviours were produced in response to external stimuli, not by internal, unobservable cognitive or emotional processes.

Byron Review A 2009 report to the British Government, by psychologist Professor Tanya Byron, about the risks for children in using digital media and the Internet. See Chapter 4.

Child Rescue A nineteenth-century movement to rescue abandoned children from the streets and to improve the lot of poor children generally. See Chapters 2 and 3.

Child Study movement A nineteenth-century movement, partly pioneered by Charles Darwin, in which children's growth and development were studied and measured scientifically, producing large amounts of data from which 'norms' of development could be derived. See Chapter 3.

Cultivation theory A theory of media effects, pioneered by Professor George Gerbner and his colleagues at the Annenberg School for Communication in Philadelphia. The theory proposes that it is the sheer *amount* of television exposure, particularly to prime-time drama, that affects people's attitudes (and possibly their behaviour). The constant effect of 'heavy-viewing' gives people a 'mean world' view towards other people. See Chapter 5.

Cultural relativism An argument that many human behaviours and 'norms', that we may think of as natural and inevitable, are culturally derived and can vary across time and place.

Developmental norms See Child Study movement.

Digital divide A lack of access by disadvantaged groups to digital media and their benefits. This lack may be due to poverty, or incompetence with technology, or age, or geographical lack of access to e.g. broadband provision.

Effects research tradition A tradition seeking to establish, usually through experiments, that watching particular acts on film or TV can result in imitation of those acts; it is particularly concerned with the effects of violence.

Enlightenment A political and intellectual movement arising from the 'Age of Reason' (the eighteenth century in Europe). It proclaimed human equality, the innate goodness of humanity (as revealed in the innocence of children), the possibility of progress and freedom from ignorance and superstition.

The Gilded Age A period in American life at the end of the nineteenth century, as lived particularly by prosperous upper middle-class people, and portrayed in the work of artists such as John Singer Sargent. (See Chapter 6.)

'Golden Age' A term frequently used to describe 'the good old days', inevitably in the past rather than the present, and often applied to childhood.

Human rights See Enlightenment (also Chapter 2).

Inoculation A view, based on the principle that giving a small dose of something protects against a larger lethal dose (as in vaccination against disease). Children can thus be protected from media effects by being taught about how they work.

Media literacy A broadly accepted definition, as stated in Ofcom's 'Report on UK Children's Media Literacy' (Ofcom 2007) is: 'the ability to access, understand and create communications in a variety of contexts'. Media literacy is sometimes seen as a defence mechanism for children, in dealing with the proliferation and easy accessibility of new media. See Chapter 4.

Moral panic A term used to describe public excitement – usually generated or accelerated by media reports – about problems such as violent videos or Internet pornography. This is usually prompted by high-profile criminal cases, such as child murders. See Chapter 5.

Nature/nurture A debate about the relative contributions of heredity or environment to human development and behaviour.

Nielsen This company carries out audience measurements for broadcasting in the USA – see BARB, above. [http://www.nielsenmedia.com/nc/portal/site/Public/]

New Sociology of Childhood A group of sociologists who have written about childhood as a 'cultural construct', rather than as a biological state, pointing out the wide cultural and historical differences in children's experiences. See Chapter 3.

Ofcom The telecommunications and media regulator in the United Kingdom, also responsible for a range of consumer concerns, including promoting Media Literacy. See [www.ofcom.org] and Chapter 4.

Paternalism An attitude of mind, deriving from a patriarchal insistence that 'father knows best' – leading to a possibly over-protective attitude towards the young.

Psychoanalysis A procedure pioneered by Sigmund Freud (see Chapter 3) in which adult patients suffering from neurotic symptoms were encouraged to explore deep-rooted, often unconscious experiences and feelings, through talking to a specially trained doctor. The roots of these anxieties were deemed often to be in early childhood.

Psychological/medical An approach to the study of childhood, based on scientific measurements of large groups of children's growth and development, with a view to identifying norms. It is the basis of modern paediatric and child psychological health and educational services.

Public service broadcasting (PSB) Broadcasting systems, or broadcast material, which are non-commercial in the sense that their goal is to educate, entertain or inform, not primarily to profit financially from these activities. Public service broadcasting usually includes children's programmes, especially indigenous (country of origin) drama, factual and educational material.

Romanticism A period in the late eighteenth and early nineteenth century in Europe, during which the importance of individual emotions, and of personal expression in the arts, was allied with national movements for independence and cultural sovereignty. The innocence of childhood was seen as a key marker of emotional integrity and children increasingly figured in cultural material. (See Chapters 3 and 6.)

Save Kids TV A group of activists in the UK, comprising producers, educators, academics, trade unionists and individual citizens, campaigning for the cultural value of children's television, and to save the local industry from disappearing.

Social modelling A psychological theory of human behaviour proposing that children model their activities on significant role models, particularly those closest to them, such as parents. The theory has been applied to the media.

Social networking Internet sites on which young people (children under 11 less so) can interact with each other and share personal and other information.

Street children Abandoned children, usually in the cities of developing countries, who live, and precariously survive (or fail to) without the care of adults.

The Troubles A period between 1969 and the late 1990s in Northern Ireland, a part of the island of Ireland in the UK, during which several thousand people were killed or maimed. It started with a Civil Rights campaign, and became a battle between paramilitary groups who either wanted to become part of a united Ireland (the IRA) or who wanted to stay British ('Loyalist' groups such as the Ulster Volunteer Force, UVF). The British Army was also involved. In 1998, the Belfast Agreement was reached, enabling the differing factions to form a power-sharing, local Assembly, still as part of the UK, but recognizing the relationship with the Republic of Ireland.

UN Convention on the Rights of the Child Ratified by 191 nations of the world in 1989, drawing on the Geneva Convention of 1924 and 'entering into force' on 2 September 1990 [http://www.unhchr.ch/html/menu3/b/k2crc.htm]. It states that children – defined as 'persons under the age of 18' – 'by virtue of [their] physical and mental immaturity, need special safeguards and care'. It has 54 detailed Articles on family life; education; health; child labour; warfare; literacy; communications and media, stating what these safeguards should be (a child-friendly version is shown on page 26).

World Summits on Children and Media A movement for promoting the production of indigenous media for children in countries around the world and asserting the rights of children to be considered as cultural citizens. (See Chapter 4.)

BIBLIOGRAPHY

Aldridge, J. and Cross, S. (2008) Young people today: news media, policy and youth justice, *Journal of Children and Media*, 2(3): 203–16.

Allen, R. (2003) Psychoanalytic film theory, in T. Miller and R. Stam (eds) *A Companion to Film Theory*. Oxford: Blackwell.

Anderson, D.R., Huston, A.C., Schmitt, K.L., Linebarger, D.L. and Wright, J.C. (2001) Early childhood televiewing and adolescent behavior, *Monographs of the Society for Research in Child Development*, 66(1): 119–34.

Aries, P. ([1962] 1996) *Centuries of Childhood*, trans. R. Baldick. London: Pimlico.

Baldwin, C. (2008) *Broadcasting Britishness? Identity, Diversity and the Role of the National Media: Conference Report*. Oxford: Said Business School, University of Oxford.

Bandura, A., Ross, D. and Ross, R. (1963) Imitation of film-mediated aggressive models, *Journal of Abnormal and Social Psychology*, 66(1): 3–11.

Barker, M. and Petley, J. (eds) (1997) *Ill Effects: The Media Violence Debate*. London: Routledge.

Barrett, L., Dunbar, R. and Lycett, J. (2002) *Human Evolutionary Psychology*. London: Palgrave Macmillan.

Bartlett, F. ([1932] 1995) *Remembering: A Study in Experimental and Social Psychology*. Cambridge: Cambridge University Press.

Barwise, P. (2004) Independent review of the BBC Digital Television Services, DCMS, www.culture.gov.uk/images/publications/IndependentReviewoftheBBCsDigital TelevisionServices.pdf (accessed 22 Nov. 2009).

Bazalgette, C. (ed.) (1988) *Primary Media Education*. London: BFI.

Bazalgette, C. and Staples, T. (1995) Unshrinking the kids: children's cinema and the family film, in D. Buckingham and C. Bazalgette (eds) *In Front of the Children*, 92–126.

Beentjes, J.W., de Koning, E. and Huysmans, F. (2001) Children's comprehension of visual formal features in television programmes, *Applied Developmental Psychology*, 22: 623–8.

Bernstein, B.B. ([1971] 2003) *Class, Codes and Control: Applied Studies Towards a Sociology of Language*. London: Routledge.

Bettelheim, B. (1976) *The Uses of Enchantment: The Meaning and Importance of Fairy Tales*. London: Thames and Hudson.

Bignell, J. (2005) Familiar aliens: *Teletubbies* and postmodern childhood, *Screen* 6(3): 373–87.

Binet, A. and Simon T. (1905) *Méthodes nouvelles pour le diagnostic du niveau intellectuel des anormaux*. L'Année psychologique, Paris, 11: 191–244. *Le développement de l'intelligence chez les enfants*. L'Année psychologique, Paris, 1908, 14: 1–94. *La mesure du développement de l'intelligence chez les jeunes enfants*. Paris, A. Coneslant, 1911.

Blumler, J.G. (1992) *Children's Television in Britain: An Enquiry for the Broadcasting Standards Council*. London: BSC.

Bowlby, J. (1969) *Attachment*, Vol. 1 of *Attachment and Loss*. London: Hogarth Press.

Briggs, S. (1998) Television in the home and family, in A. Smith and R. Patterson (eds) *Television: An International History*. Oxford: Oxford University Press, 109–21.

British Film Institute (1999) *Making Movies Matter*. London: BFI.

Brown, S. (2005) *Wizard! Harry Potter's Brand Magic*. London: Cyan Press.

Bruce, B. (2009) Reflections on youth, media and democracy, in J. Petterson (ed.) *Youth, Media, Democracy: Perceptions of New Literacies*. Dublin: Centre for Social and Educational Research, Dublin Institute of Technology, 36–42.

Bu Wei (2008) Girls' issues, gender and the media: feminist activisms in China, in S. Livingstone and K. Drotner (eds) *The International Handbook of Children and Media*. London: Sage.

Buckingham, D. (1995) The commercialisation of childhood? The place of the market in children's media culture, in P. Drummond (ed.) *Changing English*, Vol. 2.

Buckingham, D. (1996) *Moving Images*. Manchester: Manchester University Press.

Buckingham, D. (2000) *The Making of Citizens: Young People, News and Politics*. London: Routledge.

Buckingham, D. (ed.) (2002) *Small Screens: Television for Children*. Leicester: Continuum/Leicester University.

Buckingham, D. (2009) Beyond technology: re-thinking learning in the age of digital culture, in J. Petterson (ed.) *Youth, Media, Democracy: Perceptions of New Literacies*. Dublin: Centre for Social and Educational research, Dublin Institute of Technology, 36–42.

Buckingham, D. and Bazalgette, C. (eds) (1995) *In Front of the Children*. London: BFI.

Buckingham, D., Davies, H., Jones, K. and Kelley, P. (1999) *Children's Television in Britain*. London: BFI.

Buckingham, D., Whiteman, N., Willett, R. and Burn, A. (2008) 'The Impact of the media on children and young people with a particular focus on computer games and the Internet', academic literature review for the Byron Review. Available at http://www.dcsf.gov.uk/byronreview/pdfs/Buckingham%20Impact%20of%20Media%20Literature%20Review%20for%20the%20Byron%20Review.pdf (accessed 21 Nov. 2009)

Bushman, B.J. and Huesmann, L.R. (2001) Effects of televised violence on aggression, in D.G. Singer and J.L. Singer (eds) *Handbook of Children and the Media*. Thousand Oaks, CA: Sage, 223–54.

Butterworth, G. and Harris, M. (2003) *Principles of Developmental Psychology*. Hove: Psychology Press.

Byron, T. (2008) *Safer Children in a Digital World*, Report to the Department of Children, Schools and Families, http://www.dcsf.gov.uk/byronreview/ (accessed 22 Nov. 2009).

Carpenter, H. (1985) *Secret Gardens: A Study of the Golden Age of Children's Literature*. London: George Allen and Unwin.

Carter, A. (ed.) (1990) *The Virago Book of Fairy Tales*. London: Virago Press.

Carter, C. (2007) Talking about my generation: a critical examination of children's BBC *Newsround* web site discussions about war, conflict, and terrorism, in D. Lemish and M. Goetz (eds) *Children and Media in Times of War and Conflict*. Cresskill, NJ: Hampton Press.

Carter, S. (2009) *Digital Britain*, UK Department of Culture, Media and Sport, http://www.culture.gov.uk/images/publications/digitalbritain-finalreport-jun09.pdf (accessed 21 Nov. 2009).

Carter, C. and Messenger Davies, M. (2005) 'A fresh peach is easier to bruise': children and traumatic news, in S. Allan (ed.) *Journalism: Critical Issues*. Maidenhead and NY: Open University Press, 224–35.

Carter, C., Messenger Davies, M., Allan, S., Mendes, K., Milani, R. and Wass, L. (2009) *What Do Children Want from the BBC? Children's Content and Participatory Environments in an Age of Citizen Media*. AHRC/BBC, Cardiff University, http://www.bbc.co.uk/blogs/knowledgeexchange/cardifftwo.pdf (accessed 21 Nov. 2009).

Cassell, J. and Jenkins, J. (2000) *From Barbie to Mortal Kombat: Gender and Computer Games*. Cambridge, MA: MIT Press.

Chernin, A. (2008) The effects of food marketing on children's preferences: testing the moderating roles of age and gender, *Annals of the American Academy*, 615: 102–18.

Chomsky, N. (1959) A review of B.F. Skinner's *Verbal Behavior*, in *Language*, 35(1): 26–58.

Claridge, J. (2008) *At What Age Can I? A Guide to Age-Based Legislation*. The Children's Legal Centre, University of Essex, UK.

Cole, C.F., Richman, B.A. and McCann Brown, S.A. (2001) The world of *Sesame Street* research, in S.M. Fisch and R.T. Truglio (eds) *'G is for Growing': Thirty Years of Research on Children and Sesame Street*. Mahwah, NJ: Lawrence Erlbaum Associates.

Collins, A. (2008) The trouble with Harry, *Radio Times*, 4–10 October.

Comstock, G.A. and Paik, H. (1994) The effects of television violence on antisocial behavior: a meta-analysis, *Communication Research*, 21: 516–46.

Comstock, G. and Scharrer, E. (2007) *Media and the American Child*. Burlington, MA: Elsevier.

Cook, D.T. (2004) *The Commodification of Childhood: The Children's Clothing Industry and the Rise of the Child Consumer*. Durham, NC and London: Duke University Press.

Corcoran, F. (2004) *RTE and the Globalisation of Irish Television*. Bristol: Intellect Books.

Cross, G. (1997) *The Demon Headmaster Takes Over*. Oxford: Oxford University Press.

Crystal, D. (2008) *txtng: the gr8 db8*. Oxford: Oxford University Press.

Darwin, C. (1859) *The Origin of Species*. London: John Murray.

Darwin, C. (1877) A biographical sketch of an infant, *Mind*, 2: 285–329.

Davies, H., Buckingham, D. and Kelley, P. (2000) 'In the worst possible taste': children, television and cultural value, *European Journal of Cultural Studies*, 3 (1): 5–25.

Davis, A. (2006) *Good Girls and Wicked Witches: Women in Disney's Feature Animation*. Eastleigh: John Libbey.

Davis, A. et al. (2003) MFA Highlights: American Painting, available at www.mfashop.com/mfa-publications.html, Museum of Fine Arts, Boston (accessed 22 Nov. 2009).

Dayer Gallati, B. (2004) *Children of the Gilded Era: Portraits by Sargent, Renoir, Cassatt and their Contemporaries*. London, New York: Merrell.

De Beauvoir, S. (1949/1988) *The Second Sex* trans. H.M. Parshley. London: Picador.

De Fleur, M. and Ball-Rokeach, S. (1988) *Theories of Mass Communication*. New York and London: Longman.

De Saussure, F. (1916, English edition 2006) *Course in General Linguistics*. Oxford: Oxford University Press.

Drotner, K. (1992) Modernity and modern media panics, in M. Skovmand and K. Shroder (eds) *Media Cultures: Reappraising Transnational Media*. London: Routledge, 42–62.

Encyclopedia of Children and Childhood in History and Society, http://www.faqs.org/childhood/In-Ke/Infant-Mortality.html (accessed 1 May 2009).

Freedman, D. (2008) *The Politics of Media Policy*. Cambridge: Polity.

Freud, S. (1938) Three contributions to the theory of sex, in A.A. Brill (ed.) *The Basic Writings of Sigmund Freud*. New York: Random House.

Fuchs, C. (2009) Social networking sites and the surveillance society. A critical case study of the usage of StudiVZ, Facebook, and My Space by students in Salzburg in the context of electronic surveillance. Salzburg and Vienna: Research Group, Unified Theory of Information.

Gauntlett, D. (1995) *Moving Experiences*. Eastleigh: John Libbey.

Gerbner, G. and Gross, L. (1976): Living with television: the violence profile, *Journal of Communication*, 26(2): 172–99.

Gesell, A., Ilg, F., Ames, L.B. and Bullis, G. ([1946] 1977) *The Child from Five to Ten*. New York: Harper and Row.

Goswami, U. (2008) Annex to Byron Review, 2008: Literature review of cognitive development, Byron Review on the Impact of New Technologies on Children: A Research Literature Review: Child Development, www.dcsf.gov.uk/byronreview/pdfs/Goswami%20Child%20Development%20Literature%20Review%20for%20the%20Byron%20Review.pdf (accessed 22 Nov. 2009).

Götz, M., Bulbulia, F., Fisch, S. et al. (2005) 'Is that funny anywhere else?' An international comparison of humour in children's programmes, *Televizion*, 19/2006/E, http://www.bronline.de/jugend/izi/english/publication/televizion/19_2006_E/19_2006_E.htm (accessed 22 Nov. 2009).

Götz, M., Lemish, D., Aidman, A. and Moon, H. (2005) *Media and the Make Believe Worlds of Children: When Harry Potter Meets Pokemon in Disneyland*. Mahwah, NJ: Laurence Erlbaum.

Götz, M., Hofmann, O., Brosius, H.-B., et al. (2008) 'Gender in children's television worldwide', Munich: IZI, www.bronline.de/jugend/izi/english/publication/televizion/21_2008_E/21_2008_E.htmonline.de/jugend/izi/english/publication/televizion/21_ 2008_E/21_2008_E.htm (accessed 22 Nov. 2009).

Gripsrud, J. (2004) Broadcast television: the chances of its survival in a digital age, in L. Spigel and J. Olssen (eds) *Television after TV: Essays on a Medium in Transition*. Durham, London: Duke University Press, 210–23.

Groebel, J. (1998) The UNESCO global study on media violence: report presented to the Director General of UNESCO, in U. Carlsson and C. von Feilitzen (eds) *Children and Media Violence*. Goteburg: UNESCO International Clearinghouse on Children and Violence on the Screen, 181–99.

Gunter, B. and Furnham, A. (1998) *A Psychological Analysis of the Young People's Market*. London: Routledge.

Hardyment, C. ([1983] 2008) *Dream Babies: Child Care Advice from John Locke to Gina Ford* 2nd edn. London: Frances Lincoln.

Harlow, H.F. (1959) Love in infant monkeys, *Scientific American*, 200: 68, 70, 72–4.

Harrison, K. (2000) The body electric: thin-deal media and eating disorders in adolescents, *Journal of Communication*, 50: 119–43.

Harrison, K. and Cantor, J. (1997) The relationship between media consumption and eating disorders, *Journal of Communication*, 47(1): 40–67.

Hartley, J. (1998) Juvenation: news, girls and power, in C. Carter, G. Branston and S. Allan (eds) *News, Gender and Power*. London: Routledge, 47–70.

Hasebrink, U., Livingstone, S. and Haddon, L. (2008) Comparing children's online opportunities and risks across Europe: cross-national comparisons for EU Kids Online. London: EU Kids Online (Deliverable D3.2).

Heller, M. (2008) Games and the media: the acquisition of social structure and social rules, in S. Livingstone and K. Drotner (eds) *The International Handbook of Children, Media and Culture*. London: Sage, 271–2.

Hilton, M. (ed.) (1996) *Potent Fictions: Children's Literacy and the Challenge of Popular Culture*. London: Routledge.

Hilton, T. and Messenger Davies, M. (1990) *The Great Ormond Street Book of Child Health and Development*. London: Bodley Head.

Himmelweit, H., Oppenheim, A.N. and Vince, P. (1958) *Television and the Child: An Empirical Study of the Effect of Television on the Young*. Oxford: Nuffield Foundation/Oxford University Press.

Hobbs, R. (2008) Debates and challenges facing new literacies in the 21st century, in S. Livingstone and K. Drotner (eds) *The International Handbook of Children, Media and Culture*. London: Sage, 431–47.

Hodge, R. and Tripp, D. (1986) *Children and Television*. Cambridge: Polity Press.

Holland, P. (2004) *Picturing Childhood: The Myth of the Child in Popular Imagery*. London, New York: I.B. Tauris.

Holland, P. (2008) The child in the picture, in S. Livingstone and K. Drotner (eds) *The International Handbook of Children, Media and Culture*. London: Sage, 36–54.

Home, A. (1993) *Into the Box of Delights*. London: BBC.

Horn, P. (1997) *The Victorian Town Child*. Stroud: Sutton Publishing.

Huesmann, L.R., Moise-Titus, J., Padolski, C. and Eron, L. (2003) Longitudinal relations between children's exposure to TV violence and violent behavior in young adulthood, *Developmental Psychology*, 39(2): 201–22.

Hunt, P. (1992) (ed.) *Literature for Children: Contemporary Criticism*. London: Routledge.

Hunt, P. (1994) *An Introduction to Children's Literature*. Oxford: Oxford University Press.

James, Allison and James, Adrian (2005) *The Politics of Childhood*. Basingstoke: Palgrave Macmillan.

James, A. and Prout, A. ([1997] 2005) *Constructing and Reconstructing Childhood*. London: Falmer Press.

Jenkins, H. (2006) *Convergence Culture: Where Old and New Media Collide*. New York and London: New York University Press.

Jenkins, H. with Clinton, K., Purushotma, R., Robison, A.J., and Weigel, M. (2007) Confronting the Challenges of Participatory Culture: Media Education for the 21st Century. The MacArthur Foundation. http://www.digitallearning.macfound.org/atf/cf/%7B7E45C7E0-A3E0-4B89-AC9C-E807E1B0AE4E%7D/JENKINS_WHITE_PAPER.PDF (accessed 26 May 2009).

Johnson, M.H. (2008) Brain development in childhood: a literature review and synthesis for the Byron Review on the impact of new technologies on children, 2008, http://www.dcsf.gov.uk/byronreview/pdfs/Johnson%20Brain%20Development%20Literature%20Review%20for%20the%20Byron%20Review.pdf (accessed 28 May 2009).

Kaiser Family Foundation (2005) Generation M: Media in the lives of 8–18 year olds, www.kff.org/entmedia/entmedia030905pkg.cfm (accessed 22 Nov. 2009).

Kaiser Family Foundation (2003) Zero to Six: electronic media in the lives of infants, toddlers and preschoolers, http://www.kff.org/entmedia/upload/Zero-to-Six-Electronic-Media-in-the-Lives-of-Infants-Toddlers-and-Preschoolers-PDF.pdf (accessed 1 May 2009).

Kapur, Y. (1999) Television and the transformation of childhood, in Kinder, M. (ed.) *Kids Media Culture*. Durham and London: Duke University Press, 122–36.

Kerr, A. (2006) *The Business and Culture of Digital Games: Gamework/Gameplay*. London: Sage.

Kidd, D. (2007) Harry Potter and the functions of popular culture, *Journal of Popular Culture*, 40(1): 69–89.

Kinder, M. (1991) *Playing with Power in Movies, Television and Video Games: From Muppet Babies to Teenage Mutant Ninja Turtles*. Berkeley, CA: University of California Press.

Kinder, M. (1999) Ranging with power on the Fox Kids Network: or where on earth is children's educational television? in M. Kinder (ed.) *Kids Media Culture*. Durham, NC and London: Duke University Press, 177–203.

Kitzinger, S. (1994) *Ourselves as Mothers*. Jackson, TN: Perseus Books.

Kleeman, D. (2006) *Sesame Street* to *Sponge Bob*: North American humour and children's TV in *Televizion*, 19/2006/E, 24–6.

Kline, S. (1993) *Out of the Garden: Toys, TV and Children's Culture in the Age of Marketing*. London: Verso.

Klopfer, E., Osterweil, S. and Salen, K. (2009) *Moving Learning Games Forward: Obstacles, Opportunities and Openness*. Cambridge, MA: Education Arcade, MIT.

Kodaira, S.I. (2005) Children's television trends around the world, *NHK Broadcasting Studies*, 53/103(1): 104–30.

Kubey, R. (ed.) (2001) *Media Literacy in the Information Age: Current Perspectives*. New Brunswick, NJ & London: Transaction.

Kuhn, T. (1962/1996) *The Structure of Scientific Revolutions*. Chicago: University of Chicago Press.

Kunkel, D. and Goette, U. (1997) Broadcasters' response to the Children's Television Act, *Communication Law and Policy*, 2: 289–308.

Kunkel, D. and Wilcox, B. (2001) Children and media policy, in D.G. Singer and J.L. Singer (eds) *Handbook of Children and the Media*. Thousand Oaks, CA: Sage, 589–604.

Lemish, D. (2007) *Children and Television: A Global Perspective*. Malden MA: Blackwell.

Lemish, D. and Götz, M. (eds) (2007) *Children and Media in Times of War and Conflict*. Cresskill, NJ: Hampton Press, 163–76.

Lesser, G. (1974) *Children and Television: Lessons from Sesame Street*. New York: Random House.

Lewis, J. (1980) *The Politics of Motherhood*. London: Croom Helm.

Liebert, R. and Baron, R. (1972) Short-term effects of televised aggression on children's aggressive behavior, in J. Murray, E. Rubinstein and G. Comstock (eds) *Television and Social Behavior: Vol. II. Television and Social Learning*. Washington, DC: US Government printing office.

Ling, R. and Haddon, L. (2008) Children, Youth and the mobile phone, in S. Livingstone and K. Drotner (eds) (2008) *International Handbook of Children, Media and Culture*. London: Sage, 137–51.

Livingstone, S. (2002) *Young People, New Media: Childhood and the Changing Media Environment*. London: Sage.

Livingstone, S. (2007) The challenge of engaging youth online: contrasting producers' and teenagers' interpretations of websites, *European Journal of Communication*, 22(2): 165–84.

Livingstone, S. (2009) *Children and the Internet: Great Expectations, Challenging Realities*. Cambridge: Polity Press.

Livingstone, S. and Bovill, M. (1999) *Young People, New Media: Report of the Research Project, Children, Young People and the Changing Media Environment*. London: LSE.

Livingstone, S. and Drotner, K. (eds) (2008) *The International Handbook of Children, Media and Culture*. London: Sage.

Livingstone, S. and Helsper, E. (2006) Does advertising literacy mediate the effects of advertising on children? A critical examination of two linked research literatures in relation to obesity and food choice, *Journal of Communication*, 56: 560–84.

Lurie, A. (1990) *Don't Tell the Grownups: Subversive Children's Literature*. London: Bloomsbury.

Lurie, A. (2002) *Boys and Girls Forever: Children's Classics from Cinderella to Harry Potter*. London: Vintage.

Lury, K. (2005) Introduction, *Screen* (special issue 'The Child in Film and Television', 46(3): 307–14.

Lusoli, W. and Miltgen, C. (2009) *Young People and Emerging Digital Services: An Exploratory Survey on Motivations, Perceptions and Acceptance of Risk*. Seville: European Commission Joint Research Centre (JRC), Institute for Prospective Technological Studies (IPTS).

McFarlane, A., Thornham, H. and Millner, J. (2009) *Alone Together: Social Learning in BBC Blast*. AHRC/BBC, University of Bristol: http://www.bbc.co.uk/blogs/knowledgeexchange/bristol.pdf (accessed 22 Nov. 2009).

McGown, A.D. and Doherty, M.J. (2003) *The Hill and Beyond: Children's Television Drama, An Encyclopedia*. London: British Film Institute.

McRobbie, A. (1990) *Feminism and Youth Culture*. London: Routledge.

Mangan, L. (2009) Book corner: building a brilliant children's library, *Guardian*, 10 April. www.guardian.co.uk/books/2009/apr/10/charlotte's-web (accessed 20 Nov. 2009).

Marsh, J., Brooks, G., Gillott, J. et al. (2005) Digital beginnings: Young children's use of popular culture, media and new technologies, Sheffield: Literacy Research Centre, University of Sheffield, http://www.digitalbeginnings.shef.ac.uk/DigitalBeginningsReport.pdf (accessed 18 June, 2009).

Mendes, K., Carter, C. and Messenger Davies, M. (2009) Young citizens and the news, in S. Allan (ed.) *The Routledge Companion to News and Journalism Studies*. London and New York: Routledge, 450–9.

Messenger Davies, M. (1997) *Fake, Fact and Fantasy: Children's Understanding of Television Reality*, Mahwah, NJ: Laurence Erlbaum.

Messenger Davies, M. (2001a) *Dear BBC: Children, Television Storytelling and the Public Sphere*. Cambridge: Cambridge University Press.

Messenger Davies, M. (2001b), 'A bit of earth': sexuality and the representation of childhood in text and screen versions of *The Secret Garden*, *The Velvet Light Trap: Critical Journal of Film and Television*, 48: 48–58.

Messenger Davies, M. ([1989] 2001c) *Television is Good for Your Kids*. London: Hilary Shipman.

Messenger Davies, M. (2002) Classics with clout: costume drama in British and North American children's television, in D. Buckingham (ed.) *Small Screens: Television for Children*. Leicester: Continuum/Leicester University Press, 120–40.

Messenger Davies, M. (2005a): 'Crazyspace': the politics of children's screen drama, *Screen*, 46(3): 389–99.

Messenger Davies, M. (2005b) 'Just that kids' thing': the politics of 'Crazyspace', children's television and the case of *The Demon Headmaster*, in S. Lacey and J. Bignell (eds) *Popular Television Drama: Critical Perspectives*, Manchester: Manchester University Press.

Messenger Davies, M. (2006a) *The Secret Garden* in film and television, in J. Ridgman and F. Collins (eds) *Turning the Page: Children's Literature in Performance*. Bern: Peter Lang, 83–104.

Messenger Davies, M. (2006b) Do mention the war: children and media coverage of traumatic events, in J. Gunning and S. Holm (eds) *Ethics, Law and Society: Volume 2*. Aldershot, Burlington VT: Ashgate, 117–23.

Messenger Davies, M. (2007) 'And what good came of it at last?' Ethos, style and sense of audience in the reporting of war by children's news programs, in D. Lemish and M. Götz (eds) (2007) *Children and Media in Times of War and Conflict*. Cresskill, NJ: Hampton Press, 163–76.

Messenger Davies, M. (2008) Reality and fantasy in the media: can children tell the difference and how do we know? In S. Livingstone and K. Drotner (eds) *International Handbook of Children, Media and Culture*. London: Sage, 121–36.

Messenger Davies, M. (2009) Children, news media and citizenship: a study with 9–15 year olds in Northern Ireland, in J. Petterson (ed.) 'Youth, media, democracy: perceptions of new literacies', Dublin: Centre for Social and Educational Research, Dublin Institute of Technology, www.csr.ie (accessed 10 May, 2009).

Messenger Davies, M. and Corbett, B. (1997) *The Provision of Children's Television in the UK: 1990–1995*. London: Broadcasting Standards Commission.

Messenger Davies, M., Creely, M. and Morrey, J.P.R. (2007) 'Public Service Broadcasting, Global Media and the Rights of Children', no 5 in Policy Briefing Document series, Centre for Media Research, University of Ulster, http://cmr.ulster.ac.uk/pdf/policy/publicserv.pdf (accessed 1 December 2008).

Messenger Davies, M., Lloyd, E. and Scheffler, A. (1987) *Baby Language*. London: Allen and Unwin.

Messenger Davies, M. and Mosdell, N. (2001) *Consenting Children? The Use of Children in Non-fiction Television Programmes*. London: Broadcasting Standards Commission, online at http://cmr.ulster.ac.uk/pdf/policy/consenting_children.pdf and http://www.ofcom.org.uk/static/archive/bsc/pdfs/research/cchildren.pdf (accessed 22 Nov. 2009).

Messenger Davies, M. and Mosdell, N. (2005) The representation of children in the media: aspects of agency and literacy, in J. Goddard, McNamee S., Adrian James and Allison James (eds) *The Politics of Childhood: International Perspectives, Contemporary Developments*. Manchester: Palgrave/Macmillan, 208–25.

Messenger Davies, M., O'Malley, K. and Corbett, B. (1997) Children and television drama: an empirical study with children aged 5–13 years in England and Wales. London: London College of Printing (unpublished report commissioned by the BBC).

Moore, E.S. (2006) For the Kaiser Family Foundation, 'It's child's play: advergaming and the online marketing of food to children', www.kff.org (accessed 21 Nov. 2009).

Neumann, S. (1995) *Literacy in the Television Age*. Ablex.

Nikken, P. and van der Molen, J. (2008) Operation Iraqui freedom in children's news, in D. Lemish and M. Götz (eds) *Children and Media in Times of War and Conflict*. Cresskill, NJ: Hampton Press, 177–200.

Noble, G. (1975) *Children in Front of the Small Screen*. London: Constable.

Ofcom (2004) Ofcom's strategy and priorities for the promotion of media literacy. London: Ofcom.

Ofcom (2007a) Television advertising of food and drink products to children: full statement, www.ofcom.org.uk/consult/condocs/foodads_new/statement/statement.pdf

Ofcom (2007b) The future of children's broadcasting in the UK, www.ofcom.org (accessed 22 Nov. 2009).

Ofcom (2008) Media Literacy Audit: Report on UK children's media literacy, www.ofcom.org.uk/advice/media_literacy/medlitpub/medlitpubrss/ml_childrens08/mlchildrens08.pdf (accessed 22 Nov 2009).

Ofcom (2009) How children are consuming media, presentation by James Thickett to seminar, 'Trends in children's media', BBC, London, 6 February 2009, http://www.ofcom.org.uk/advice/media_literacy/medlitpub/ (accessed 22 Nov. 2009).

Opie, I. (1993) *The People in the Playground*. Oxford: Oxford University Press.

Opie, I. and Opie, P. ([1951] 1997) *The Oxford Dictionary of Nursery Rhymes*. Oxford: Oxford University Press.

Opie, I. and Opie, P. ([1959] 1986) *The Lore and Language of Schoolchildren*. Oxford: Clarendon Press.

Opie, I. and Opie, P. (eds) ([1969] 1988) *Children's Games in Street and Playground*. Oxford: Oxford University Press.

Opie, I. and Opie, P. ([1974] 1992) *The Classic Fairy Tales*. Oxford: Oxford University Press.

Orme, N. (2001) *Medieval Childhood*. New Haven and London: Yale University Press.

Palmer, E.L. (1994) *Television and America's Children: A Crisis of Neglect*. Oxford: Oxford University Press.

Palmer, P. (1986) *The Lively Audience*. Sydney: Allen and Unwin.

Palmer, S. (2006) *Toxic Childhood*. London: Orion Press.

Pearce, P. ([1958] 1979) *Tom's Midnight Garden*. Harmondsworth: Puffin.

Piaget, J. (1923) *The Language and Thought of the Child*. London: Kegan Paul.

Piaget, J. (1937) *The Construction of Reality in the Child*. New York: Basic Books.

Piaget, J. and Szeminska, A. (1941) *The Child's Conception of Number*. London: Routledge and Kegan Paul.

Postgate, O. ([2003] 2008) 'We made mountains in the cowshed and space in the barn', *The Guardian*, 10 December www.guardian.co.uk/media/2008/dec/10/postgate-bagpuss-animation-television (accessed 22 Nov. 2009).

Postman, N. (1994) *The Disappearance of Childhood*. New York: Allen and Unwin.

Propp, V. ([1928] 1968) *The Morphology of the Folk Tale*. Austin, TX: University of Texas Press.

Prout, A. (2008) Culture – Nature and the construction of childhood, in S. Livingstone and K. Drotner (eds) *The International Handbook of Children, Media and Culture*. London: Sage, 21–35.

Rahman, M. (2001) The globalisation of childhood and youth: new actors and networks in protecting street children and working children in the South, in H. Helve and C. Wallace (eds) *Youth, Citizenship and Empowerment*. Aldershot, UK and Burlington Vt: Ashgate.

Rich, M. (2008) Music videos: media of the youth, by the youth, for the youth, in P.H. Jamieson and D. Romer (eds) *The Changing Portrayal of Youth in the Media and Why it Matters*. Oxford: Oxford University Press, 78–102.

Rideout, V., Roberts, D.F. and Foehr, U.G. (2005) *Generation M: Media in the Lives of 8–18 Year Olds*. Menlo Park, CA: Kaiser Family Foundation.

Rose, J. (1993) *The Case of Peter Pan, or, The Impossibility of Children's Fiction*. Philadelphia: University of Pennsylvania Press.

Schramm, W., Lyle, J. and Parker, E.B. (1961) *Television in the Lives of Our Children*. Stanford, CA: Stanford University Press.

Scott, A.O. (1999) Harry Potter is the new *Star Wars*, Slate, 23 August http://www.slate.com/id/2000111/entry/1003472/ (accessed 6 May 2009).

Seiter, E. and Pincus, M. (2004) 'A protective silence': US children and the Iraq war, *Televizion*, 17/2004 E http://www.br-online.de/jugend/izi/english/publication/televizion/17_2004_E/17_2004_E.htm (accessed 21 Nov. 2009).

Sefton Green, J. (2002) Children's TV goes online, in D. Buckingham (ed.) *Small Screens: Television for Children*. Leicester: Leicester University Press/Continuum, 185–226.

Selwyn, N. (2003) Doing IT for the kids: re-examining children, computers and the information society, *Media Culture and Society*, 25(3): 351–78.

Shanahan, J. and Morgan, M. (1999) *Television and its Viewers: Cultivation Theory and Research*. Cambridge: Cambridge University Press.

Sheridan, M. ([1973] 2009) *From Birth to Five Years: Children's Developmental Progress*, 3rd edn. London: Routledge.

Shuler, C. (2009) *Pockets of Potential: Using Mobile Technologies to Promote Children's Learning*. New York: Joan Ganz Cooney Center.

Signorielli, N. (1990) Children, television and gender roles, *Journal of Adolescent Health Care* 11(1): 50–8.

Signorielli, N. (2001) Television's gender role images and contribution to stereotyping: past, present, future, in D.G. Singer and J.L. Singer (eds) *Handbook of Children and the Media*. Thousand Oaks, CA: Sage, 341–58.

Silver, N. (2006) *Age, Text, Location*. Colchester: txtcafé, http://www.txtcafe.com

Smith, R., Anderson, D.R. and Fisher, C. (1985) Young children's comprehension of montage, *Child Development*, 56, 962–71.

Spigel, L. and Olssen, J. (2004) *Television after TV: Essays on a Medium in Transition*. Durham, London: Duke University Press.

Springhall, J. (1998) *Youth, Popular Culture and Moral Panics: Penny Gaffs to Gangsta Rap*. Basingstoke: Macmillan.

Staksrud, E., Livingstone, S., and Haddon, L. (eds) (2007) EU Kids Online: What do we know about children's use of online technologies? A report on data availability and research gaps in Europe. EU Kids Online deliverable D1.1 data availability for the EC Safer Internet Plus programme. EU Kids Online, London.

Starker, S. (1989) *Evil Influences: Crusades Against the Mass Media*. Edison, NJ: Transaction.

Steemers, J. (2004) *Selling Television: British Television in the Global Marketplace*. London: BFI.

Steemers, J. (2008) 'Between commerce and creativity: licensing and the production of preschool television', presentation to Conference on Making television for young children: Future prospects and issues', University of Westminster, 21 September 2008.

Strelitz, L. and Boshoff, P. (2008) The African reception of global media, in S. Livingstone and K. Drotner (eds) *The International Handbook of Children and Media*. London: Sage, 237–53.

Tanner, J. M. (1990) *Foetus into Man: Physical Growth from Conception to Maturity*. Cambridge, MA: Harvard University Press.

Tatar, M. (2003) *The Hard Facts of the Grimms' Fairy Tales*. Princeton, NJ: Princeton University Press.

Thickett, J. (2008) 'Perspectives on the audience', Broadcasting Britishness Conference, Said Business School, University of Oxford, 17 June.

Thornham, H. (2008) 'It's a boy thing': gaming, gender and geeks, *Feminist Media Studies*, 8(2): 127–42.

Trotta, L. (2001) Children's advocacy groups: a history and analysis, in D.G. Singer and J. L. Singer (eds) *Handbook of Children and the Media*. Thousand Oaks, CA: Sage, 699–720.

Tucker, N. (1992) Good friends or just acquaintances? The relationship between child psychology and children's literature, in P. Hunt (ed.) *Literature for Children; Contemporary criticism*. London: Routledge, 156–73.

Twain, M. (1884, Penguin Classic, 1986) *Huckleberry Finn*. New York: Penguin.

UNICEF (2008) *The State of the World's Children: 2008*. New York: UNICEF.

UNICEF (2007) *Report Card 7: Child Poverty in Perspective: An Overview of Child Well-being in Rich Countries*, released 14 February, 2007, New York: UNICEF.

Unnikrishnan, N. and Bajpai, S. (1996) *The Impact of Television Advertising on Children*. New Delhi: Sage.

Ward, C. (1978, reprinted 1990) *The Child in the City*, Harmondsworth: Penguin.

Warner, M. (1995) *From the Beast to the Blonde*. London: Vintage.

Wartella, E. and Robb, M. (2007) Young children, new media, *Journal of Children and Media*, 1(1): 35–44.

Wasko, J., Phillips, M. and Meehan, E.R. (eds) (2001) *Dazzled by Disney: The Global Disney Audiences Project*. London and New York: Leicester University Press.

Wells, K. (2008) Child saving or child rights: depictions of children in international NGO campaigns on conflict, *Journal of Children and Media*, 2(3): 235–50.

Williams, R. (1976) *Keywords: A Vocabulary of Culture and Society*. Oxford: OUP.

Williams, T.B. (1986) *The Impact of Television*. New York: Academic Press.

Wimmer, R.D. and Dominick, J.R. (2006) *Mass Media Research: An Introduction*, 8th edn. Florence, KY: Cengage Learning.

Winn, M. (2002) *The Plug-in Drug: Television, Computers and Family Life*. New York: Penguin.

Wober, M. (1986) *Patterns of Viewing Perceptions and Personality Among Children: Some Preliminary Findings*. IBA Research Department Working Paper, London: IBA.

Zipes, J. (1986) *Don't Bet on the Prince: Contemporary Feminist Fairy Tales in North America and England*.

Zipes, J. (2002) *Sticks and Stones: The Troublesome History of Children's Literature from Slovenly Peter to Harry Potter*. New York, London: Routledge.

FILMOGRAPHY/TELEVISION

Dates given are dates of first release

3rd and Bird (2008) Television, United States and United Kingdom; Little Airplane Productions, New York and London.

The Animated Shakespeare (1992) Television, Wales; Dave Edwards Studio, Cardiff.

Arthur (1996) Television, United States of America; WGBH, Boston, Massachusetts.

Animated Tales of the World (2001) Television, United States of America; HBO, New York.

Battlestar Galactica (2004) Television, Canada; David Eick Productions, NBC Universal Television, R&D TV, Stanford Pictures (II), Universal Media Studios, United States of America.

Beauty and the Beast (1991) Film, United States of America; Walt Disney Feature Animation, California.

Ben Ten (2005) Television, United States of America; Warner Bros. Village Roadshow Pictures, Melbourne and Los Angeles.

Bob the Builder (1999) Television, United Kingdom; HiT Entertainment, London.

Byker Grove (1989) Television, United Kingdom; British Broadcasting Corporation, London.

Children's Ward (The Ward) (1989) Television, United Kingdom; Granada Television, Manchester.

Chuggington (2008) Television, United Kingdom; Ludorum, London and Chicago.

Cinderella (1950) Film, United States of America; Walt Disney Productions, California.

City of God (2002) Film, Brazil; O2 Films, Brazil.

Degrassi Junior High (1987) Television, Canada; Playing with Time, Toronto.

The Demon Headmaster (1996) Television, United Kingdom; British Broadcasting Corporation, London.

Doctor Who (1963–present) Television, United Kingdom; British Broadcasting Corporation, London.

The Face at the Window (2003) Television, United Kingdom; British Broadcasting Corporation, London.

Grange Hill (1978) Television, United Kingdom; British Broadcasting Corporation, London.

Hannah Montana (2006) Television, United States of America; It's A Laugh Productions, California.

Harry Potter and the Goblet of Fire (2005) Film, United Kingdom; Warner Bros. Pictures, California.

Harry Potter and the Sorcerer's Stone (2001) Film, United Kingdom; Warner Bros. Pictures, California.

Heroes (2006) Television, United States of America; NBC Universal Television, United States of America.

Horrible Histories (2009) Television, United Kingdom; Lion Television, Glasgow and London.

Ivor the Engine (1958) Television, United Kingdom; Smallfilms, Kent.

Jeugdjournaal (1981) Television, Netherlands; NOS, Netherlands.

Little Miss Sunshine (2006) Film, United States of America; Fox Searchlight Pictures, Los Angeles.

The Little Mermaid (1989) Film, United States of America; Walt Disney Pictures, California.

Lizzie Maguire (2001) Television, United States of America; Stan Rogow Productions, California.

M.I. High (2007) Television, United Kingdom; Kudos Film and Television, London.

My Parents are Aliens (1999) Television, United Kingdom; Granada Media, Manchester.

My So-called Life (1994) Television, United States of America; ABC Productions, California.

Panorama (1953–present) Television, United Kingdom; British Broadcasting Corporation, London.

Play School (1964) Television, United Kingdom; British Broadcasting Corporation, London.

Play Days (1988) Television, United Kingdom; British Broadcasting Corporation, London.

Postman Pat (1981) Television, United Kingdom; Woodland Animations, Manchester.

The Prince and the Pauper (1996) Television, United Kingdom; British Broadcasting Corporation, London.

The Secret Garden (1975) Television, United Kingdom; British Broadcasting Corporation, London.

The Secret Garden (1993) Film, United States of America; American Zoetrope, San Francisco.

That Summer Day (2006) Television, United Kingdom; Hat Trick Productions, London.

The Story of Tracy Beaker (2002) Television, United Kingdom; British Broadcasting Corporation, London.

Sesame Street (1969) Television, United States of America; Sesame Workshop, New York.

Sesame Tree (2008) Television, United Kingdom; Sixteen South, Belfast.

Shaun the Sheep (2007) Television, United Kingdom; Aardman Animations, Bristol.

The Simpsons (1989) Television, United States of America; Twentieth Century Fox Television, Los Angeles.

Slumdog Millionaire (2008) Film, India; Celador Films, London.

Spongebob Squarepants (1999) Television, United States of America; Nicktoons, California.

Star Trek (1966) Television, United States of America; Desilu Productions, California.

Teletubbies (1997) Television, United Kingdom; Ragdoll Productions, Buckinghamshire.

Thomas the Tank Engine (2003) Television, United Kingdom; HiT Entertainment, London.

The Tomorrow People (1992) Television, United Kingdom; Central Independent Television, Surrey.

Tractor Tom (2003) Television, United Kingdom; E1 Entertainment, London.

CHILDREN'S LITERATURE

Alcott, L.M. ([1868] 2008) *Little Women*. London: Penguin.

Briggs, R. ([1978] 2009) *The Snowman*. London: Penguin.

Burningham, J. (1978) *Mr Gumpy's Outing*. London: Penguin.

Burningham. J. (1979) *Mr Gumpy's Motor Car*. London: Penguin.

Collodi, C. ([1892] 2002) *Pinocchio*. London: Penguin.

Cross, G. ([1997] 2004) *The Demon Headmaster Takes Over*. Oxford: Oxford University Press.

Dr Seuss ([1957] 20090 *The Cat in the Hat*. Collins.

Grahame, K. ([1908] 2005) *Wind in the Willows*. London: Penguin.

Grimm, J. and Grimm, W. ([1948] 1972, translated Stern, M.) *Nursery and Household Tales*. London: Routledge & Kegan Paul.

Hoban, R. (2005) *The Mouse and his Child*. London: Faber.

Hodgson Burnett, F. ([1886] 1994) *Little Lord Fauntleroy*. London: Penguin.

Hodgson Burnett, F. ([1911] 2008) *The Secret Garden*. London: Penguin.

Milne, A.A. ([1929] 2009) *Winnie the Pooh*. London: Egmont.

Montgomery, L.M. ([1908] 2007) *Anne of Green Gables*. Oxford: Oxford University Press.

Nesbit, E. ([1906] 2005) *The Railway Children*. London: Penguin.

Norton, M. ([1952] 2003) *The Borrowers*. London: Penguin

Rowling, J.K. (1997) *Harry Potter and the Philosopher's Stone*. London: Bloomsbury.

Rowling, J.K. (1998) *Harry Potter and the Chamber of Secrets*. London: Bloomsbury.

Rowling, J.K. (1999) *Harry Potter and the Prisoner of Azkaban*. London: Bloomsbury.

Rowling, J.K. (2000) *Harry Potter and the Goblet of Fire*. London: Bloomsbury.

Rowling, J.K. (2003) *Harry Potter and the Order of the Phoenix*. London: Bloomsbury.

Rowling, J.K. (2006) *Harry Potter and the Half Blood Prince*. London: Bloomsbury.

Rowling, J.K. (2007) *Harry Potter: The Deathly Hallows*. London: Bloomsbury.

White, E.B. ([1952] 2008) *Charlotte's Web*. London: Penguin.

Williams, M. ([1922] 1998) *The Velveteen Rabbit*. Philadelphia, PA: The Running Press.
Wilson, J. (2005) *Clean Break*. London: Doubleday.

Websites

American Academy of Child and Adolescent Psychiatry, http://www.aacap.org/cs/root/
    facts_for_families/children_and_video_games_playing_with_violence (accessed 28
    May 2009).
CBeebies, http://www.bbc.co.uk/cbeebies/
Centre for Media Research, University of Ulster, policy documents: http://cmr.ulster.
    ac.uk/pdf/policy/publicserv.pdf (accessed 21 Nov. 2009).
The Children's Television Charter http://www.nordicom.gu.se/clearinghouse.php?
    portal=linkdb&main=ctc4.php& (accessed 22 Nov. 2009).
Fictionalley.org – Harry Potter fan fiction and artwork, www.fictionalley.org (accessed
    22 Nov. 2009).
First World Summit on Children and Television, Melbourne, Australia, 1995, http://
    www.wsmcf.com/past_summits/pdf/finrep1.pdf (accessed 18 June 2009).
Home Office, UK http://www.gro.gov.uk/gro/content/ (accessed 22 Nov. 2009).
The Imperial War Museum, London, http://www.iwmcollections.org.uk/qryFilm.asp
    (accessed 22 Nov. 2009).
Newsround (http://news.bbc.co.uk/cbbcnews/hi/teachers/default.stm) (accessed 21 Nov.
    2009).
Ofcom, UK Children's Media Literacy, 2008, http://www.ofcom.org.uk/advice/media_
    literacy/medlitpub/medlitpubrss/ml_childrens08/ml_childrens08.pdf   (accessed
    21 Nov. 2009).
Save Kids TV, http://www.savekidstv.org.uk/ (accessed 21 Nov. 2009).
Sesame Street, http://www.sesamestreet.org/home (accessed 22 Nov. 2009).
UN Convention on the Rights of the Child, http://www.unhchr.ch/html/menu3/b/
    k2crc.htm (accessed 17 June 2009).
Viacom (Nickelodeon, the children's channel) http://www.viacom.com/ourbrands/
    medianetworks/mtvnetworks/Pages/nickelodeon.aspx (accessed 16 June 2009).
World Summits for Children and Media, http://www.wsmcf.com/ (accessed 18 June
    2009).
World Wide Kids' Art Gallery, http://www.theartgallery.com.au/kidsart.html (accessed
    17 June 2009).

INDEX

Related books from Open University Press
Purchase from www.openup.co.uk or order through your local bookseller

---

MEDIA CONVERGENCE

Tim Dwyer

- How will people access digital media content in the future?
- What combination of TV, computer or mobile device will be employed?
- Which kinds of content will become commonplace?

Rapid changes in technology and the media industries have led to new modes of distributing and consuming information and entertainment across platforms and devices. It is now possible for newspapers to deliver breaking news by email alerts or RSS feeds, and for audiovisual content to be read, listened to or watched at a convenient time, often while on the move.

This process of 'media convergence', in which new technologies are accommodated by existing media industries, has broader implications for ownership, media practices and regulation. Dwyer critically analyses the political, economic, cultural, social, and technological factors that are shaping these changing media practices.

There are examples of media convergence in everyday life throughout, including IPTV, VoIP and Broadband networks. The impacts of major traditional media players moving into the online space is illustrated using case studies such as the acquisition of the social networking site MySpace by News Corporation, and copyright issues on Google's YouTube.

This informative resource is key reading for media studies students, researchers, and anyone with an interest in media industries, policy and regulation.

Contents

Introduction – Interpreting Media Convergence – Traditional Media Moves Online – Media Ownership and the Nation-State – Audiences Of Neoliberal Imaginaries – Living At The Network Edge – Conclusion – Glossary Of Key Terms – References – Index

2010   208pp
978–0–335–22873–7 (Paperback)   978–0–335–22872–0 (Hardback)

TELEVISION, AUDIENCES AND EVERYDAY LIFE
Matt Briggs

Television is commonplace in developed societies, an unremarkable and routine part of most people's everyday lives, but also the subject of continued concern from academia and beyond. But what do we really know about television, the ways that we watch it, the meanings that are made, and its relationship to ideology, democracy, culture and power?

Television, Audiences and Everyday Life draws on an extensive body of audience research to get behind this seemingly simple activity. Written in a clear and accessible style, key audience studies are presented in ways that illuminate critical debates and concepts in cultural and media studies.

Key topics and case studies include:

- News, debate and the pubic sphere
- Reality television, talk shows and media ethics
- Soap opera, play and gossip
- The uses of television in the home
- Television, identity and globalization
- Textual analysis, discourse and semiotics

Each chapter makes a compelling case for the importance of audience research in our thinking about television texts. The case studies introduce important new terms in the study of television, such as play, semiosis and modality, while also throwing new light on familiar terms, such as decoding, ideology and the public sphere.

Television, Audiences and Everyday Life is essential reading for undergraduate students on media, cultural studies and sociology courses, or anybody who wants to understand television, its genres, and their place in everyday life.

Contents
Introduction: Doing Things with Audience Research – Television, News & the Public Sphere – Reality Television, Audiences & Ethics – Soap Opera & Play – Television & Domestic Space – Television, Identity & Global Audiences Conclusion: Television & Ethics – Glossary – Bibliography

2009   192pp
978–0–335- 22869–0 (Paperback)   978–0–335- 22868–3 (Hardback)